The A.C.E. Spelling Dictionary

Find words quickly
and
improve your spelling

The A.C.E. Spelling Dictionary
By David Moseley and Catherine Nicol

Acknowledgements

The authors would like to thank all those who took part in the field trials in England, Northern Ireland, Scotland and Wales. Special thanks are due to Ronald Beresford for his expert phonetic advice and to George Macbride for helping us to meet the needs of Scottish users.

Learning Development Aids
Duke Street
Wisbech
Cambs. PE13 2AE
England

The A.C.E. Spelling Dictionary
LD425
© David Moseley & Catherine Nicol

First Published 1986
Second Edition 1986
Third Edition 1987
Fourth Edition 1988
Fifth Edition 1989
Sixth Edition 1990
Reprinted 1991, 1992

ISBN 1 85503 106 X

Printed in Great Britain by
Ebenezer Baylis & Son Ltd
The Trinity Press, Worcester and London

CONTENTS

INTRODUCTION

This spelling dictionary is designed for writers of all ages. It is intended for both school and home use. It is easy to use, even if you find spelling difficult. You will soon be able to find any word you need in just a few seconds. All you have to do is to look at the index, turn to the page you need and then scan down a single column.

The index gives the alphabet across the page and is the key to the different sections. Within each section the words are arranged in alphabetical order. Once you have understood how to use the index, you should never again have to ask someone else how to spell a word. Later, when you know where the different sections are, you will be able to do without the index and find words even more quickly.

Before starting to use the dictionary it is important to understand what you have to do. The first two sections of this introduction should be studied carefully; and you should practise looking up the words given as examples. Children may need an adult to help them at this stage. Perhaps the most important thing to understand is that you have to *listen* to the way you say a word. Try to think not of vowel letters but of vowel sounds.

English spelling does not obey simple rules. Although a proportion of words can be called 'regular', there are very many exceptions and uncommon patterns. The vowel sounds present the biggest problem. There are more than two hundred different vowel spellings associated with the eighteen basic English vowel sounds. This can cause delay and frustration when looking up words in an ordinary dictionary. The vowel sound classification used in this Aurally Coded English dictionary is, however, an efficient and powerful aid. You will be able to find words very quickly, as most columns are short. Every time you look down a column for a word you will see how different written symbols are used to represent the same spoken sound.

This ACE dictionary consists of three main parts, each including five or six sections. All the words in a section have the same or nearly the same vowel sound. Vowel sounds are made with the voice, with the mouth open.

The first five sections of 'short' vowel sounds are printed on white paper. These sounds, as a rule, are the ones taught at school:

PART 1
a   as in cat
e   as in elephant
i   as in pig
o   as in dog
u   as in duck   & oo   as in woodpecker

The 'alphabet-name' vowel sounds are printed on blue paper. These are 'long' vowel sounds:

PART 2
ae   as in snail
ee   as in eagle
ie   as in lion
oe   as in goat
ue   as in newt   & oo   as in smooth

The last six sections include spellings with the letter 'r' and two double sounds. These are printed on white paper and are also 'long' vowel sounds:

PART 3
ar   as in shark
air   as in bear
er   as in worm
or   as in horse
oi   as in oyster
ou   as in owl

As this is a spelling dictionary, word meanings are given only if two or more words sound the same or nearly the same. However, using the ACE dictionary to look up spellings will make it easier for you to use other dictionaries for looking up meanings. It should also improve your spelling. You will think of long words as made up of smaller parts, often corresponding to spoken syllables. As you become more aware of the common patterns, unusual spellings will stand out from the others and hold your attention. It is a good idea to write down unusual spellings in a personal spelling book, noting the 'tricky' part or parts and using the 'look-cover-write-check' routine.

HOW TO USE THE SPELLING DICTIONARY

HOW TO USE THE DICTIONARY

To find a word in the dictionary you have to do two things:
(1) pick out the first strong or the first clear vowel sound
(2) decide on what you think is the first letter in the word

The index tells you where to find any one of 16,000 words. You will soon be able to link each vowel sound with its spelling symbol. The animal pictures and the word examples will help you to do this. A word will nearly always be where you think it is, even if you are wrong about the first letter. Sometimes you have to turn over to the next page and sometimes you will be asked to look on another page.

When you have turned to the right page, you only have to run down one of the columns. So, if you are looking for the word 'sub-mar-ine' on page 130 you look in the column of three-syllable words. The number of stars at the top of the column is the same as the number of syllables. Every syllable contains a vowel sound, and you can tell how many syllables are in a word if you say it slowly and tap at the same time. This rhyme may help:

> "One tap for 'fun'
> And two for 'be-gun'
> Three taps for 'sta-di-um'
> And four for 'gym-na-si-um'."

Longer words containing four or more syllables are to be found on the right hand side of each page. The longest word in the dictionary has eight syllables.

This is the full routine

TO LOOK UP   submarine

SAY 'sub . . .' >

Say the first syllable.
Say it really slowly.
Find the vowel sound.

SAY 'u' >

Say the vowel sound
on its own.

GO TO INDEX >

See pages x-xi
or the separate sheet.

FIND u (as in duck) >

Find the spelling
symbol for the vowel
sound, at one side of
the index page.

FIND S >

Scan through the
alphabet across the
page for the first letter
in the word.

IT'S PAGE 130! >

Find this with one
finger, while pointing
at the letter S.

P. 130 IS IN
PART 1 /

This part contains
words with 'short'
vowel sounds, printed
on white paper.

OPEN BOOK IN
PART 1 /

u is the last sound
in Part 1.

FIND PAGE 130 >

All pages with even
numbers are on the
left hand side.

TAP OUT
sub-ma-rine
TAP-TAP-TAP /

Say the word slowly
and tap out the
syllables.

LOOK UNDER * * * >

You won't have to
turn to the next
page this time!

DIRECT HIT!

This is the basic routine:

TO LOOK UP   rhinoceros

SAY 'rhi . . .'>

SAY 'ie'>

GO TO INDEX>

FIND ie (as in lion)>

FIND R>

IT'S PAGE 189!>

PAGE 189 is in Part 2>

OPEN BOOK IN PART 2>

FIND PAGE 189>

TAP OUT rhi-no-ce-ros TAP-TAP-TAP-TAP>

LOOK UNDER ****>

GOT IT!

Now try it yourself!

Here are some more words for you to find, using the basic routine. Start by saying the word quite normally, not by 'sounding out'. The vowel sounds are given for you in these practice examples:

monster	(SHORT o)
friend	(SHORT e)
bicycle	(LONG ie)
noise	(LONG oi)
accident	(SHORT a)
fright	(LONG ie)
multiplication	(SHORT u)
fortune	(LONG or)
squirrel	(SHORT i)
nose	(LONG oe)
beautiful	(LONG ue)
name	(LONG ae)
farther	(LONG ar)
burglary	(LONG er)
hour	(LONG ou)
hairdresser	(LONG air)

Neutral vowel sounds

If you find it hard to tell which is the first strong vowel sound in a word, take the first one you can hear clearly, as long as it is in the first or second syllable. Suppose you want to look up 'supposed'. Here the strong vowel sound is the 'oe' sound in the second syllable, and the word is under 'S' on page 207. However, if you pick out the 'u' sound, you will find the word on page 132, after the other words in the 'neutral vowel' box. So, if you cannot see a word where you think it should be, see if it is in a neutral vowel box. You will soon notice that neutral vowels sound rather like a quiet grunt. They are never strong sounds.

Listen to the way you pronounce 'balloon', for example:

| SAY 'ba . . . .' ⟩ | SAY 'a' ⟩ | A NEUTRAL SOUND! ⟩ |

Start to say the word, at a normal speed.

You can hardly hear this sound in the word.

It's not like the a sound in cat.

So, to find 'balloon' in the dictionary, listen for the strong vowel sound (in the second syllable):

| SAY 'balloo . .' ⟩ | SAY 'oo' ⟩ | GO TO INDEX ⟩ |

In all of the following words the strong vowel sound is in the second syllable, but you will probably succeed in finding the words all the same if you try to identify the letters used for the neutral vowel sound. However, as neutral vowels all sound much the same it is easier to go by the strong vowel.

IV

WORD	STRONG VOWEL	WORD	STRONG VOWEL
above	SHORT u	guitar	LONG ar
absurd	LONG er	infectious	SHORT e
advertisement	LONG er	laboratory	SHORT o
amazing	LONG ae	magician	SHORT i
apart	LONG ar	manouevre	LONG oo
appearance	LONG ee	observer	LONG er
appendicitis	SHORT e	occurred	LONG er
applause	LONG or	opponent	LONG oe
approach	LONG oe	particular	SHORT i
association	LONG oe	performer	LONG or
because	SHORT o	pollution	LONG oo
before	LONG or	position	SHORT i
circumference	SHORT u	potatoes	LONG ae
collection	SHORT e	prepared	LONG air
collision	SHORT i	production	SHORT u
conceited	LONG ee	remarkable	LONG ar
conclusion	LONG oo	remain	LONG ae
conductor	SHORT u	report	LONG or
confetti	SHORT e	request	SHORT e
describing	LONG ie	revenge	SHORT e
deserve	LONG er	reverse	LONG er
despair	LONG air	surrender	SHORT e
destroy	LONG oi	surroundings	LONG ou
discuss	SHORT u	survivor	LONG ie
disgusting	SHORT u	tonight	LONG ie
effect	SHORT e	towards	LONG or
emotional	LONG oe	trapeze	LONG ee
encouragement	SHORT u	tremendous	SHORT e
enough	SHORT u	velocity	SHORT o
exhaust	LONG or	vocabulary	SHORT a

GETTING THE MOST OUT OF THE DICTIONARY

Looking up words in order to spell them correctly is only one way of using the ACE Dictionary. Other ways of using it can be just as valuable and can help to increase your speed of word-recognition as well as your knowledge about words. You can do this by timing yourself as you look for words of a certain type. You might like to work with someone else and take turns in looking up words. The words can be chosen by topic, by use, by length, by stress pattern, by sound, by features of spelling or by grammatical function. It can also be fun to think of combinations of these – for example, to find as many long words as possible that can be used to express enjoyment of food, picking out only those where the stress is (greedily) placed on the first syllable.

The authors hope that many more ideas for actively exploring the dictionary will be thought of by those who use it. What is provided here is a more detailed account of some of the rules that have been followed by the authors, especially those that relate to alphabetical order and to the inclusion of different forms of the same word. You do not need to understand all of these before you start to use the dictionary, but you may need to refer to them at times and they may also suggest some useful activities.

Alphabetic grouping of words

Within each section, words are grouped by initial letter, taken in alphabetical order. A letter is omitted if there are no words beginning with it in that section.

Within each column of words, there are smaller sets, each beginning with the same two letters. This makes the columns easier to scan, and cuts down word search time. It does not take long to learn that 'sc' is near the top of a column of words beginning with S, that 'sm' is about half way down and that 'sw' is near the bottom.

Some words are entered in more than one place. This happens when the first sound in the word does not uniquely determine what is the first letter. For example, words beginning with a silent letter (like 'knife' and 'gnome') are entered according to initial sound as well as spelling. Words like 'ceiling' and 'chassis' are entered under both S and C. Words like 'kangaroo' and 'karate' are entered under C and well as under K. Smaller print is used for double-entered words when they begin with a different letter from the rest of the words in a column.

In certain cases, cross-reference pointers are used instead of double or multiple entries. A cross-reference is always provided from K to C within the same section, instead of repeating a long list of C words under K. Dropped H's, confusion between initial E and I and between F and TH as well as uncertainty about the spelling of words beginning with QU are also taken care of by the use of cross-reference pointers.

Meaning

In cases where two words sound the same (or nearly the same) but have different meanings, you need to check that you have found the right word. All such words have an asterisk (*) against them and their meanings are given in brackets. These words are called homonyms (words with the same sound but with different meanings). Some of them are also homographs (words with the same spelling but with different meanings).

If the meaning or meanings do not fit the word you are looking for, all you have to do is to try another similarly-sounding word with an asterisk against it.

Plurals

If the plural form of a noun is not shown, it is safe to assume that you simply add an 's'. So, if you find 'journey', you will be able to spell 'journeys'.

All 'es' and '-ies' plurals are shown, for example 'box(es)' and 'baby(-ies)'. Where, as in 'baby(-ies)' there is a dash before the ending, it means that part of the word has to be removed before the plural ending is added. The most common pattern is for a final 'y' to be removed before adding '-ies'. Irregular forms such as 'calves' are treated in a similar way: 'calf(-ves)'.

Present participles

These are given for the more common words and in all cases where a final consonant is doubled before 'ing' is added (for example, 'swim' and 'swimming').

When the present participle form (ending in 'ing') is not given, you can be sure that the spelling falls into one of two patterns:

(a) for words not ending in 'e', add 'ing'
(b) for words ending in 'e', remove the 'e' before adding 'ing'.

Past tenses

The past tense form is given for the more common words and whenever a final consonant is doubled before 'ed' is added (for example, 'skid' and 'skidded').

In all words where the final 'ed' has the sound 't' (as in 'ticked') the ending is given in brackets: tick(ed).

All irregular past tense forms are given in full. They are entered in the appropriate sections, but are also included, enclosed in square brackets, immediately below the corresponding present tense form:

bring   buy
[brought]   [bought]

Comparatives and superlatives

These are given in full for the more common words and whenever a final consonant is doubled (as in 'bigger' and 'biggest'). Where a final 'y' is changed to '-ier' or to '-iest' this is also always shown (for example, 'saucy(-ier, -iest)'.

If you cannot find a particular word with the ending 'er' or 'est', you can be sure that the spelling falls into one of two patterns:

(a) for words not ending in 'e', add 'er' or 'est'
(b) for words ending in 'e', remove the 'e' before adding 'er' or 'est'.

DIALECTS

The vowel sound sections are based on 'BBC' pronunciation, but regional differences have been taken into account. Particular care has been taken to make the dictionary suitable for use in Scotland. Trials have taken place throughout the British Isles and wherever systematic shifts in the pronunciation of vowels have been noted, words have been entered in more than one section. Wherever a dash appears next to a word it means that for some speakers the word is pronounced with the same vowel sound as the other words in the section.

In the 'a' section words pronounced in a 'BBC' accent with an 'ar' sound have a dash against them. These words are pronounced with an 'a' in Scotland, and in most cases in the north of England. In the 'o' section the words with a dash against them belong there only for Scottish speakers. In the short vowel 'u' and 'oo' section, two 'BBC' sounds have been put together, with a dash against the 'oo' sound words. In the north of England there may be no difference in pronunciation between the two groups. In the section containing words with the long 'oo' sound, the words with a dash against them belong there only for Scottish speakers. In parts of the Midlands the sounds 'air' and 'er' are pronounced in the same way. The 'air' words therefore also entered in the 'er' section, a feature which also makes sense for some of the words as pronounced in Scotland.

A major feature of Scottish speech is the rolled 'r' following a vowel. This has important implications for Scottish users of the dictionary, since the 'BBC' ar, air, er and or sounds are pronounced differently in Scotland. 'Thistle-sign' cross-reference pointers are used in the appropriate sections, but these will not be needed if users learn to refer to the third part of the book for words with vowels followed by an 'r'. This applies for all of the short vowels, and for the long vowels ae and oe. It does not, however, apply for the long vowels ee, ie and ue.

The following table is provided for the benefit of Scottish users:

WORDS WITH	SECTION	EXAMPLES
SHORT a followed by 'r'	ar	shark, article
SHORT e followed by 'r'	er	early, nervous
SHORT i followed by 'r'	er	bird, firmly
SHORT o followed by 'r'	or	horse, warning
SHORT u followed by 'r'	er	hurt, worm
LONG ae followed by 'r'	air	rare, airport
LONG ee followed by 'r'	ee	clear, steer
LONG ie followed by 'r'	ie	wire, tyre
LONG oe followed by 'r'	or	hoarse, bored
LONG ue/oo followed by 'r'	ue/oo	pure, poor

HOW THE WORDS WERE CHOSEN

Both British and American sources have been used in compiling the ACE Spelling Dictionary. Also, words have been added as a result of field trials in which users kept records of words they needed but were unable to find.

When work started in 1967 on the first version of the ACE Dictionary, the two main sources of vocabulary were 'Words Your Children Use' by Edwards and Gibbon and Schonell's Essential Spelling List. Later, words were added from the Thornike—Lorge list and from the adult reading vocabulary list of Kucera and Francis. However, the most recent and comprehensive source is the American Heritage Word Frequency Book. This contains no fewer than 86,741 words types (words and word forms) from books used in schools by children in the age-range 8 to 14. The complete range of school subjects is covered.

Unless they were judged to be unfamiliar to British users, all words (but not all word forms) occurring in the first 23,000 word types of the American Heritage list are included in the ACE Dictionary. This is equivalent to excluding words only if they are used less than once in every 2,000,000 words of text. As explained above, plurals, present participles, past tense forms, comparatives and superlatives have not always been included if they are straightforward to spell.

In order to meet the needs of British students, the authors have also included lists supplied by subject teachers for all areas of the curriculum. Particular care has been taken to cover scientific, technical and mathematical vocabulary. The Evans Technical Dictionary and a list of mathematical terms published by the Scottish Examination Board are among the sources used.

A list of the publications from which words have been taken is given below:

Carroll, J. B., Davies, P. and Richman, B. (1971) *The American Heritage Word Frequency Book*. Boston, Houghton Mifflin.

Edwards, R. P. A. and Gibbon, V. (1964) *Words Your Children Use*. London, Burke.

Evans Technical Dictionary. (1982) London, Evans.

Kucera, H. and Francis, W. N. (1967) *Computational Analysis of Present-Day American English*. Providence, Brown University Press.

Schonell, F. J. (1932) *The Essential Spelling List*. London, Macmillan.

Scottish Examination Board (1984). Scottish Certificate of Education, Standard Grade.

Arrangements in Mathematics for Foundation, General and Credit Levels in and after 1986.

INDEX

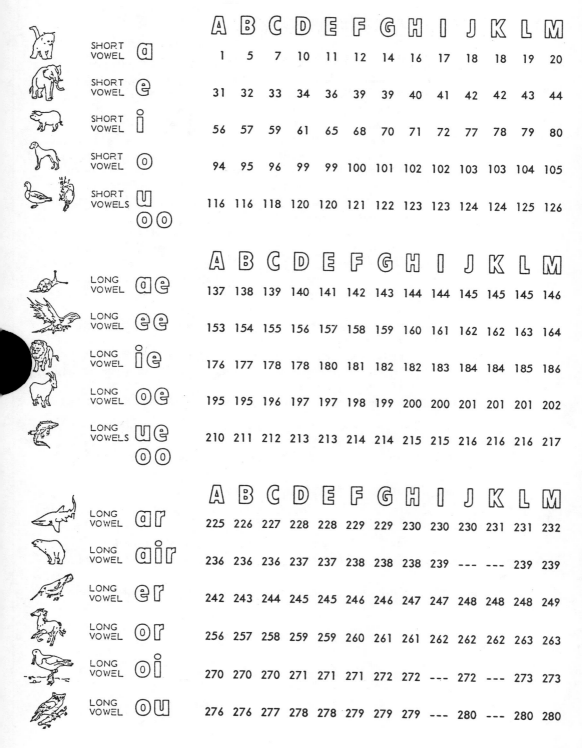

Permission to photocopy

© LDA

© LDA

∗	∗ ∗	∗ ∗ ∗	∗ ∗ ∗ ∗ [∗ ∗]
act	-aardvark	abacus(es)	abnormally
		abandon(ed)	aboriginal
add	abbess(es)	abdomen	aborigines
*adds (does add)	abbey	abnormal(ly)	absolutely
*adze (tool)	abbot	absentee	
	absence	absolute	academic(ally)
-aft	absent		academy(-ies)
	abstract	accident	accessory(-ies)
-alms (gift to		accurate	accidental(ly)
charity)	accent	acetate	accuracy(-ies)
Alps	access(ed)	acrobat	accurately
	acid	actively	accusation
am	acrid	actual(ly)	acquisition
	acted		acrobatic(ally)
an	acting	adapter/adaptor	activity(-ies)
and	action	additive	actually
*ant (insect)	active	addressee	
	actor	adequate	adaptable
apt	actress(es)	adjective	adaptation
	actual(ly)	admirable	adjectival(ly)
as		admiral	admirable
ash(es)	adapt	-advancement	admiration
-ask(ed)	added	-advancing	adolescence
ass(es)	addend	-advantage(d)	adolescent
	adder	advertise(d)	advantageous
at	addict	advocate	adverbial(ly)
	adding		
-aunt (relative)	adult	affluence	Afghanistan
	-advance(d)	affluent	
axe(d)	advent	Africa	aggravation
	adverb	African	agitation
	adverse	-afternoon	agoraphobia
		-afterwards	agoraphobic
	affix(es)		agricultural(ly)
	Afghan	aggravate	agriculture
	-after	agitate	
		agonise(d)	alabaster
	-aghast	ze	alcoholic
	agile	agony(-ies)	algebraic(ally)
			Algeria
	alas	Alaska	alimentary
	album	albatross(es)	allegretto
	alcove	alchemy	alligator
	algae	alcohol	alphabetical(ly)
	Allah	algebra	altimeter
	alley	alibi	aluminium
	alloy(ed)	alkali	-see next page
	ally(-ies)	alkaline	
	(allied)	allergy(-ies)	
	-almond	alphabet	
	alpha	Alsatian	
	-see next page	altitude	
		-see next page	

for H ...
see page 16

for a-r
see page 225

In these words you can hear the vowel sound a as in cat

1

* *

amass(es)
amassed
amber
amble(d)
ambling
ambush(es)
ambushed
ampere
ample

anchor
anger(ed)
angle(d)
*angler (person who
    fishes with hook
    and line)
angling
angry(-ier,-iest)
anguish(ed)
ankle
annexe(d)
annual(ly)
anode
-answer(ed)
anthill
anthrax
*antics (strange
    behaviour)
antique
*antiques (very old
    objects)
antlers
anvil
anxious

aphid/aphis
apple

Arab
arid
arrow(ed)

ashtray
-asking
aspect
asphalt
aspirin
asset
aster
asthma
-see next page

* * *

amalgam
amateur
ambition
ambitious
ambulance
amethyst
ammeter
amplify(-ies)
    (amplified)
amplitude
amputate

anagram
analogue
analyse(d)
    ze
ancestor
ancestry(-ies)
anchorage
andante
Anglican
angrier
angriest
angrily
*angular (with sharp
    corners)
animal
aniseed
annual(ly)
anodise(d
    ze
anorak
-answering
antarctic
anteater
antelope
antenna(e)
anthracite
anthropoid
antifreeze
antonym
anxiously

aperture
apparent
appetite
applicant
apprehend
aptitude
-see next page

* * * * [* *]

amalgamate
ambassador
ambidextrous
ambiguous
ammunition
amphibian
amphibious
amphitheatre
amplification
amplifier

anachronism
anaesthesia/
anesthesia
anaesthetic/
anesthetic
analogy(-ies)
analysis(-es)
analytic(ally)
anatomical(ly)
anatomy(-ies)
Anglo-Saxon
animation
anniversary(-ies)
annually
antagonise(d)
    ze
antagonism
Antarctica
antecedent
anthology(-ies)
anthropologist
anthropology
antibiotic
antibody(-ies)
anticipate
anticipation
antimony
antiquity(-ies)
antiseptic(ally)
antitoxin
anxiety(-ies)
-see next page

for H ...
see page 16

for a-r
see page 225

In these words you can hear the vowel sound a as in cat

*: *:

athlete
atlas(es)
atoll
atom
attach(es)
attached
attack(ed)
attic
attract

-Auntie/Aunty

average(d)

*axes (more than one
    axe or axis)
*axis (fixed or
    imaginary line)
axle

azure

impasse

* * *

aquatic
aqueduct

Arabic
arable
arrogance
arrogant
arrowhead

asbestos
aspirin
assassin
assonance
asterisk
asteroid
astronaut

athletic(ally)
Atlantic
atmosphere
attitude
attracted
attraction
attractive
attributes

avalanche
avant-garde
avenue
average(d)

axiom

* * * * [* *]

apostolic(ally)
apparatus
apparently
apparition
application
apposition
apprehension

aquamarine

aristocracy(-ies)
aristocrat
arithmetically

asparagus
aspiration
assassinate
assassination

athletically

for H . . .
see page 16

for a-r
see page 225

In these words you can hear the vowel sound α as in cat

In these words the first letter 'a' and the 'ae' are neutral vowels.

'AMAZING' WORDS

abate
abbreviation
abeyance
abide
[abode]
ability(-ies)
ablaze
aboard
abode
abolish(es)
abolished
abominable
abominate
abortion
abound
about
above
abrasive
abreast
abroad
abrupt
abscond
absorb(ed)
absorber
absorption
abstain(ed)
absurd
abundance
abundant
abuse(d)
abysmal(ly)
abyss(es)
accelerate
acceleration
accelerator
accept(able)
acceptance
accepting
accessible
accessory(-ies)
acclaim(ed)
accommodate
accommodation
accompaniment
accompany(-ies)
 (accompanied)
accomplish(es)
accomplished
accomplishment
accord(ance)
according(ly)
accordion
account
accrue(d)
accumulate
accumulation
accumulator
accuse(d)
accustom(ed)
acetylene
achieve(d)
achievement
acknowledge(d)
acknowledgement/
acknowledgment

acknowledging
across
acquaint(ance)
acquire(d)
acute
addicted
addiction
addictive
additional(ly)
address(es)
addressed
adhere(d)
adhesive
adieu
adjacent
adjoining
adjourn(ed)
adjust(ed)
adjuster
adjustment
administer(ed)
administrate
administration
administrator
admire(d)
admission
admit(ted)
admittance
admitting
adopt
adorable
adore(d)
adorn(ed)
adrenalin
adsorption
adrift
advance(d)
advancement
advancing
advantage(d)
adventure
adventurous
adverbial(ly)
adversity(-ies)
advertisement
advice
advisable
advise(d)
adviser
advisory
Aegean
aesthetic(ally)
afar
affair
affect(ed)
affection
affectionate(ly)
affiliate
affirm(ed)
affix(es)
affixed
affliction
afford
afloat
afoot

afraid
again
against
agenda
aggression
aggressive
aggressor
aghast
agility
ago
agog
agree(d)
agreement
agreeable
ahead
ahoy!
ajar
alarm(ed)
Alaska
alert
alight
alignment
alike
alive
allegiance
allegro
allergic
alliance
alliteration
allot(ted)
allotting
allotment
allow(ed)
allowance
alluvial
alluvium
aloft
alone
along(side)
aloof
aloud
amalgam
amalgamate(d)
amaze(d)
amazing
amenable
amend(ment)
America(n)
amid(st)
amino
amiss
ammonia
ammonium
amoeba
among(st)
amount
amuse(d)
amusement
anaemia/anemia
anaemic/anemic
anaesthetist/
anesthetist
anemone
anneal(ed)
annihilate

announce(d)
announcement
announcer
annoy(ed)
annoyance
anoint
anon(ymous)
another
apart
apartheid
apartment
apostle
apologetic(ally)
apologise(d)
       ze
apology(-ies)
apostrophe
appal(led)
appalling
appeal(ed)
appear(ed)
appearance
append
appendicitis
appendix(-ces)
applaud
applause
appliance
apply(-ies)
  (applied)
appoint(ment)
appreciate
apprentice(d)
apprenticeship
approach(es)
approached
approaching
appropriate
approval
approve(d)
approximate(ly)
approximation
aquarium
Arabia
arena
arise
[arose]
[arisen]
arithmetic
aroma
around
arouse(d)
arrange(d)
arrangement
array(ed)
arrest
arrival
arrive(d)
ascend(ing)
ascension
ascent
ashamed
ashore
aside
asleep

assault
assemble(d)
assembly(-ies)
assent
assert(ion)
assertive
assess(es)
assessed
assessment
assign(ed)
assignment
assimilate
assimilation
assist(ance)
assistant(s)
associate
association
associative
assorted
assortment
assume(d)
assumption
assurance
assure(d)
astern
astigmatism
astonish(es)
astonished
astonishment
astounded
astounding
astray
astrology
astronomer
astronomy
asylum
atone(d)
atonement
atrocious
attain(ed)
attainment
attempt(ed)
attend(ed)
attendance
attendant(s)
attention
attentive
attribute
aurora
Australia
avail(ed)
availability
available
avenge(d)
avoid(ed)
await
awake(d)
[awoke]
awaken(ed)
award
aware
away
awhile
awoke(n)
awry

✻   ✻ ✻   ✻ ✻ ✻   ✻ ✻ ✻ ✻

back(ed)	backbone	bachelor	bacteria
*bad (not good)	background	badminton	ballerina
*bade (did bid)	backwards	-Bahamas	
badge	badger(ed)	balcony(-ies)	botanical
bag(ged)	badly	balloted	
ban(ned)	baffle(d)	-banana	
*band (strip of	baffling	Bangladesh	
material /	baggage	banishment	
stripe / group)	bagging	banister	
bang(ed)	baggy(-ier,-iest)	baptism	
*banned (forbidden)	bagpipes	baritone	
*bands (more than	balance(d)	barrelling	
one band)	ballad	barricade	
bang(ed)	ballast	barrier	
bank(ed)	*ballet (dance)	barrister	
*banns (announcement	*ballot(ed) (voting)	-basketball	
in church of plan	-balmy	bathysphere	
to marry)	bamboo	battalion	
bash(es)	bandage(d)	battery(-ies)	
bashed	bandit	battlefield	
-bask(ed)	bandy(-ies)	battleship	
bat(ted)	(bandied)		
batch(es)	banger		
-bath(ed)	bangle	blackberry(-ies)	
	banish(es)	blanketed	
black(ed)	banished		
blank(ed)	banjo(es/s)	brassière	
-blast	banker		
	bankrupt		
-bra	banner		
brad	banning		
brag(ged)	banquet		
bran	bantam		
-branch(es)	baptise(d)		
-branched	ze		
brand	*baron (lord)		
-brass(es)	barrack(ed)		
brat	barracks		
	barrage(d)		
	barrel(led)		
	*barren (not fertile)		
	barrow(ed)		
	basalt		
	-basket		
	-bastard		

-see next page

for a-r
see page 226

* *

-bathroom
*baton (short stick)
*batted (did bat)
*batten (board)
 batter
*battered (did
    batter)
 batting
 battery(-ies)
 battle(d)
 battling

 began
-behalf

 blackbird
 blackboard
 blacken(ed)
 blackmail(ed)
 blacksmith
 bladder
 blanket(ed)

 bracket
 bradawl
 braggart
 bragging
 bramble
-branches
 brandish(es)
 brandished
 brandy(-ies)
 brassière

for a-r
see page 226

In these words the first letter 'a'
is a neutral vowel. It.. er... er...
sounds like the 'a' in 'astonish'.

baboon	basalt
Bahamas	bazaar
balloon(ed)	bazooka
banana	blancmange
barometer	Brazil

In these words you can hear the vowel sound a as in cat

cab
cadge(d)
-calf(-ves)
-calve(d) (produce
    a calf)
-calm(ed)
camp(ed)
can(ned)
-can't
cap(ped)
cash(es)
cashed
-cask
*-cast (throw /
    mould / decide
    parts in a
    play / squint)
-[cast]
*-caste (social
    class)
cat
catch(es)
[caught]

champ(ed)
*-chance (lucky
    event / risk)
-chanced
-chant
*-chants (does
    chant / more
    than one chant)
chap
chapped
chat(ted)

clad
clam(med)
clamp(ed)
clan
clang(ed)
clank(ed)
clap(ped)
clash(es)
clashed
-clasp(ed)
-class(es)
-classed
-see next page

for Qu ...
see page 24

cabbage
cabin
cackle(d)
cackling
cactus(es/-i)
*caddie (person paid
    to carry golf clubs)
*caddy(-ies) (caddie /
    box to hold tea)
    (caddied)
cadging
café
caffeine
callous
camber(ed)
camel
camera
campaign(ed)
camper
*campers (people in a
    camp)
camphor
camping
*campus(es) (college
    or university
    grounds)
camshaft
canal
cancel(led)
cancer
*candid (frank)
*candied (sugar-
    coated)
candle
candy
canning
*cannon (gun / stroke
    in billiards)
cannoned
cannot
canny(-ier,-iest)
*canon (musical
    round /rank in
    church /laws /
    list of works)
canteen
canter(ed)
*canvas (cloth)
*canvass(ed) (seek
    opinions and/or
    support)
*canyon (deep and
    narrow valley)
-see next page

* * *

cabinet
cadmium
calcium
calculate
calendar
calibrate
calico
callipers
calorie
camera
camouflage
Canada
cancelling
candidate
candlelight
candlestick
cannibal
canopy(-ies)
capital
caramel
caravan
caribou
carolling
carrier
carrion
carrycot
carrying
casserole(d)
castanets
-castaway
casually
casualty(-ies)
catalogue(d)
catalyst
catapult
cataract
category(-ies)
catholic
Catholic
cavalier
cavalry
cavity(-ies)

ceramic
-see next page

* * * * [* * *]

cafeteria
calamity(-ies)
calculation
calculator
Cambodia
cantilever(ed)
capacitor
capacity(-ies)
capitalise(d)
    ze
Caribbean
caricature(d)
casually
casualty(-ies)
catastrophe
catastrophic(ally)
category(-ies)
caterpillar

championship
chandelier
characterise(d)
    ze
characteristic(ally)
charioteer
charitable
chrysanthemum

classically
classification

collapsible
comparative
comparison
compassionate
compatible
congratulate
congratulations
constabulary(-ies)
contaminate
contamination

for a-r
see page 227

In these words you can hear the vowel sound a as in cat

*

crab
crack(ed)
-craft
crag
cram(med)
cramp(ed)
crank(ed)
crash(es)
crashed

* *

capping
capstan
capsule
captain(ed)
captive
captor
capture(d)
*carat (measure of
   purity of gold)
carol(led)
carriage
*carrot (vegetable)
carry(-ies)
   (carried)
cascade
cashew
cashier(ed)
*caster/castor
   (caster sugar /
   swivelling wheel)
-casting
-castle
*-castor (castor oil)
casual(ly)
catching
cathode
catholic
Catholic
catkin
cattle
catty(-ier,-iest)
cavern

chaffinch(es)
chalet
challenge(d)
champagne
chandler
channel(led)
chapel
chapter
-charade
chasm
chassis
*chatted (had a chat)
chatter
*chattered (talked
   quickly and too
   much / rattled)
chatty(-ier,-iest)
*-chorale (hymn tune)
   -see next page

* * *

champion(ed)
-chancellor
channelling
-chapati
character
chariot
charity(-ies)
chatterbox(es)

clarinet
clarify(-ies)
   (clarified)
clarity
classical(ly)
classify(-ies)
   (classified)

combatted
combatting
-commander
-commandment
companion
compassion
contraction
contractor
contralto(s)
contraption

kangaroo
-karate

for Qu ...
see page 24

for a-r
see page 227

In these words you can hear the vowel sound a as in cat

* *

cladding
clamber(ed)
clamming
clammy
clamour(ed)
clanger
clanking
clapper
clapping
classic(ally)
-classmate
-classroom
clatter(ed)

collapse(d)
combat(ted)
-command
compact
contract
-contrast
*-corral (enclosure
    for cattle and
    horses)

cracker
crackle(d)
crackling
-craftsman
craggy
cramming
crankshaft
cranny(-ies)
crevasse

-khaki

-Koran

for Qu ...
see page 24

for a-r
see page 227

In these words the first letter 'a' is a neutral vowel.

cacao	canoe(d)	caress(es)	chameleon
cadet	capillary(-ies)	caressed	chapati
Canadian	capricious	catarrh	charade
canary(-ies)	career(ed)	cathedral	charisma

In these words you can hear the vowel sound a as in cat

*	* *	* * *	* * * * [*]

dab(bed)
dad
-daft
*dam (water-
   barrier / mother
   of animal)
dammed
*damn (swear word /
   condemn)
damned
damp(ed)
-dance(d)
dank
dash(es)
dashed

drab
*-draft (rough plan /
   selected group)
drag(ged)
drank
*-draught (current of
   air / depth of
   ship in water /
   piece in game)
-draughts

dabbing
dabble(d)
dabbling
dachsund
daddy
dagger
dally(-ies)
   (dallied)
damage(d)
damsel
damson
-dancer
-dancing
dandruff
dandy(-ies)
dangle(d)
dangling
dapple(d)
dashboard
dazzle(d)
dazzling

decamp(ed)
-demand
*despatch(es) (send
   off)
despatched
detach(es)
detached
detract

*dispatch(es)
   (despatch /
   message)
dispatched
distract
divan

dragging
dragon
-drama
drastic(ally)
-draughty(-ier,-iest)

daffodil
dalmatian
damaging

-demanded

-disaster
-disastrous
dismantle(d)
dismantling
distraction
distractor

dragonfly(-ies)
dramatic(ally)
dramatise(d)
   ze
drastically

dandelion

dilapidated
dissatisfy(-ies)
   (dissatisfied)

dramatically
drastically

for a-r
see page 228

In these words you can hear the vowel sound a as in cat

*

** **

*** *** ***

**** **** **** **** [*]

*	**	***	**** [*]
	elapse(d)	ecstatic(ally)	ecstatically

enact
encamp(ed)
-enchant
-entrance(d)

elaborate
elastic(ally)

elaborate
elaboration
elastically
elasticity

er- or -ir- ?

embankment
embarrass(es)
embarrassed

es- or is- ?

em- or im- ?

embarrassing
embarrassment

exact
expand
expanse
extract

enamel(led)
enamour(ed)
-enchanting
entangle(d)
entangling
-entrancing

em- or im- ?

enamelling

en- or in- ?

en- or in- ?

erratically

erratic(ally)

er- or -ir- ?

er- or ir- ?

establishment

et- or it- ?

establish(es)
established

evacuate
evacuation
evacuee
evaluate
evaluation
evaporate
evaporation

es- or is- ?

exactly
examine(d)
-example
expanded
expanding
expansion
expansive
extraction
extractor

exaggerate
exaggeration
examination
expandable
explanatory
extrapolate
extravagance
extravagant
extravaganza

for H ...
see page 16

for I ...
see page 17

for a-r
see page 228

In these words you can hear the vowel sound a as in cat

F

*

fact
fad
fag(ged)
fan(ned)
fangs
-fast
fat(ter,test)
fax(ed)

flag(ged)
flan
flange(d)
flank(ed)
flap(ped)
flash(es)
flashed
-flask
flat(ted,ter,test)
flax

*franc (French coin)
-France
*frank (plain and
    honest)
  franked

for th ...
see page 28

* *

fabric
factor
factory(-ies)
factual(ly)
faddy
fagging
faggots
fallow
famine
famish(es)
famished
fanbelt
fancy(-ies)
fancied
fanning
fascist
fashion(ed)
-fasten(ed)
-faster
-fastest
*-father (male parent)
-fathered
fathom(ed)
fatten(ed)
fattening
fatter
fattest
fatty(-ier,-iest)

finance(d)

flabby(-ier,-iest)
flagging
flagpole
flannel(led)
flapper
flapping
flappy
flasher
flashing
*flatted (made flat)
flatten(ed)
flatter(ed)
*flattered (did
    flatter)
flattest
flatting
-see next page

* * *

fabulous

factorise(d)
    ze
factory(-ies)
factual(ly)
faculty(-ies)
Fahrenheit
fallacy(-ies)
family(-ies)
fanciful
fantastic(ally)
fantasy(-ies)
fascinate
fascism
-fastener
fattening

*-fiancé (male engaged
    to be married)
*-fiancée (female
    engaged to be
    married)
financial(ly)

flanelling

fractional(ly)
frantically

* * * * [*]

fabricated
fabrication
factually
fantastically
fascinating
fascination
fashionable
-father-in-law

financially

flabbergasted

fractionally
frantically

philatelist

for a-r
see page 229

In these words you can hear the vowel sound **a** as in **cat**

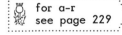

* *

forbade

fraction
fracture(d)
fragile
fragment
frantic(ally)

for th ...
see page 28

for a-r
see page 229

phantom

In these words the first letter 'a'
is a neutral vowel. It.. er... er...
sounds like the 'a' in 'astonish'.

facility(-ies)	fatigue(d)
fallacious	flamingo(es/s)
familiar	

In these words you can hear the vowel sound a as in cat

G

‹

gag(ged)
gang
gap(ped)
gas(es)
gassed
gash(es)
gashed
-gasp(ed)

glad(der,dest)
-glance(d)
gland
-glass(es)

gnash(es)
gnashed
gnat

grab(bed)
gram
grand
-grant
-graph(ed)
-grasp(ed)
-grass(es)
-grassed

✫ ✫

gadget
gagging
gallant
*galleon (ship)
galley
*gallon (measure)
gallop(ed)
gallows
gambit
*gamble(d) (risk)
gambler
*gambling (taking
    risks)
*gambol(led) (frisk)
gamma
gammon
gander
gangling
gangplank
gangster
gangway
gannet
gapping
garage(d)
garret
gasket
gassing
gather(ed)

-Ghana
-ghastly(-ier,-iest)

-giraffe

gladden(ed)
gladder
gladdest
glamour
-glasses
  -see next page

✫ ✫ ✫

galaxy(-ies)
gallery(-ies)
galvanise(d)
        ze
*gambolling (frisking)
garrison

-Ghanaian

*glacier (mass of
    slow-moving ice)
glamorous
glandular

gradual(ly)
graduate
gramophone
grandchildren
grandfather
grandmother
grandparent
-grasshopper
gratitude
gravelling
gravity(-ies)

guarantee(d)

-gymkhana
gymnastics

✫ ✫ ✫ ✫

gasometer

gladiator

gradually
graduation
gravitation

 for a-r see page 229

14

In these words you can hear the vowel sound a as in cat

※ ※

grabber
grabbing
gradual(ly)
grammar
grandad/granddad
grandeur
grandma
grandpa
grandstand
granite
granny(-ies)
-granted
graphite
grapple(d)
grappling
-grasslands
gravel(led)

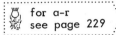

for a-r
see page 229

In these words the first letter 'a'
is a neutral vowel. It.. er... er...
sounds like the 'a' in 'astonish'.

galena   gazelle   graffiti
galoshes   gradation

In these words you can hear the vowel sound a as in cat

15

*

hack(ed)
had
-half(-ves)
-halve(d)
ham(med)
hand
hang
[hung]
hanged
has
hash(ed)
hat
hatch(es)
hatched
hath
have
[had]

* *

habit
haddock
hadn't
halal
hallo
hammer(ed)
hamming
hammock
hamper(ed)
hamster
hamstring(ed)
[hamstrung]
handbag
handbrake(d)
handcuff(ed)
handed
handful
handle(d)
handling
*hand-made (made by hand)
*handmaid (servant)
*handsome (good-looking)
*hangar (building to house planes)
*hanger (means of hanging)
hanging
hanky(-ies)
*hansom (cab)
happen(ed)
happy(-ier,-iest)
harass(ed)
harrow(ed)
hasn't
hatchet
hatter
haven't
having
havoc
hazard

hello

* * *

habitat
Halloween
hamburger
handicap(ped)
handicraft
handiwork
handkerchief(s)
handlebar
handwriting
happening
happier
happiest
happily
happiness
harassment
haversack
Hawaii
Hawaiian
hazardous

* * * *

habitation
handicapping

for a-r
see page 230

In this word 'a' is a neutral vowel.

habitual(ly)

In these words you can hear the vowel sound a as in cat

*

* *

* * *

* * * * [*]

impasse	il- or el- ?	il- or el- ?
intact	imagine(d)	imaginary
		imagination
in- or en- ?	im- or em- ?	imaginative
		immaculate
-Iran	inhabit(ed)	-impassable
-Iraq		implacable
	in- or en- ?	impractical
-Islam		
	-Iraqi	im- or em- ?
ix- or ex- ?		
	Islamic	inaccurate
		inadequate
	is- or es- ?	inflammable
		inflammatory
	Italian	inhabitant
	italic	inhabited
		inhabiting
	ix- or ex- ?	insanitary
		insanity
		intransitive
		in- or en- ?
		irrational(ly)
		ir- or er- ?
		is- or es- ?
		italicise(d)
		ze
		iv- or ev- ?
		ix- or ex- ?

for E . . .
see page 11

17

In these words you can hear the vowel sound a as in cat

J

*

jab(bed)
jack(ed)
*jam (fruit boiled
  with sugar /
  crush / block)
jammed
*jamb (side post of
  door or window)
jazz(ed)

* *

-giraffe

gymnast

jabber(ed)
jabbing
jackal
jackdaw
jacket
jack-knife
jagged
jamjar
jamming
jampot
jangle(d)
jangling
Japan
jasper

* * *

-gymkhana
  gymnastics

jaguar
jamboree
Japanese
javelin

* * * *

January

for a-r
see page 230

In these words the first letter 'a'
sounds like the 'a' in 'astonish'.

Jacuzzi   Jamaica

K

*

knack

for C . . .
see page 7

for Qu . . .
see page 24

* *

-khaki

knapsack

-Koran

* * *

kangaroo
-karate

* * * *

In these words the first letter 'a'
sounds like the 'a' in 'astonish'.

kaleidoscope   karate

In these words you can hear the vowel sound a as in cat

L

※

lack(ed)
*lacks (does lack)
lad
lag(ged)
lamb(ed)
lamp
-lance(d)
land
lap(ped)
Lapp
lash(es)
lashed
lass(es)
-last
latch(es)
latched
-laugh(ed)
*lax (slack)

※ ※

lacquer(ed)
ladder(ed)
lagging
lambing
lamp-post
lampshade
landed
landing
landlord
landmark
landscape
language
languid
languor
lanky(-ier,-iest)
lantern
Lapland
lapping
larynx
lasso(ed)
-lasted
-lather(ed)
Latin
latter
lattice(d)
-laughter
-lava
lavish(ed)

-llama

※ ※ ※

Labrador
lacerate
laminate
Lancashire
landlady(-ies)
landowner
lariat
lasagne
lateral(ly)
latitude
lavatory(-ies)
lavender
laxative

※ ※ ※ ※

laminated
laryngitis
laterally
lavatory(-ies)

legality

🌸 for a-r see page 231

In these words the first letter 'a' is a neutral vowel. It.. er... er... sounds like the 'a' in 'astonish'.

laboratory(-ies)   lament
laconic(ally)   lapel
lagoon   lasagne

In these words you can hear the vowel sound a as in cat

*	* *	* * *	* * * * [* *]
ma'am	mackerel	macabre	macaroni
mad(der,dest)	*Madam (English)	mackerel	magically
mall	*Madame (French)	mackintosh	magnesium
man(ned)	madden(ed)	Mademoiselle	magnetically
Manx	madder	magazine	magnetism
map(ped)	maddest	magical(ly)	magnificent
mash(ed)	madness	magistrate	maladjusted
-mask(ed)	maggot	magnetic(ally)	malnutrition
mass(es)	magic(ally)	magnetise(d)	manageable
massed	magma	ze	manageress(es)
-mast	*magnate (wealthy	magnetite	manifesto
*mat (small rug)	businessman)	magnify(-ies)	mannerism
match(es)	*magnet (iron which	(magnified)	manometer
matched	attracts iron)	magnitude	manually
*matt (not shiny)	malice	majesty(-ies)	manufacture(d)
	mallard	malleable	manufacturer
	mallet	management	manufacturing
	mammal	manager	marijuana
	mammoth	managing	marionette
	manage(d)	mandolin	masturbation
	mandrel	manganese	mathematical(ly)
	mangle(d)	manicure(d)	mathematician
	mangling	manifest	mathematics
	mango(es/s)	manifold	
	manhood	*mannequin (model)	mechanical(ly)
	mankind	*mannikin (dwarf)	menagerie
	*manner (way)	manslaughter	metabolism
	mannered	mantelpiece	
	manning	manual(ly)	miraculous
	*manor (large house	manuscript	
	with land)	marathon	morality(-ies)
	mansion	marigold	
	*mantel (frame round	mariner	
	fire)	maritime	
	*mantle (cloak)	mascara	
	manual(ly)	masculine	
	mapping	masquerade	
	marriage	massacre(d)	
	married	-masterpiece	
	marrow	-mastery	
	marry(-ies)	mastodon	
	(married)	masturbate	
	mascot	matador	
	massage(d)	matinee	
	masseur	maximum	
	masseuse		
	*massif (highlands)	meander(ed)	
	*massive (huge)	mechanic(ally)	
	-master(ed)	medallion	
	-see next page		
		Mohammed	
		molasses	

for a-r
see page 232

In these words you can hear the vowel sound a as in cat

* *

matches
matching
*matted (twisted in
  a thick mass)
matter
*mattered (did
  matter)
matting
mattress(es)

meringue

-morale
-moustache(d)

for a-r
see page 232

In these words the first letter 'a' is a neutral vowel.

'MAJESTIC' WORDS

machine(d)	mahogany	malaria	mama	maroon(ed)
machinery	majestic(ally)	Malaysia	manipulate	material(ly)
machinist	Majorca	malicious	manoeuvre(d)	mature(d)
magician	majority(-ies)	malignant	manure(d)	maturity

N

*

gnash(es)
gnashed
gnat

knack

nag(ged)
nap(ped)

* *

knapsack

nagging
nana
nanny(-ies)
napkin
napping
nappy(-ies)
narrow(ed)
-nasty

* * *

narrative
nasturtium
national(ly)
natural(ly)
naturalist
navigate

nomadic

* * * * [*]

nationality(-ies)
nationally
nationalism
naturalist
naturally
navigable
navigation
navigator

In these words the first letter 'a'
sounds like the 'a' in 'astonish'.
    narrate   nasturtium
    narrator   nativity

for a-r
see page 232

In these words you can hear the vowel sound a as in cat

✴

pack
*packed (tightly
    filled)
*pact (agreement)
pad(ded)
pal
-palm(ed)
pan(ned)
pang
pant
pants
-pass(es)
*-passed (went by)
*-past (time that
    has passed /
    beyond)
pat(ted)
patch(es)
patched
-path

plaid
plait
plan(ned)
plank(ed)
-plant

pram
-prance(d)
prank

-psalm

✴ ✴

package(d)
packet
packing
padded
padding
paddle(d)
paddling
paddock
paddy
padlock(ed)
pageant
palace
*palate (taste)
*palette (board for
    mixing colours)
*pallet (mattress /
    tool)
pally(-ier,-iest)
pampas
pamper(ed)
pamphlet
pancake
*panda (animal)
*pander(ed) to
    (encourage by bad
    example or taste)
panel(led)
panic
panicked
panning
pansy(-ies)
panther
panties
pantry(-ies)
parish(-es)
parrot
parry(-ies)
    (parried)
passage
-passing
passion
passive
-passport
-password
pasta
*pastel (crayon /
    soft colour)
*pastille (sweet)
-pasture(d)
pasty(-ies)
-see next page

✴ ✴ ✴

-Pakistan
Palestine
pancreas
panelling
panicking
pantograph
pantomime
parable
parachute
paradise
paradox(es)
paraffin
paragraph(ed)
parakeet
parallel(ed)
paralyse(d)
        ze
paranoid
parasite
parasol
paratroop
parody(-ies)
passageway
passenger
-passers-by
passionate
pasteurise(d)
        ze
-pastoral(ly)
patronage
patronise
        ze

pianist
piano(s)
-piranha

planetary
plantation
plasticine
platinum
platypus(es,-i)

practical(ly)
practising
protractor

-pyjamas

. ✴ ✴ ✴ ✴ [✴ ✴]

-Pakistani
palaeontologist/
paleontologist
palaeontology/
paleontology
panorama
papier-mâché
parabola
parallelogram
paralysis(-es)
paralytic
paramecium
paraphernalia
parasitical(ly)
pastorally
pathological(ly)
patronising

philatelist

pianoforte

planetary

practically

for a-r
see page 233

* *

patchwork
patchy(-ier,-iest)
patent
*patted (did pat)
patter
*pattered (did
    patter)
pattern(ed)
patting
patty(-ies)

perhaps

phantom

pianist
piano(s)

placard
placid
planet
plankton
planner
planning
-planted
-planter
-planting
plasma
-plaster(ed)
plastic
plateau
platen
platform
platter
-plaza

*practice (action)
*practise(d) (do or
    act / repeat for
    improvement)

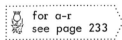
for a–r
see page 233

In these words the first letter 'a' is a neutral vowel.
It... er.... er.... er.... sounds like the 'a' in 'astonish'.

'PATHETIC' WORDS

| Pacific | papa | parenthesis(-es) | pathology(-ies) | patrolling |
| palatial(ly) | parade | pathetic(ally) | patrol(led) | pavilion |

*

quack(ed)

* *

quango(s)

* * *

* * * *

R

*

rack(ed)
-raft
rag(ged)
ram(med)
ramp
ran
-ranch(es)
rang
rank(ed)
*rap (knock)
*rapped (knocked)
*rapt (entranced)
rash(es)
-rasp(ed)
rat(ted)

*wrap (cover)
*wrapped (covered)

* *

rabbi
*rabbit (animal)
*racket (racquet /
   din / dishonest
   way of making
   money)
*racquet (bat with
   strings)
radish(es)
raffle(d)
-rafter
ragged
ragging
rally(-ies)
   (rallied)
ramble(d)
rambling
ramming
rampart
rancid
random
ransack(ed)
ransom(ed)
rapid
*rapping (knocking)
*rarebit (cheese
   on toast)
-rascal(ly)
rasher
-raspberry(-ies)
ratchet
-rather
ration(ed)
ratted
ratting
rattle(d)
rattling
ratty(-ier,-iest)

-see next page

* * *

rabbitted
rabbitting
radical(ly)
raffia
Ramadan
ramshackle
randomise(d)
         ze
rapidly
-raspberry(-ies)
rational(ly)
rattlesnake
ravenous

reaction
reactor
refraction
regatta

romantic(ally)

* * * * [*]

radically
Rastafarian
rationalise(d)
         ze
rationally
ravioli

reactionary(-ies)
reality(-ies)

romantically

for a-r
see page 233

In these words you can hear the vowel sound a as in cat

* *

react
refract
relax(es)
relaxed

romance(d)

for a-r
see page 233

wrangle(d)
wrangling
wrapper
*wrapping (covering)

In these words the 'a' is neutral.

raccoon/racoon
rapidity
ravine

S

*	* *	* * *	* * * * [*]
-psalm	chalet	ceramic	chandelier
	champagne		
*sac (pouch)	-charade	saccharine	sacrificial(ly)
*sack (large bag /	chassis	sacrifice(d)	salutary
plunder / dismiss		-safari	salutation
from a job)	sabbath	-Sahara	sanatorium
sack(ed)	sadden(ed)	-salami	sanctuary(-ies)
sad(der,dest)	sadder	salaried	sanitary
sag(ged)	saddest	salary(-ies)	sanitation
sand	saddle(d)	salutary	satisfaction
sang	sadly	salvation	satisfactory
sank	sagging	sanctify(-ies)	saturated
sash(es)	salad	(sanctified)	saturation
sat	salmon	sanctuary(-ies)	
	salvage(d)	sandpaper	Scandinavian
scab	-sample(d)	sandpiper	scantiest
scalp(ed)	-sampler	sanitary	
scamp	-sampling	sanity	-Somalia
scan	sanction	satellite	
*scanned (did scan)	sandal(led)	satisfy(-ies)	statically
*scant (hardly	sander	(satisfied)	statistician
enough)	sandstone	saturate	strangulation
scrap(ped)	sandwich(es)	Saturday	
scratch(es)	sandwiched	savanna	substantially
scratched	sapphire	saveloy	
-see next page	sapwood	saxophone	syllabically
	satchel		
	satin	scaffolding	
	satire		
	Saturn	-soprano(s)	
	savage(d)		
	Saxon	spatula	
	-see next page	-see next page	

for a-r
see page 234

In these words you can hear the vowel sound a as in cat

25

*

shack
-shaft
shag
shall
sham(med)
shank
shrank

slab(bed)
slack(ed)
slam(med)
slang
-slant
slap(ped)
slash(es)
slashed

smack(ed)
smash(es)
smashed

snack
snap(ped)
snatch(es)
snatched

spank(ed)
span
spanned
spat
splash(es)
splashed
sprang
sprat

stab(bed)
stack(ed)
-staff(ed)
stag
stamp(ed)
-stance
stand
[stood]
stank
strand
strap(ped)

swag
swam
swank(ed)

* *

scabbard
scabby
scaffold
scallop(ed)
scalpel
scamper(ed)
scanner
scanning
scanty(-ier,-iest)
scatter(ed)
scavenge(d)
scrabble
scrabbling
scraggy
scramble(d)
scrambling
scrapbook
scrapping
scrappy(-ier,-iest)
scrapyard
scratchy(-ier,-iest)

shabby(-ier,-iest)
shadow(ed)
shaggy(-ier,-iest)
shallow
shambles
shamming
shampoo(ed)
shamrock
shandy(-ies)
shanty(-ies)
shatter(ed)
shrapnel

slamming
slapping

smasher
smashing

snapping
snappy(-ier,-iest)

Spaniard
spaniel
Spanish
spanner
spanning
sparrow
spastic

-see next page

* * *

-staccato
stalactite
stalagmite
stamina
standardise(d)
            ze
statically
statuesque
stratagem
strategy(-ies)
stratosphere

substantial(ly)
subtracting
subtraction
-sultana

syllabic(ally)

for a-r
see page 234

In these words you can hear the vowel sound a as in cat

* *

stabbing
stagger(ed)
stagnant
stallion
stammer(ed)
stampede
standard
standing
standpoint
standstill
stanza
static(ally)
statue
stature
straggle(d)
straggling
stranded
strangle(d)
strangling
strapping
-stratum(strata)

subtract
-surpass(ed)

swagger(ed)

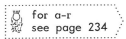

for a-r
see page 234

In these words the first letter 'a'
is a neutral vowel. It.. er... er...
sounds like the 'a' in 'astonish'.

safari   saloon   statistics
Sahara   salute   statistically
salami   samosa   strategic(ally)
salinity   satirical(ly)
saliva   spaghetti

In these words you can hear the vowel sound a as in cat

tab	tabby(-ies)	tabulate	tabulation
tack	tableau	tactfully	tabulator
*tacked (did tack)	tablet	taffeta	tachometer
*tacks (more than	tackle(d)	tambourine	Tanzania
one tack)	tackling	tangerine	tapioca
*tact (skill in	tacky(-ier,-iest)	tangible	tarantula
putting things	tactful(ly)	tantalise(d)	Tasmania
to people)	tactics	ze	
tag(ged)	tactless	tapestry(-ies)	theatrical(ly)
tan(ned)	tadpole	taxation	
tank	tagging	taxpayer	tobacconist
tap(ped)	talcum		
-task	talent	thankfully	trafficator
*tax(es) (money	tally(-ies)		tragically
taken by	(tallied)	tobacco(s)	trampolining
government)	tamper(ed)	-tomato(es)	tranquillity
taxed	tampon		tranquilliser
	tangent	trafficker	zer
than	tangle(d)	trafficking	transatlantic
thank(ed)	tangling	tragedy(-ies)	transferable
that	tango(s)	tragically	transformation
thatch(es)	tangoed	trampoline(d)	transistorised
thatched	tankard	tranquilly	zed
that's	tanker	transaction	transitional(ly)
*thrash(es) (beat)	tanner	transcription	transitory
thrashed	tanning	transferring	transmutation
*thresh(es) (beat	tantrum	transformer	transparency(-ies)
corn)	tappet	transfusion	transpiration
threshed	tapping	transistor	transportation
	tariff	transition	transubstantiation
track	tarry(-ies)	transitive	
*track(ed) (did	(tarried)	transitory	tyrannical(ly)
track)	tassel(led)	translation	tyrannosaurus
*tract (pamphlet)	tattered	translator	
tram	tattoo(ed)	translucent	
tramp(ed)	tavern	transmission	
-trance	taxi(s)	transmitted	
trap(ped)		transmitter	
trash	thankful(ly)	transmitting	
	that'd	transparent	
twang(ed)	that'll	transversal	
		transvestite	
	tracksuit	trapezoid	
	traction	traveller	
	tractor	travelling	
	traffic		
	trafficked		
	tragic(ally)		
	trample(d)		
	trampling		
	-see next page		

for a-r
see page 235

In these words you can hear the vowel sound a as in cat

* *

tranquil(ly)
*transact (make a
  deal)
transcribe(d)
*transect (cut
  across)
transept
transfer(red)
transfix(es)
transfixed
transform(ed)
transit
translate
transmit(ted)
transpire(d)
transplant
transport
transpose(d)
transverse
trapper
trapping
trappings
travel(led)
traverse(d)

for a-r
see page 235

In these words the 'a' is neutral.

tattoo(ed)   trajectory(-ies)
trachea   trapeze
traditional(ly)

V

*

van
valve(d)
-vase
-vast
vat

* *

vaccine
vacuum(ed)
valiant
valid
valley
value(d)
vampire
vandal
vanish(es)
vanished
vanquish(es)
vanquished
-vantage

* * *

vacillate
vaccinate
valentine
valiant
validate
valium
valuable
vandalise(d)
vanity(-ies)
vaseline
Vatican

verandah

-vibrato

* * * * [*]

vacillation
vaccination
validation
valuable
valuation
vandalism

vocabulary(-ies)

vulgarity(-ies)

for a-r
see page 235

In these words the
first 'a' is neutral.

vacate
vacation
validity
vanilla
variety(-ies)

In these words you can hear the vowel sound a as in cat

W

*

wag(ged)
wax(ed)

whack(ed)

*wrap (cover)
*wrapped (covered)
-wrath

* *

wagging
waggle(d)
wagon
wagtail

wrangle(d)
wrangling
wrapper
*wrapping (covering)

* * *

* * * *

Y

*

yank(ed)
yap(ped)

* *

yapping

* * *

* * * *

for a-r
see page 235

Z

*

* *

* * *

Zambia

-Zimbabwe

* * * *

In these words you can hear the vowel sound a as in cat

✳

✳ ✳

✳ ✳ ✳

✳ ✳ ✳ ✳ [✳]

abreast

*accept (take
   something offered)

address(es)
addressed

*affect (alter)

again
against

ahead

amend

annexe(d)
any

arrest

ascend
*ascent (climb)
*assent (agree)
assess(es)
assessed

attempt
attend

avenge(d)

acceptance
accepting

adventure

aesthetic(ally)

affected
affection

agenda
aggression
aggressive
aggressor

allegro
already

amendment

anyhow
anyone
anything
anyway
anywhere

appendix(-ces)
apprentice(d)

ascension
assemble(d)
assembly(-ies)
assessment

attempted
*attendance (those
   present / rate of
   attending)
attendant
*attendants (servants)
attended
attention
attentive

authentic(ally)

accelerate
acceleration
accelerator
acceptable
accessory(-ies)
acetylene

adrenalin
adventurous

aesthetically

affectionate
affectionately

America
American

anemone
anybody

appendicitis
apprenticeship

authentically

 for e-r
see page 242

   *

bed(ded)
beg(ged)
*bell (instrument)
*belle (beauty)
belt
bench(es)
bend
[bent]
best
bet(ted)
[bet]

bled
blend
bless(es)
blessed
[blest]

*bread (food)
*breadth (width)
breast
*breath (air passing
  in and out of
  lungs)
*bred (produced
  young / reared)

   * *

beckon(ed)
bedding
bedrock
bedroom
bedside
bedtime
befell
befriend
beggar
begging
behead
beheld
Belgian
Belgium
bellow(ed)
belly(-ies)
bending
benzene
bereft
*beret (flat, round
  cap)
*berry(-ies) (fruit)
beset
[beset]
betted
better
betting
bevel(led)
beverage

blessed
blessing

breakfast
breastbone
breathless
brethren

*bury(-ies) (place
  deep down)
  (buried)

   * * *

benefit(ed)
besetting
bevelling
beverage

breathalyse(d)
breathtaking

burial

   * * * * [*]

beneficial(ly)
benefited
benefiting
benevolent

breathalyser

In these words the first letter 'e'
is pronounced like the 'i' in 'pig'.

'BENEVOLENT' WORDS

became	behave(d)	beseech(es)
because	behaviour	beseeched
become	behead	[besought]
[became]	beheld	beset(ting)
[become]	behind	[beset]
becoming	behold	beside
befall	[beheld]	besides
[befell]	belief	besiege(d)
[befallen]	believe(d)	bestow(ed)
before(hand)	belong(ed)	betray(ed)
befriend	belonging	between
begin	beloved	betwixt
[began]	below	beware
[begun]	beneath	bewilder(ed)
beginner	benevolent	bewitch(es)
beginning	bereave(d)	bewitched
behalf	bereft	beyond

---

for e-r
see page 243

In these words you can hear the vowel sound e as in elephant

✼

*cell (unit)
*cent (money / hundred)
*cents (money)

ce- or se- ?

*check(ed) (stop / test)
chef
*cheque (order to bank)
chess
chest

clef
cleft
cleanse(d)
clench(es)
clenched

crept
cress(es)
crest

kelp
kept
ketch(es)

for Qu ...
see page 47

✼ ✼

cadet
caress(es)
cassette

*cellar (underground storage room)
cello(s)
Celtic
cement
*censer (pan for burning incense)
*censor(judge of what may not be published)
census(es)
centaur
central(ly)
centre

ce- or se- ?

checking
chemist
cherish(es)
cherished
cherry(-ies)
chestnut

cleansing
clever

collect
commence(ed)
compel(led)
compress(es)
compressed
condemn(ed)
condense(d)
confess(es)
confessed
connect
consent
contempt
contend
content
contest
correct

credit(ed)
crescent
crevice
-see next page

✼ ✼ ✼

celandine
celebrate
celery
celestial
cellophane
cellular
celluloid
cellulose
Celsius
cemetery(-ies)
censorship
centigrade
centipede
centrally
century(-ies)
cerebral
cerebrum

ce- or se- ?

chemical(ly)
chemistry

cleanliness

collecting
collection
collective
collector
compelling
complexion
compression
compressor
concentric
conception
concession
condenser
confession
confessor
confetti
conjecture(d)
connected
connecting
connection
connector
consensus
contestant
contention
convention
corrected
correction
correctly
-see next page

✼ ✼ ✼ [✼ ✼]

celebrated
celebration
celebrity(-ies)
celestial
centenary(-ies)
centimetre
centrifugal(ly)
centurion
cerebellum
ceremonial(ly)
ceremony(-ies)

ce- or se- ?

chemically
cholesterol

commemorate
commemoration
competitive
competitor
confectioner
confectionery
confessional
congenital(ly)
consecutive
contemporary(-ies)
contemptible
contemptuous
conventional(ly)

crematorium

Czechoslovakia

for e-r
see page 244

33

In these words you can hear the vowel sound e as in elephant

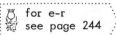
※ ※

kennel
kestrel
ketchup
kettle

※ ※ ※

credible
credited
creditor
crescendo(s)

> In these words the first letter 'e'
> is pronounced like the 'i' in 'pig'.
>
> | | | |
> |---|---|---|
> | celestial | cremate | crescendo(s) |
> | cement | cremation | crevasse |

for e-r
see page 244

D

※	※ ※	※ ※ ※	※ ※ ※ ※ [※ ※]
dead	deaden(ed)	deafening	decimetre
deaf	deadly	debited	declaration
dealt	deafen(ed)	December	decorated
death	debit(ed)	deception	dedication
debt	debris	deceptive	definitely
deck(ed)	debtor	decimal	definition
den	debut/début	decorate	delegation
*dense (closely	*decade (ten years)	dedicate	delicacy(-ies)
packed / stupid)	deckchair	defective	democratic(ally)
dent	defect	defector	demonstration
*dents (more than	defence	defendant	dependable
one dent)	defend	defender	dependency(-ies)
depth	deflect	defensive	deprivation
desk	delta	deflection	derivation
	deluge(d)	definite	designated
dread(ed)	denim	delegate	desolation
dreamt	Denmark	delicate	desperation
dredge(d)	dental	democrat	destination
dregs	dentist	demonstrate	devastation
drench(es)	depend	density(-ies)	developer
drenched	depot	*dependant (person	developing
dress(es)	depress(es)	who depends)	development
dressed	depressed	*dependants (people	
	derrick	who depend)	digestible
dwell(ed)	descant	depended	directory(-ies)
[dwelt]	descend	*dependence (reliance)	
	*descent (way down)	*dependent (relying /	-see next page
	desert	hanging)	
	desperate	depression	
	detect	depressive	
	detest	deputy(-ies)	
	devil(led)		
	-see next page	-see next page	

for e-r
see page 245

In these words you can hear the vowel sound **e** as in **elephant**

☆ ☆	☆ ☆ ☆	☆ ☆ ☆ ☆ [☆]
digest	derelict	domestically
direct	descendant	domesticate
dispense(d)	descended	
*dissent	designate	dyslexia
(disagreement)	desolate	
distress(es)	desperate	
distressed	destiny(-ies)	
	destitute	
dreaded	detection	
dreadful(ly)	detective	
dredger	detector	
dredging	detention	
dresser	*deterrence (prevention	
dressing	by causing fear)	
	deterrent	
dwelling	*deterrents (more than	
	one deterrent)	
	devastate	
	develop(ed)	
	digestion	
	dilemma	
	dimension	
	directed	
	direction	
	directive	
	directly	
	director	
	discretion	
	displeasure	
	distressing	
	domestic(ally)	
	dreadfully	
	dyslexic	

In these words the first letter 'e' is pronounced like the 'i' in 'pig'.

'DELIGHTFUL' WORDS

debate	deficient	depend(ed)	desire(d)	detain(ed)	deterrent
decamp(ed)	define(d)	dependable	despair(ed)	detect(ion)	deterring
decay(ed)	deflation	dependant	despatch(es)	detective	detest
decease(d)	deflect(ion)	dependants	despatched	detector	detract
deceit	deform(ed)	dependence	despise(d)	detention	develop(ed)
deceive(d)	defy(-ies)	dependency(-ies)	despite	deter(red)	developer
December	(defied)	dependent	dessert	detergent	developing
deception	degree	deport	destroy(ed)	deteriorate	development
deceptive	delay(ed)	deposit(ed)	destroyer	deterioration	device
decide	delete	depositing	destruction	determination	devise(d)
deciduous	deliberate(ly)	depreciate	destructive	determine(d)	devote(d)
decipher(ed)	delicious	depreciation	detach(es)	determining	devotion
decision	delight(ed)	depress(es)	detached	deterrence	devour(ed)
decisive	delightful(ly)	depressed			
declare(d)	delirious	depression			
decline(d)	deliver(ed)	depressive			
decree(d)	deliverance	deprive(d)			
decry(-ies)	delivery(-ies)	derail(ed)			
(decried)	demand(ed)	derivative			
deduce(d)	democracy(-ies)	derive(d)			
deduction	demobbed	descend(ed)			
deductive	demolish(es)	descendant			
defeated	demolished	descent			
defect(or)	denial	describe(d)			
defective	denomination	describing			
defence	denominator	description			
defend(ant)	denote	descriptive			
defender	denounce(d)	desert(ed)			
defensive	deny(-ies)	deserve(d)			
defiance	(denied)	design(ed)			
defiant	depart(ure)	designer			
deficiency(-ies)	department	desirable			

for e-r
see page 245

*	* *	* * *	* * * * [* * * *]
ebb(ed)	any	aesthetic(ally)	aesthetically
edge(d)	echo(ed)	anyhow	anybody
		anyone	
egg(ed)	eddy(-ies)	anything	eccentrically
	(eddied)	anyway	economical(ly)
elf(-ves)	edging	anywhere	economics
elm	edit(ed)		ecstatically
else		eccentric(ally)	ecumenical(ly)
	effect	ecstasy(-ies)	
end	effort	ecstatic(ally)	editorial(ly)
		Ecuador	educated
etch(es)	eject	eczema	education
etched			educational(ly)
	elbow(ed)	edible	Edwardian
	elder	edited	
	eldest	editor	effectively
	elect	educate	effervescence
	elsewhere		effervescent
		effective	
	ember	effervesce(d)	electoral(ly)
	emblem	effigy(-ies)	electorate
	empire		electrical(ly)
	empress(es)	ejection	electricity
	empty(-ies)	ejector	electrocute
			electrolysis
	em- or im-	elderly	electrolyte
		election	electrolytic(ally)
	ending	electors	electromagnetic(ally)
	endless	electric(ally)	electronic(ally)
	engine	electrode	elementary
	enter(ed)	electron	elevated
	entrance	elegance	elevation
	entry(-ies)	elegant	eligible
	envy(-ies)	element	elocution
	(envied)	elephant	
	enzyme	elevate	el- or il- ?
		eleven(th)	
	en- or in- ?	eloquent	embryonic(ally)
		-see next page	emigration
	erect		empirical(ly)
	errand		
	error		em- or im- ?
			-see next page
	escort		
	esquire		
	essay		
	essence		
	-see next page		

See also E on page 65

for H ... see page 40

for I ... see page 41

for e-r see page 245

In these words you can hear the vowel sound e as in elephant

* *

etching
ethics
ethnic(ally)

et- or it- ?

event
ever
every

excel(led)
*except (not
    including)
*excerpt (selected
    passage)
excess(es)
exempt
exhale(d)
exhort
exile
exit
expect
expel(led)
expense
expert
exploit
export
express(es)
expressed
extend
extent
extra
extract

See also E
on page 65

for H ...
see page 40

for I ...
see page 41

* * *

embedded
embellish(es)
embellished
embezzle(d)
embryo(s)
emerald
emery
emigrate
eminence
eminent
emperor
emphasis
emphasise(d)
        ze

em- or im- ?

endeavour(ed)
endocrine
enemy(-ies)
energy(-ies)
engineer(ed)
entering
enterprise
entertain(ed)
envelope
envious

en- or in- ?

epilogue
episode
epithet

equinox(es)

erection

escalate
escapade
Eskimo(s)
esplanade
essential(ly
estimate
estuary(-ies)

ethical(ly)
ethnical(ly)
etiquette
-see next page

* * * [* * *]

energetic(ally)
engineering
entertainment
entertainer

en- or in- ?

epicyclic(ally)
epidemic(ally)
epilepsy(-ies)
epileptic(ally)

equatorial(ly)
equilibrium
escalator
especially
essentially
estimated
estimation

ethically
ethnically
etymological(ly)
etymology

eventually
everlasting
everybody

excavation
excellency(-ies)
exceptionally
exclamation
execution
executive
exemplary
exhibition
exhortation
-see next page

for e-r
see page 245

In these words you can hear the vowel sound e as in elephant.

In these words the first letter 'e' is pronounced like the 'i' in 'pig'.

'EFFECTIVE' WORDS

ecclesiastical(ly)	endorse(d)	excelling
eclipse(d)	endow(ed)	except(ionally)
ecology	endurance	excess(es)
edition	endure(d)	excessive
effect(ively)	enfold	exchange(d)
efficient	enforce(d)	exchequer
Egyptian	enforcement	excite(d)
eject(ion)	engage(d)	excitedly
ejector	engagement	excitement
elaborate	engrave(d)	exciting
elaboration	engraving	exclaim(ed)
elastic(ally)	engulf(ed)	exclamation
elasticity	enjoy(ed)	exclude
elect(ion)	enjoying	exclusion
elector(ate)	enjoyment	exclusive(ly)
electoral(ly)	enlarge(d)	excretion
electrical(ly)	enlighten(ed)	excuse(d)
electricity	enlist	excursion
electrocute	enquire(d)	exemplary
electrode	enquiry(-ies)	exempt
electrolysis	enormous	exert(ion)
electrolyte	enough	exhaust(ed)
electrolytic(ally)	enrage(d)	exhaustion
electromagnetic(ally)	enrich(es)	exhibit(ed)
electron	enriched	exhibiting
electronic(ally)	enrol(led)	exist(ed)
eleven(th)	enrolment	existence
elicit(ed)	enslave(d)	exotic(ally)
eliciting	ensure(d)	expandable
eliminate	entangle(d)	expand(ed)
elimination	enthusiasm	expanding
Elizabethan	enthusiastic(ally)	expansion
ellipse	entire(ly)	expansive
elliptical(ly)	entitle(d)	expect(ed)
elope(d)	entrancing	expectant(ly)
elusive	entrust	expel(led)
emancipate	enumerate	expelling
emancipation	environment(ally)	expenditure
embankment	envisage(d)	expense
embark(ed)	equality	expensive
embarrass(es)	equation	experience(d)
embarrassed	equator	experiment(ally)
embarrassing	equip(ped)	explain(ed)
embarrassment	equipment	explaining
embedded	equipping	explanatory
embedding	equivalence	explicit
embellish(es)	equivalent	explode
embellished	erase(d)	explore(d)
embellish(es)	eraser	explorer
embellished	erect(ion)	exploring
embezzle(d)	erode	explosion
embroider(ed)	erosion	explosive
embroidery	erotic(ally)	exponent
emerge(d)	erratic(ally)	export
emergence	erupt(ed)	expose(d)
emergency(-ies)	eruption	exposure
emission	escape(d)	express(es)
emit(ted)	escarpment	expressed
emitter	especially	expressing
emitting	essential(ly)	expression
emotional(ly)	establish(es)	expressive
emotive	established	exquisite
empirical(ly)	establishment	extend(ed)
employ(ed)	estate	extending
employee	estrange(d)	extension
employer	eternal(ly)	extensive
employment	evacuate	extent
emulsion(ed)	evacuation	exterior
enable(d)	evacuee	exterminate
enabling	evade	external(ly)
enact	evaluate	extinct(ion)
enamel(led)	evaluation	extinguish(ed)
enamelling	evaporate	extinguisher
enamour(ed)	evaporation	extract(ion)
encamp(ed)	evasion	extractor
encase(d)	event	extraordinarily
enchant(ing)	eventual(ly)	extraordinary
encircle(d)	evict	extrapolate
enclose(d)	evolve(d)	extravagance
enclosure	exact(ly)	extravagant
encounter(ed)	exaggerate	extravaganza
encourage(d)	exaggeration	extreme(ly)
encouragement	exalt(ed)	extrusion
encyclopedia	examination	exuberance
endanger(ed)	examine(d)	exuberant
endear(ed)	example	
endearment	exceed(ingly)	
endeavour(ed)	excel(led)	

eventual(ly)
evergreen
everyone
everything
everywhere
evidence
evident

excavate
excellence
excellent
excelling
exception
excessive
exchequer
execute
exemption
*exercise (practice / use)
*exercise(d) (take exercise / use)
*exorcise(d) (cast out devil)
expectant
expected
expelling
expensive
expressing
expression
expressive
exquisite
extended
extending
extension
extensive
external(ly)

expectantly
expectation
expedition
expenditure
experiment
experimental(ly)
explanation
exploitation
exploration
exponential(ly)
exposition
externally

for e-r
see page 245

See also E
on page 65

for H ...
see page 40

for I ...
see page 41

In these words you can hear the vowel sound e as in elephant

F

*

fed
fell
*fell(ed) (cut down)
*felt (did feel /
    type of cloth)
fend
fence(d)
fetch(es)
fetched

fleck(ed)
fled
flesh(ed)
flex(es)
flexed

French
fresh
fret(ted)
friend

phlegm

* *

feather
feldspar
fellow
ferment
ferret(ed)
ferry(-ies)
   (ferried)
fester(ed)
festive
fetter(ed)

fledgeling/fledgling
Flemish

foretell
forget
forwent/forewent

freckles
Frenchman
fretsaw
fretted
fretting
friendly
friendship

pheasant

* * *

February
federal(ly)
fellowship
feminine
ferreted
ferreting
festival

fiesta

flexible
fluorescent

forgetful(ly)
forgetting

freshwater

phonetic(ally)

> for th ...
> see page 52

* * * *

February
federally
federation
festivity(-ies)

flexibility

forgetfully

phonetically

> for e-r
> see page 246

> In these words the
> letter 'e' sounds
> like the 'i' in 'pig'.
>
> ferocious
> ferocity

G

*

gem
get
[got]

glen

guess
*guessed (did guess)
*guest (person
    invited)

jest
jet(ted)

> In this word the
> 'e' sounds like
> 'a' in 'astonish'.
>
> guerilla/guerrilla

* *

gazelle

general(ly)
generous
gentle
gently
gesture(d)
getting

ghetto(es/s)

jealous
jelly(-ies)
   (jellied)
jemmy(-ies)
jester
jetted
jetty(-ies)

* * *

general(ly)
generalise(d)
generate
generous
genetic(ally)
gentleman
gentlemen
genuine
gestation

jealousy(-ies)
jellyfish
jettison(ed)

> In these words the first 'e'
> has a short 'i' sound.
>
> genetic(ally)
> geranium

* * * * [* *]

generalisation
    zation
generalise(d)
    ze
generally
generation
generator
generosity
genetically
gesticulate

> for e-r
> see page 246

In these words you can hear the vowel sound **e** as in **elephant**

✲

head
health
hedge(d)
held
hell
helm
help(ed)
hem(med)
hemp
hen
hence
Herr

✲ ✲

head-dress(es)
headed
heading
headlamp
headland
headlight
headline(d)
headphones
healthy(-ier,-iest)
heather
heaven
heavy(-ier,-iest)
heckle(d)
heckling
hectare
hectic(ally)
hedgehog
hedgerow
hedging
hefty(-ier,-iest)
heifer
hello
helmet(ed)
helper
helpful(ly)
helping
helpless
hemming
henceforth
herald
heron
herring
herself

himself

✲ ✲ ✲

haematite/hematite
haemorrhage/
hemorrhage(d)
headmaster
headmistress(es)
headquarters
headwaters
healthier
healthiest
heavier
heaviest
heavily
hectically
helical(ly)
helmeted
helpfully
hemisphere
heraldry
heritage
*heroin (drug)
*heroine (female hero)
hesitate
hexagon

hysterics

✲ ✲ ✲ ✲ [✲]

hectically
helically
helicopter
helter-skelter
hereditary
heredity
heroism
hesitation
hexagonal(ly)

hysterically

for e-r
see page 247

In this word the letter 'e'
sounds like the 'i' in 'pig'.

heroic(ally)

In these words you can hear the vowel sound e as in **elephant**

☆ ☆

if- or ef- ?

ij- or ej- ?

il- or el- ?

immense
impel(led)
impress(es)
impressed

im- or em- ?

incense(d)
indent
infect
inject
inspect
instead
intend
*intense (extreme)
intent
*intents (purposes)
invent
invest

ir- or er- ?

is- or es- ?

itself

iv- or ev- ?

ix- or ex- ?

☆ ☆ ☆

ic- or ec- ?

if- or ef- ?

ij- or ej- ?

il- or el- ?

impeller
impelling
impregnate
impression
impressive

im- or em- ?

incessant
indented
indenture(d)
infection
infectious
inherent
inherit(ed)
injection
inspection
inspector
intensive
intention
intestine
invention
inventive
inventor
investment
investor

in- or en- ?

is- or es- ?

iv- or ev- ?

ix- or ex- ?

☆ ☆ ☆ ☆ [☆ ☆]

ic- or ec- ?

if- or ef- ?

illegible

il- or el- ?

immensity
impeccable
imperative
impregnable
impressionism
impressionist

incredible
indefinitely
inedible
inevitable
inflexible
inheritance
inherited
inheriting
insecticide
insensitive
integrity
intelligence
intelligent
intensify(-ies)
  (intensified)
intensity(-ies)
intentional(ly)
interrogate
interrogation
investigate
investigation
investigator

irregular
irregularity(-ies)

is- or es- ?

iv- or ev- ?

ix- or ex- ?

for E . . .
see page 36

for e-r
see page 247

In these words you can hear the vowel sound **e** as in **elephant**

J

*	* *	* * *	* * * * [* *]
gem	general(ly)	general(ly)	generalisation
	generous	generalise(d)	zation
jest	gentle	ze	generalise(d)
jet(ted)	gently	generate	ze
	gesture(d)	generous	generally
		genetic(ally)	generation
	jealous	gentleman	generator
	jelly(-ies)	gentlemen	genetically
	(jellied)	genuine	gesticulate
	jemmy(-ies)	gestation	
	jester		
	jetted	jealousy(-ies)	
	jetty(-ies)	jellyfish	
		jettison(ed)	

for e-r
see page 248

K

*	* *	* * *	* * * *
kelp	kennel		
kept	kestrel		
ketch(es)	ketchup		
	kettle		
knelt			

for C ...
see page 33

for e-r
see page 248

for Qu ...
see page 47

In these words you can hear the vowel sound **e** as in **elephant**

L

*

*lead (metal)
*leant (did lean)
leapt
*led (showed/shown
  the way)
ledge
left
leg(ged)
lend
*[lent] (did lend)
Lent
length
lens(es)
less
let
[let]
let's

* *

lament
lapel

leather(ed)
lecture(d)
legend
leggings
leisure(d)
lemon
leopard
leper
*lessen(ed) (make
  less)
lesser
*lesson (period of
  instruction)
letter(ed)
letting
lettuce
level(led)
levy(-ies)
levied

* * *

Lebanese
Lebanon
lecturer
legendary
legislate
lemonade
leprechaun
leprosy
lesbian
letterbox(es)
lettering
levelling

lieutenant

* * * *

legendary
legislation
levitation

for e-r
see page 248

In these words the first letter 'e'
is pronounced like the 'i' in 'pig'.

legality   legitimate

In these words you can hear the vowel sound e as in elephant

*	* *	* * *	* * * * [* *]
meant	many	majestic(ally)	majestically
melt			
[molten]	meadow	measurement	mechanism
men	measure(d)	measuring	medically
mend	*medal (award /	medical(ly)	medication
mesh(es)	memento)	megaphone	medieval
meshed	*meddle(d) (interfere)	megaton	mediterranean
mess(es)	*meddler (person who	melody(-ies)	melancholy
messed	interferes)	membership	Melanesia
met	meddling	memento(es/s)	memorable
	medicine	memorable	memorandum
	*medlar (fruit)	memorise(d)	menstruation
	medley	ze	mentality(-ies)
	mellow(ed)	memory(-ies)	metabolism
	melon	meniscus(es/-i)	metallurgy
	melted	menstruate(d)	metamorphic
	melting	mentally	metamorphosis(-es)
	member	merrily	methylated
	membrane	merriment	metrically
	memoirs	mesmerise(d)	metropolitan
	menace(d)	ze	
	mental(ly)	messenger	molecular
	mention(ed)	metaphor	
	menu	metrical(ly)	
	merit(ed)	metronome	
	merry	Mexican	
	message	Mexico	
	messieux		
	messy(-ier,-iest)	momentum	
	*metal(led) (mineral		
	substance)		
	method		
	metric(ally)		
	*mettle (courage)		

misdealt
misled
misspell(ed)
[misspelt]
misspend
[misspent]

🌹 for e-r
see page 249

In these words the first letter 'e'
is pronounced like the 'i' in 'pig'.

mechanic(ally)	memento(es/s)	meridian
melodic(ally)	memorial	meticulous
melodious	meniscus(es/-i)	mnemonic

In these words you can hear the vowel sound e as in elephant

N

*	* *	* * *	* * * * [*]
knelt	necklace	nebula	necessarily
	nectar	nebulous	necessary
neck(ed)	neglect	necessary	necessity(-ies)
nest	nephew	negative	neglectfully
net(ted)	nestle(d)	neglectful(ly)	negligible
next	nestling	Netherlands	nevertheless
	netball		
	netted	November	
	netting		
	nettle(d)		
	network(ed)		
	never		

for e-r see page 249

In these words the first letter 'e' is pronounced like the 'i' in 'pig'.

necessity(-ies)	neglectful(ly)
negation	negotiate

O

*	* *	* * *	* * * * [*]
	object	already	authentically
	obsess(es)		
	obsessed	authentic(ally)	objectionable
			obsessional(ly)
	offence	objection	
	offend	objective	
	oppress(es)	obsession	
	oppressed	obsessive	
		offensive	
		oppression	
		oppressive	
		oppressor	

for e-r see page 249

In these words you can hear the vowel sound e as in elephant

✲

✲ ✲

✲ ✲ ✲

✲ ✲ ✲ ✲ [✲ ✲]

peck(ed)
peg(ged)
pelt
pen(ned)
pence
pest
pet(ted)

phlegm

pledge(d)

press(es)
pressed

peasant
pebble
*pedal (foot lever)
pedalled
*peddle(d) (carry and
   try to sell)
peddler
peddling
pegboard
pegging
pellet
penance
pencil(led)
pendant
penguin
pennant
penning
penny(-ies)
pension(ed)
pepper(ed)
perfect
peril
perish(es)
perished
perplex(es)
perplexed
pester(ed)
pestle
petal(led)
*petrel (sea-bird)
*petrol (fuel)
petting

pheasant

pleasant
pleasure
pledging
plenty

possess(es)
possessed
-see next page

pathetic(ally)

pedalling
pedestal
pedigree
pelican
penalty(-ies)
pendulum
penetrate
penniless
pensioner
pentagon
peppermint
percentage
perception
perceptive
perceptual(ly)
perfection
perilous
periscope
perpetual(ly)
perplexing
perspective
pessimist
petrify(-ies)
   (petrified)
petticoat

phonetic(ally)

plentiful(ly)

possession
possessive
potential(ly)

*precedence (priority)
precedent
*precedents (previous
   examples)
precipice
predator
predatory
predicate
preferably
preference
pregnancy(-ies)
prejudice(d)
premature
premier
-see next page

parenthesis(-es)
pathetically

pedestrian
penetration
penicillin
*peninsula (land
   almost surrounded
   by water)
*peninsular (of/like a
   peninsula)
perceptually
perennial(ly)
perishable
perpetually
pessimistic(ally)

phonetically

pleasurable
plentifully

potentially

predatory
preferably
preparation
preposition
prepositional(ly)
presentable
presentation
preservation
presidential(ly)
professional(ly)

pterodactyl

for e-r
see page 250

In these words you can hear the vowel sound e as in elephant

** **

precious
preference
pregnant
prelude
premier
*presence (being present)
present
*presents (gifts)
pressing
pressure(d)
prestige
pretence
pretend
prevent
profess(es)
professed
progress(es)
progressed
project
propel(led)
prospect
protect
protest

*** ***

presented
presenting
presently
president
pretended
prevalent
prevention
preventive
procession
profession
professor
progression
progressive
projectile
projection
projector
propelling
propeller
prospective
prospector
prospectus(es)
protected
protection
protective
protector

 for e-r see page 250

In these words the first letter 'e' sounds like the 'i' in 'pig'.

'PHENOMENAL' WORDS

peculiar
pedestrian
peninsula
peninsular
perimeter
petition(ed)
petroleum
phenomena

phenomenal(ly)
phenomenon
precaution
precede(d)
preceding
precipitate
precipitation
precise(ly)

precision
precocious
predict(ion)
predictable
predominantly
prefer(red)
preferring
preliminary(-ies)

prepare(d)
preparing
prescribe(d)
prescription
present(ed)
presentable
presenting
preserve(d)

preside
presumably
presume(d)
pretence
pretend(ed)
prevail(ed)
prevent(ion)
preventive

*

quell(led)
quench(es)
quenched
quest

** **

quelling
question(ed)
quintet

*** ***

questionnaire

**** ****

questionable

In these words you can hear the vowel sound e as in elephant

47

*	* *	* * *	* * * * [* *]
*read (looked at and understood)	ready(-ier,-iest)	readier	receptacle
realm	rebel(led)	readiest	recitation
*red (colour)	recess(es)	readily	recognition
rend	recessed	readiness	recollection
[rent]	reckon(ed)	rebelling	recommendation
rent	record	rebellion	recreation
*rest (repose / ones left over)	rector	rebellious	rectangular
*retch(es) (try to vomit)	redden(ed)	reception	referendum
retched	redder	receptive	regimental(ly)
	reddest	recession	registration
wreck(ed)	reddish	recessive	regretfully
wren	redskin	recipe	regularity(-ies)
wrench(es)	redwood	recognise(d)	regularly
wrenched	reference	ze	regulation
*wrest (seize)	reflect	recollect	relatively
*wretch(es) (unhappy creature)	refresh(es)	recommend	relativity(-ies)
	refreshed	reconcile(d)	relegation
	refuge	rectangle	remembering
	reggae	rectify(-ies) (rectified)	reminiscence
	regret(ted)	rectory(-ies)	reminiscent
	reject	referee	repetition
	relent	reference(d)	repetitive
	relic	reflected	representation
	remnant	reflection	representative
	render(ed)	reflector	represented
	rental	reflexive	representing
	repel(led)	refreshment	reputation
	repent	refugee	resentfully
	reptile	regiment	reservation
	request	register(ed)	residential
	rescue	registrar	resignation
	*resent (feel angry at)	registry(-ies)	resolution
	resin	regretful(ly)	respectable
	respect	regretted	respectfully
	rested	regretting	respectively
	resting	regular	respiration
	restless	regulate	respiratory
	revenge(d)	rejection	restoration
	reverence	relative	revelation
	*reverend (deserving respect)	relegate	revolution
	*Reverend (title)	relentless	revolutionary(-ies)
	*reverent (feeling or showing reverence)	relevance	
		relevant	
		remedy(-ies) (remedied)	
	rosette	remember(ed)	
		remembrance	
	wreckage	Renaissance	
	wrestle(d)	-see next page	
	wrestler		
	wrestling		
	wretched		

for e-r
see page 251

In these words you can hear the vowel sound e as in elephant

> **In these words the first letter 'e' is pronounced like the 'i' in 'pig'.**
>
> 'REFRESHING' WORDS
>
> | | | |
> |---|---|---|
> | react(ion) | regard(ed) | republic(an) |
> | reactionary(-ies) | regardless | repudiate |
> | reactor | regatta | repulsive |
> | reagent | regret(ted) | request |
> | real | regretful(ly) | require(d) |
> | realise(d) | regretting | requirement |
> | ze | rehearsal | research(es) |
> | realism | rehearse(d) | researched |
> | realistic(ally) | reject(ion) | researcher |
> | reality(-ies) | rejoice(d) | resemblance |
> | really | rejoin(ed) | resemble(d) |
> | rearm(ed) | relate(d) | resembling |
> | rebel(led) | relation(ship) | resent |
> | rebelling | relax(es) | resentful(ly) |
> | rebellion | relaxed | resentment |
> | rebellious | release(d) | reserve(d) |
> | rebound | relent(less) | resign(ed) |
> | recall(ed) | reliable | resist(ance) |
> | receding | reliability(-ies) | resistor |
> | receipt | reliance | resolve(d) |
> | receive(d) | relief | resort |
> | receiver | relieve(d) | resource(d) |
> | receiving | religion | respect(able) |
> | receptacle | religious | respectful(ly) |
> | reception | reluctant(ly) | respective(ly) |
> | receptive | rely(-ies) | respire(d) |
> | recess(es) | (relied) | respond |
> | recessed | remain(ed) | response |
> | recession | remainder | responsibility(-ies) |
> | recessive | remaining | responsible |
> | reciprocal(ly) | remark(ed) | responsive |
> | reciprocate | remarkable | restore(d) |
> | recital | remember(ed) | restrain(ed) |
> | recite | remembering | restrict(ion) |
> | reclaim(ed) | remembrance | result(ed) |
> | recoil(ed) | remind(ed) | resultant |
> | record(ed) | reminder | resulting |
> | recorder | remote | resume(d) |
> | recording | removal | resuscitate |
> | recover(ed) | remove(d) | resuscitation |
> | recovery(-ies) | removing | retain(ed) |
> | recruit | Renaissance | retard(ed) |
> | reduce(d) | renew(ed) | retire(d) |
> | reduction | renown(ed) | retirement |
> | refer(red) | repair(ed) | retort |
> | referral | repay | retreat |
> | referring | [repaid] | return(ed) |
> | refine(d) | repeal(ed) | returnable |
> | refinery(-ies) | repeat(ed) | returning |
> | reflect(ed) | repeating | reveal(ed) |
> | reflection | repel(led) | revenge(d) |
> | reflector | repellent | reverberate |
> | reflexive | repelling | reverse(d) |
> | reform(ed) | repentance | reversal |
> | retract(ion) | repetitive | reversible |
> | refrain(ed) | replace(d) | review(ed) |
> | refresh(es) | replacement | revise(d) |
> | refreshed | reply(-ies) | revision |
> | refresnment | (replied) | revive(d) |
> | refrigerator | report(ed) | revolt |
> | refund | reporter | revolve(d) |
> | refuse(d) | repose(d) | revolver |
> | refusal | reproach(es) | revue |
> | regain(ed) | reproached | reward |

* * *

repelling
repentance
repertoire
represent
-researcher
resemblance
resemble(d)
resembling
resentful(ly)
resentment
reservoir
*residence (house

repellent
repelling
repentance
repertoire
represent
resemblance
resemble(d)
resembling
resentful(ly)
resentment
reservoir
*residence (house)
resident
*residents (occupiers)
residue
resolute
respectful((y)
respective
restaurant
retention
retentive
retina
revenue
reverence
*reverend (deserving
  respect)
*Reverend (title)
*reverent (feeling or
  showing reverence)

for e-r
see page 251

In these words you can hear the vowel sound **e** as in **elephant**

✲

*cell (unit)
*cent (money / hundred)
*cents (money)

chef

said
says

*scent (perfume / smell)

sect
*sects (religious groups)
self
*sell (exchange for money)
[sold]
send
[sent]
*sense (understandable pattern)
sensed
*sent (made to go)
set
[set]
*sex(es) (male/ female)
sexed

shed
[shed]
shelf(-ves)
shelved
shell(ed)
shred(ded)

sketch(es)
sketched

sledge(d)
slept
-see next page

✲ ✲

*cellar (underground storage room)
cement
*censer (pan for burning incense)
*censor (judge of what may not be published)
census(es)
central(ly)
centre(d)

sceptic
sceptre(d)
schedule(d)

second
section
sector
segment
seldom
select
selfish
*seller (person who sells)
senate
sending
señor
*sensor(detecting device)
sensual(ly)
sentence(d)
sepal
separate
session
setted
settee
setting
settle(d)
settler
settling
seven(th)
several
sexist
sextet
sexual(ly)
sexy(-ier,-iest)
-see next page

✲ ✲ ✲

celandine
celebrate
celery
celestial
cellophane
celluloid
cellulose
Celsius
cemetery(-ies)
centigrade
centipede
centrally
century(-ies)
cerebral
cerebrum

sceptical(ly)

secession
secondary(-ies)
second-hand
secretary(-ies)
secular
sedative
sediment
segregate
selected
selecting
selection
selective
selector
sellotape
semibreve
senator
señora
sensation
sensible
sensitive
sensual(ly)
sensuous
sentiment
sentinel
separate
September
serenade
settlement
-see next page

✲ ✲ ✲ ✲ [✲]

celebrated
celebration
celebrity(-ies)
celestial
centenary(-ies)
centimetre
centrifugal(ly)
centurion
ceremony(-ies)

secondary(-ies)
secretarial
secretary(-ies)
sedimentary
segregation
self-reliant
semicircle
semicircular
semicolon
semi-conductor
semi-detached
semiquaver
semolina
señorita
sensational(ly)
sensitivity(-ies)
sentimental(ly)
separated
separately
separation
seventieth
severity(-ies)
sexuality(-ies)
sexually

sincerity

specialisation zation
speciality(-ies)
specification
spectacular
speculation
spherically
-see next page

for e-r
see page 252

In these words you can hear the vowel sound e as in elephant

☆	☆ ☆	☆ ☆ ☆	☆ ☆ ☆ ☆ [☆]
smell(ed)	shedding	seventeen(th)	stegosaurus
[smelt]	shellfish	seventy(-ies)	
	shelter(ed)	several	successfully
speck	shepherd	severance	suggestible
sped	sheriff	sexism	susceptible
spell(ed)	shredded	sexual(ly)	
[spelt]	shredding		symmetrical(ly)
spend		skeleton	synthetically
[spent]	sledging		
spread	slender	spaghetti	
[spread]		specialise(d)	
	smelter	ze	
squelch(es)		specially	
squelched	special(ly)	specify(-ies)	
	speckle(d)	(specified)	
stealth	spectre	specimen	
stem(med)	spectrum(-a)	spectacle	
stench(es)	speller	spectacles	
*step (pace /	spelling	spectator	
stage)	spending	speculate	
*steppe (dry,	splendid	spherical(ly)	
treeless plain)	splendour		
stepped	spreading	steadily	
stet		steadiness	
strength	steady(-ies)	stealthier	
stress(es)	(steadied)	stealthiest	
stressed	stealthy(-ier,-iest)	stencilling	
stretch(es)	stellar	sterilise(d)	
stretched	stemming	ze	
	stencil(led)	stethoscope	
sweat	stepping	strenuous	
swell	strengthen(ed)		
[swollen]	stretcher	subjection	
swept	stretching	successful(ly)	
		succession	
	subject	successive	
	subtend	successor	
	success(es)	suggested	
	suggest	suggesting	
	suspect	suggestion	
	suspend	surrender(ed)	
	suspense	suspected	
		suspension	
	sweater		
	swelter	synthetic(ally)	

 for e-r
see page 252

In these words the first letter 'e' sounds like the 'i' in 'pig'.

'SELECTED' WORDS

secession	secure(d)	selection	settee
seclude(d)	security(-ies)	selective	severe(ly)
secrete	select(ed)	selector	severity(-ies)
secretion	selecting	sequoia	specific(ally)

In these words you can hear the vowel sound e as in elephant

tell
[told]
tempt
ten(th)
tend
*tense (form of
    verb / stretched
    tight)
tensed
tent
*tents (more than
    one tent)
tenth
test
text

theft
them
then
thence
thread(ed)
threat

tread
[trod]
[trodden]
trench(es)
trend

twelfth
twelve

technique
teddy(-ies)
telling
temper(ed)
tempest
template
temple
tempo(s)
tenant
tender(ed)
tendon
*tenner (ten pound
    note)
tennis
tenon(ed)
*tenor (male voice)
tension
tepid
terrace(d)
terrain
terror
tested
testing
testis(testes)
tether(ed)
textbook
textile
texture(d)

themselves
threaded
threaten(ed)
threshold

treadle
treasure(d)
treble(d)
trebling
trellis(ed)
tremble(d)
trembling
tremor
trendy(-ier,-iest)
trestle

twenty(-ies)

technical(ly)
telegraph(ed)
telephone(d)
telescope(d)
televise(d)
temperament
temperate
temperature
temporary
temptation
tendency(-ies)
tenderness
tenement
tentacle
tentative
terrible
terribly
terrier
terrify(-ies)
    (terrified)
territory(-ies)
terrorise(d)
        ze
tessellate
testicle
testify(-ies)
    (testified)
tetanus

therapy(-ies)

together
torrential(ly)

treacherous
treachery(-ies)
treasury(-ies)
tremendous

twentieth

pterodactyl

technically
technological(ly)
technology(-ies)
telegraphy
telephonist
telephoto
television
temperamental(ly)
temperature
temporarily
temporary
terrarium
terrestrial(ly)
territorial(ly)
territory(-ies)
terrorism
tessellation
testimonial
testimony(-ies)

torrentially

for e-r
see page 253

In these words the first letter 'e'
is pronounced like the 'i' in 'pig'.

'TERRIFIC' WORDS

telegraphy	terrestrial(ly)
telephonist	terrific(ally)
tepee	tremendous

In these words you can hear the vowel sound e as in elephant

U

*   * *   * * *   * * * *

unless

V

*   * *   * * *   * * * * [*]

Venn	vector	vegetable	vegetation
vent	velvet	venison	Venezuela
vest	vending	ventilate	ventilation
vet(ted)	vendor	ventricle	ventilator
vex(es)	vengeance	verify(-ies)	ventriloquist
vexed	venture(d)	(verified)	veterinary
	very	veteran	
	vessel		
	vestry(-ies)		
	veteran		
	vetted		
	vetting		

for e-r
see page 254

> **In this word the letter 'e'**
> **sounds like the 'i' in 'pig'.**
>
> velocity(-ies)

W

*

wealth
web(bed)
wed(ded)
[wed]
wedge(d)
weft
weld
well(ed)
Welsh
wench(es)
went
wept
west
*wet(ted,ter,test)
   (make wet / not
   dry)
[wet]

whelk
whelp(ed)
when
whence
*whet(ted) (sharpen)

wreck(ed)
wren
wrench(es)
wrenched
*wrest (seize)
*wretch(es) (unhappy
   creature)

* *

waistcoat

wealthy(-ier,-iest)
weapon
*weather (conditions
      outside / survive
      bad weather)
weathered
webbing
wedded
wedding
wedging
Wednesday
welcome(d)
welfare
Welshman
western
westward
*wetted (made wet)
wetter
wettest
*wetting (making wet)

*whether (if)
*whetted (sharpened)
*whetting (sharpening)

wreckage
wrestle(d)
wrestler
wrestling
wretched

* * *

Wednesday
wellington

whenever

for e-r
see page 255

* * * *

X

*

* *

* * *

* * * * [*]

xenophobia
xenophobic

In these words you can hear the vowel sound **e** as in **elephant**

Y

✳	✳ ✳	✳ ✳ ✳	✳ ✳ ✳ ✳
yell(ed)	yelling	yesterday	
yelp(ed)	yellow		
yen			
yes	yourself		
yet	yourselves		

for e-r
see page 255

for e-r
see page 255

Z

✳	✳ ✳	✳ ✳ ✳	✳ ✳ ✳ ✳ [✳]
Zen	zealous		xenophobia
zest	zebra		xenophobic
	zenith		
	zephyr		

In these words you can hear the vowel sound e as in elephant

✵ ✵ ✵ ✵ ✵ ✵ ✵ ✵ ✵ [✵]

abyss(es)   abysmal(ly)   ability(-ies)
                                     abysmally
admit(ted)   addicted
adrift   addiction   additional(ly)
                   addictive   administer(ed)
affix(es)   addition   administrate
affixed   admission   administration
                   admittance   administrator
amid   admitted
amidst   admitting   affiliate
amiss
                   affliction   alliteration
assist
                   ambition   arithmetic
                   ambitious
                                     assimilate
                   arisen   assimilation
                                     astigmatism
                   *assistance (help)
                   assistant   auxiliary(-ies)
                   *assistants (helpers)

                   attribute   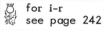 for i-r
                                     see page 242

In these words you can hear the vowel sound i as in pig

*   * *   * * *   * * * *

*been (past form of
  'be')

bib
bid
[bade]
[bid]
[bidden]
big
bill
*billed (did bill)
*bin (container)
bit
bitch(es)
bitched

blink(ed)

brick(ed)
bridge(d)
brim(med)
bring
[brought]
brink
brisk

*build (construct)
  [built]

became
because
become
[became]
[become]
befall
[befell]
[befallen]
before
befriend
begin
[began]
[begun]
behalf
behave(d)
behead
beheld
behind
behold
[beheld]
belief
believe(d)
belong(ed)
beloved
below
beneath
bereave(d)
[bereft]
beseech(es)
beseeched
[besought]
beset
[beset]
beside
besides
besiege(d)
besought
bestow(ed)
betray(ed)
between
betwixt
beware
bewitch(es)
bewitched
beyond
–see next page

becoming
befallen
beforehand
beginner
beginning
behaviour
belonging
beloved
besetting
bewilder(ed)

bishopric

bricklayer
brigadier

busier
busiest
busily
businessman

benevolent

binocular
binoculars

Bolivia

for i-r
see page 243

In these words you can hear the vowel sound i as in pig

✳ ✳

bidden
bidding
bigger
biggest
bilious
billiards
billion
billow(ed)
biscuit
bishop
*bitten (past form
    of 'bite')
bitter
*bittern (bird)
*bizarre (peculiar)

blinkered
blinkers
blister(ed)
blizzard

Brazil
breeches
bridging
brigade
brilliance
brilliant
brimming
bringing
bristle(d)
bristling
*Britain (country)
British
*Briton (British
    person)
brittle

builder
building
business
busy(-ies)
    (busied)
busy(-ier,-iest)

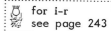
for i-r
see page 243

In these words you can hear the vowel sound i as in pig

*	**	***	**** [*]
chick	cement	capricious	capillary(-ies)
chid			
chill(ed)	chicken(ed)	celestial	celebrity(-ies)
chimp	chidden	ceramic	celestial
chin	chiffchaff		certificate
chink	chilblain	charisma	
chintz	children	chickenpox	Christianity
chip(ped)	*Chile (country)	chimpanzee	chrysanthemum
	*chilli (hot spice)	chiselling	
cinch(es)	*chilly(-ier,-iest)	chivalrous	citizenship
	(cold)	chivalry	civilisation
click(ed)	chimney	chrysalis	zation
cliff	chipboard		
cling	chipmunk	cigarette	clinically
[clung]	chipping	*cilia (more than	
clink(ed)	chisel(led)	one cilium)	commissioner
clip(ped)	christen(ed)	cilium(-a)	coniferous
	Christian	cinema	considerable
crib(bed)	Christmas	cinnamon	considerate
cringe(d)		citizen	consideration
crisp	cigar	civilian	consistency(-ies)
	cinder	civilise(d)	conspicuous
crypt	cirrus	ze	conspiracy(-ies)
	cistern	civilly	constituency(-ies)
kick(ed)	citrus		constituent
kid(ded)	city(-ies)	clinical(ly)	contingency(-ies)
kids	civic	clitoris	continual(ly)
kill(ed)	civil		continuation
kiln		collision	continuous
kilt	clinic(ally)	commission(ed)	continuum
king	clipper	commitment	contributed
kink(ed)	clipping	committed	
kiss(ed)		committee	criminally
kit(ted)	commit(ted)	committing	critically
	conflict	condition(ed)	criticism
	conscript	conscription	
	consist	consider(ed)	cylindrical
	convict	consistent	
	convince(d)	consisting	kilometre
	–see next page	continual(ly)	kindergarten
		continue(d)	
		contribute	
		conviction	
		–see next page	

for Qu ...
see page 83

for i-r
see page 244

In these words you can hear the vowel sound i as in pig

☆ ☆

☆ ☆ ☆

create
cremate
cribbing
cricket
crimson
crinkle(d)
crinkly
cripple(d)
crisscross(ed)
critic(ally)
crystal

created
creating
creation
creative
cremation
crescendo(s)
criminal(ly)
crinoline
critical(ly)
criticise(d)
 ze
crystalline
crystallise(d)
 ze

*cygnet (young swan)
*cymbals (discs to
 clash)

cylinder
Cypriot

kidded
kidding
kidnap(ped)
kidney
killer
killing
kindle(d)
kindling
kingdom
kinky(-ier,-iest)
kipper
kissing
kitchen
kitted
kitten
kitting

kidnapper
kidnapping
kilogram
kimono(s)

for Qu ...
see page 83

 for i-r
see page 244

 In these words you can hear the vowel sound i as in pig

*

did
dig(ged)
[dug]
dim(med)
din
ding
dip(ped)
disc/disk
dish(es)
ditch(es)
ditched

drift
drill(ed)
drink
[drank]
[drunk]
drip(ped)

* *

debate
*decade (ten years)
decamp(ed)
decay(ed)
*decayed (did decay)
decease(d)
deceit
deceive(d)
decide
declare(d)
decline(d)
decrease(d)
decree(d)
decry(-ies)
   (decried)
deduce(d)
defeat
defect
defence
defend
define(d)
deflect
deform(ed)
defy(-ies)
   (defied)
degree
delay(ed)
delete
delight
demand
demobbed
denote
denounce(d)
deny(-ies)
   (denied)
depart
depend
deport
depress(es)
depressed
deprive(d)
derail(ed)
derive(d)
-see next page

* * *

December
deception
deceptive
decipher(ed)
decision
decisive
deduction
deductive
defeated
defective
defector
defendant
defender
defensive
defiance
defiant
deficient
deflection
deletion
deliberate
delicious
delighted
delightful(ly)
deliver(ed)
demanded
demolish(es)
demolished
denial
department
departure
*dependant (person
   who depends)
*dependants (people
   who depend)
depended
*dependence
   (reliance)
*dependent (relying /
   hanging)
deposit(ed)
depression
depressive
descendant
descended
describing
description
descriptive
deserted
designer
destroyer
destruction
destructive
-see next page

* * * * [* *]

deciduous
deficiency(-ies)
deliberate
deliberately
delightfully
delirious
deliverance
delivery(-ies)
democracy(-ies)
denomination
denominator
dependable
dependency(-ies)
deposited
depositing
depreciate
depreciation
derivative
desirable
deteriorate
deterioration
determination
determining
developer
developing
development

dictatorial(ly)
dictionary(-ies)
differential
differently
difficulty(-ies)
digestible
digitally
dilapidated
diphtheria
diplodocus
diplomacy
diplomatic(ally)
directory(-ies)

-see next page

for i-r
see page 245

⁂ ⁂

descend
*descent (way down)
describe(d)
*desert (leave)
deserve(d)
design(ed)
desire(d)
despair(ed)
*despatch(es) (send off)
despatched
despise(d)
despite
*dessert (sweet dish)
destroy(ed)
detach(es)
detached
detain(ed)
detect
deter(red)
detest
detract
*device (gadget / plan)
*devise(d) (invent / work out)
devote
devour(ed)

dictate
diction
didn't
differ(ed)
difference
different
diffuse(d)
digest
digger
digging
digit
dimmer
dimming
dimple(d)
*dinghy(-ies) (small boat)
*dingy(-ier,-iest) (dull)
dinner
-see next page

⁂ ⁂ ⁂

detection
detective
detector
detention
detergent
determine(d)
*deterrence (preventing by causing fear)
deterrent
*deterrents (more than one deterrent)
deterring
develop(ed)
devoted
devotion

dictation
dictator
dictionary(-ies)
difference
different
differently
difficult
diffusion
digestion
digital(ly)
dignify(-ies) (dignified)
dignity(-ies)
dilemma
dimension
diminish(es)
diminished
diploma
directed
direction
directive
directly
director
disable(d)
disabling
disagree(d)
disappear(ed)
disappoint
disapprove(d)
disaster
disastrous
disbelief
disciple
discipline(d)
-see next page

⁂ ⁂ ⁂ ⁂ [⁂ ⁂]

disciplinarian
discovery(-ies)
discriminate
discrimination
disgracefully
disintegrate
disloyally
disloyalty
disobedience
disobedient
disposition
disproportion
disqualify(-ies) (disqualified)
dissatisfaction
dissatisfy(-ies) (dissatisfied)
dissimilar
distinguishable
distribution
distributive
distributor
diversity
divisibility
divisible

dysentery
dyslexia

for i-r see page 245

In these words you can hear the vowel sound i as in pig

* *

diphthong
dipper
dipping
dipstick
direct
disarm(ed)
discard
discern(ed)
discharge(d)
disclose(d)
disco(s)
discount
*discreet (careful
   not to embarrass)
*discrete (separate)
*discus(es) (disc)
*discuss(es) (debate)
*discussed (debated)
disease(d)
disgrace(d)
disguise(d)
*disgust (strong
   dislike)
dishcloth
dishes
dislike(d)
disloyal(ly)
dismal(ly)
dismay(ed)
dismiss(ed)
dismount
disown(ed)
*dispatch(es)
   (despatch /
   message)
dispatched
dispense(d)
disperse(d)
displace(d)
display(ed)
displease(d)
dispose(d)
disprove(d)
[disproven]
dispute
disrupt
*dissent
   (disagreement)
dissolve(d)
-see next page

* * *

discomfort
discontent
discotheque
discourage(d)
discover(ed)
discretion
discussing
discussion
disgraceful(ly)
disgusting
dishearten(ed)
dishonest
dishwasher
disinfect
disloyally
disloyalty
dismally
dismantle(d)
dismissal
dismissing
displacement
displeasure
disobey(ed)
disorder(ed)
disposal
disproven
disregard
disruption
disruptive
distilling
distinction
distinctive
distinguish(es)
distinguished
distraction
distractor
distressing
distribute
disturbance
divided
dividend
dividers
dividing
division
divisor

dynasty(-ies)
dysentery
dyslexic
dystrophy(-ies)

 for i-r
see page 245

In these words you can hear the vowel sound i as in pig

✼ ✼

distance(d)
distant
distil(led)
distinct
distort
distract
distress(es)
distressed
district
distrust
disturb(ed)
disused
dither(ed)
divan
diverge(d)
diverse
divert
divide
divine(d)
divorce(d)
dizzy(-ier,-iest)

dribble(d)
dribbling
drifted
driftwood
drinker
drinking
dripping
driven
drizzle(d)
drizzling

dwindle(d)
dwindling

for i-r
see page 245

In these words you can hear the vowel sound i as in pig

☆	☆ ☆	☆ ☆ ☆	☆ ☆ ☆ ☆ [☆ ☆ ☆ ☆]
	éclair	eccentric(ally)	eccentrically
	eclipse(d)		ecclesiastical(ly)
		edition	ecology
	effect		economy(-ies)
		effective	
	eject	efficient	effectively
			efficiency
	elect	Egyptian	
	ellipse		elaborate
	elope(d)	eg- or ig- ?	elaboration
			elastically
	el- or il- ?	ejection	elasticity
		ejector	electoral(ly)
	embark(ed)		electorate
	embed(ded)	elaborate	electrical(ly)
	embrace(d)	elastic(ally)	electricity
	embroil(ed)	election	electrocute
	emerge(d)	electors	electrolysis
	emit(ted)	electric(ally)	electrolyte
	employ(ed)	electrode	electrolytic(ally)
		electron	electromagnetic(ally)
	em- or im- ?	eleven(th)	electronic(ally)
		*elicit(ed) (draw out)	elicited
	enact	*elusive (hard to find)	eliciting
	encamp(ed)		eliminate
	encase(d)	el- or il- ?	elimination
	enchant		Elizabethan
	enclose(d)	embankment	elliptical(ly)
	endear(ed)	embarrass(es)	
	endorse(d)	embarrassed	el- or il- ?
	endow(ed)	embedded	
	endure(d)	embedding	emancipate
	enfold	embellish(es)	emancipation
	enforce(d)	embellished	embarrassing
	engage(d)	embezzle(d)	embarrassment
	England	embroider(ed)	embroidery
	English	emergence	emergency(-ies)
	engrave(d)	emission	emotional(ly)
	engulf(ed)	emitted	empirical(ly)
	enjoy(ed)	emitter	
	enlarge(d)	emitting	em- or im- ?
for H ... see page 71	enlist	emotion	-see next page
	enough	emotive	
	enquire/inquire(d)	employee	
	enrage(d)	employer	
	enrich(es)	employment	
for I ... see page 72	enriched	emulsion(ed)	
	enrol(led)		
	-see next page	em- or im- ?	
		-see next page	

✻ ✻

enslave(d)
*ensure(d) (make
  certain)
entire
entrance(d)
entrust

en- or in- ?

equate
equip(ped)

erase(d)
erect
erode
erupt

escape(d)
escort
estate
esteem(ed)
estrange(d)

es- or is- ?

evade
event
evict
evolve(d)

exact
exalt
exceed
excel(led)
*except (not
  including)
excess(es)
exchange(d)
excite
exclaim(ed)
exclude
excuse(d)
exempt
exert
exhaust
exhort
exist
-see next page

✻ ✻ ✻

enable(d)
enabling
enamel(led)
enamour(ed)
enchanting
encircle(d)
enclosure
encounter(ed)
encourage(d)
endanger(ed)
endearment
endeavour(ed)
endurance
enforcement
engagement
Englishman
engraving
enjoying
enjoyment
enlighten(ed)
enormous
enquiry/inquiry(-ies)
enrolling
enrolment
entangle(d)
entirely
entitle(d)
entrancing
envisage(d)

en- or in- ?

equation
equator
equipment
equipping

eraser
erection
erosion
erotic(ally)
erratic(ally)
erupted
eruption

er- or ir- ?
-see next page

✻ ✻ ✻ ✻ [✻ ✻ ✻]

enamelling
encouragement
encyclopedia
enthusiasm
enthusiastic(ally)
enumerate
environment
environmental(ly)

en- or in- ?

equality
equivalence
equivalent

erotically
erratically

er- or ir- ?

especially
essentially
establishment

eternally

evacuate
evacuation
evacuee
evaluate
evaluation
evaporate
evaporation
eventually

exaggerate
exaggeration
examination
exceedingly
exceptionally
excitedly
exclamation
exclusively
-see next page

for H . . .
see page 71

for I . . .
see page 72

In these words you can hear the vowel sound ĭ as in pig

✻ ✻   ✻ ✻ ✻   ✻ ✻ ✻ ✻ [✻ ✻ ✻]

expand   escarpment   executive
expanse   essential(ly)   exemplary
expect   establish(es)   exhibited
expel(led)   established   exhibiting
expense   exotically
explain(ed)   es- or is- ?   expandable
explode   expectantly
exploit   eternal(ly)   expenditure
explore(d)   experience(d)
export   et- or it- ?   experiment
expose(d)   experimental(ly)
express(es)   evasion   explanatory
expressed   eventual(ly)   exploratory
extend   exterior
extent   exactly   exterminate
extinct   exalted   externally
extract   examine(d)   extinguisher
extreme   example   extraordinarily
                              excellent   extraordinary
                              excelling   extrapolate
                              exception   extravagance
                              excessive   extravagant
                              exchequer   extravaganza
                              excited   exuberance
                              excitement   exuberant
                              exciting
                              exclusion
                              exclusive
                              excretion
                              excursion
                              exemption
                              exertion
                              exhausted
                              exhaustion
                              exhibit(ed)
                              existed
                              existence
                              exotic(ally)
                              expanded
                              expanding
                              expansion
                              expansive
                              expectant
                              expected
                              expelling
                              expensive
                              explaining
                              explicit
                              explorer
                              exploring
                              explosion
                              explosive

                              -see next page

for H ...
see page 71

for I ...
see page 72

In these words you can hear the vowel sound i as in pig

✻ ✻ ✻

exponent
exposure
expressing
expression
expressive
exquisite
extended
extending
extension
extensive
external(ly)
extinction
extinguish(es)
extinguished
extraction
extractor
extremely
extrusion

for H ...
see page 71

for I ...
see page 72

F

✻

fib(bed)
fifth
fig
fill(ed)
film(ed)
filth
fin(ned)
finch(es)
Finn
fiord/fjord
fish(es)
fished
fist
fit(ted)
fix(es)
fixed
fizz(es)
fizzed
-see next page

✻ ✻

fibbing
fiction
fiddle(d)
fiddler
fiddling
fidget(ed)
fifteen(th)
fifty(-ies)
figure(d)
filler
fillet
filling
filly(-ies)
filter(ed)
filthy(-ier,-iest)
-see next page

✻ ✻ ✻

familiar

ferocious

*fiancé (man engaged
    to be married)
*fiancée (woman
    engaged to be
    married)
fictional
fictitious
fidgeted
fidgeting
fidgety
fiesta
fiftieth
-see next page

✻ ✻ ✻ ✻ [✻ ✻ ✻]

facility(-ies)

ferocity
fertility

figurative
financially

phenomena
phenomenal(ly)
phenomenon

philatelist
philosophical(ly)
philosophy(-ies)
physically
physiological(ly)
physiology

for th ...
see page 90

for i-r
see page 246

In these words you can hear the vowel sound i as in pig

*

flick(ed)
flinch(es)
fling
[flung]
flint
flip(ped)
flit(ted)

fridge
frill(ed)
fringe(d)
frisk(ed)

* *

finance(d)
finger(ed)
finish(es)
finished
Finland
Finnish
fiord/fjord
fiscal
*fisher (man who
    fishes)
fishes
fishing
fission
*fissure(d) (crack)
fitness
fitted
fitting
fixture
fizzle(d)
fizzy(-ier,-iest)

flicker(ed)
flimsy(-ies)
flipper
flipping
flitted
flitting

forbid
[forbad(e)]
[forbidden]
forgive
[forgave]
[forgiven]

friction
frigate
frigid
fritter(ed)
frizzy(-ier,-iest)

fulfil(led)

physics
physique

* * *

filament
filthiest
filtration
financial(ly)
fingernail
fingerprint
fingertip
finishing
fisherman

flamingo(es/s)

forbidden
forbidding
forgiven
forgiveness

frivolous

fulfilling

physical(ly)
physician
physicist

for th . . .
see page 90

for i-r
see page 246

*

gift
gig
*gild (paint with
    gold)
*[gilt] (gilded)
gills
gin
give
[gave]
[given]

glimpse(d)
glint

grid
*grill(ed) (cook by
    direct heat /
    bars for cooking /
    food so cooked)
*grille (protecting
    set of bars in
    door or window)
grim
grin(ned)
grip(ped)
grit(ted)

*guild (association)
*guilt (responsibility
    for doing wrong)

jib(bed)
jig(ged)

* *

giggle(d)
giggling
gilded
*gilder (person who
    gilds)
gimlet
ginger(ed)
gingham
gipsy/gypsy(-ies)
giraffe
given
giver
giving

glimmer(ed)
glisten(ed)
glitter(ed)

grenade
griddle
grinning
gripping
gristle
gritting
grizzle(d)
grizzling
grizzly

*guilder (Dutch coin)
guilty(-ier,-iest)
guinea
Guinea
guitar

gymnast
gymslip
gypsy/gipsy(-ies)

jibbing
jiffy
jigging
jigsaw
jingle(d)
jingling

* * *

genetic(ally)

gibberish
Gibraltar
gingerbread

glycerine

*gorilla (ape)

*guerilla/guerrilla
    (agent of political
    violence)
guillemot
guillotine(d)

gymkhana
gymnastics
gymnosperm

* * * * [* *]

genetically
geographical(ly)
geography(-ies)
geological(ly)
geology
geometrical(ly)
geometry(-ies)
geranium

gymnasium

for i-r
see page 246

In these words you can hear the vowel sound i as in pig

*

hid
hill
*him (that male
 individual)
hinge(d)
hint
hip
his
hiss(ed)
hit
[hit]
hitch(es)
hitched

*hymn (song with
 verses sung in
 church)

* *

hiccup(ped)
hidden
hillside
hilltop
himself
hinder(ed)
hindrance
Hindu
hissing
hither
hitting

hymnal

* * *

habitual(ly)

heroic(ally)

hiccupping
hickory
hideous
historic(ally)
history(-ies)
hitherto

hypnosis
hypnotic(ally)
hypnotise(d)
      ze
hysterics

* * * * [* *]

habitually

hereditary
heredity
heroically

higgledy-piggledy
hilarious
Himalayas
hippopotamus(es/-i)
historian
historical(ly)

hypnotically
hypnotism
hysterical(ly)

*	* *	* * *	* * * * [* * *]
if	ic- or ec- ?	idiom	ic- or ec- ?
		idiot	
ill	if- or ef- ?		idiomatic(ally)
		id- or ed- ?	idiotic(ally)
imp	ignite		
	ignore(d)	if- or ef- ?	iguanodon
*in (not outside)			
inch(ed)	ij- or ej- ?	igneous	illegally
ink		ignition	illegible
*inn (small hotel)	illness(es)	ignorance	illiterate
		ignorant	illogical(ly)
is	il- or el- ?		illuminate
		ig- or eg- ?	illumination
it	image(d)		illustration
itch(es)	immense	ij- or ej- ?	illustrative
itched	immerse(d)		illustrator
*its (belonging to	immune	illegal(ly)	illustrious
it)	impact	*illicit (illegal)	
*it's (it is)	impel(led)	illusion	il- or el- ?
	implore(d)	*illusive (deceptive)	
	imply(-ies)	illustrate	imaginary
	(implied)		imagination
	import	il- or el- ?	imaginative
	impose(d)		imitation
	impress(es)	imagery	immaculate
	impressed	imagine(d)	immediate
	imprint	imitate	immediately
	improve(d)	immediate	immensity
	impulse	immersion	immigration
	impure	immigrant	immortality
		immigrate	immortally
	im- or en- ?	immobile	immovable
		immortal(ly)	immunisation
	incense(d)	immunise(d)	zation
	*incite (encourage	ze	immunity
	strong feeling or	impatience	impassable
	action)	impatient	impeccable
	incline(d)	impeachment	imperative
	include	impeller	imperial(ly)
	income	impelling	impersonal
	increase(d)	imperfect	impersonate
	indeed	impetus(es)	impersonation
	indent	implement	impertinent
	index(ed)	impolite	implacable
	indoors	importance	implication
	induce(d)	important	impossibility
	indulge(d)	impregnate	impossible
	-see next page	impression	-see next page
		impressive	
		imprison(ed)	
		-see next page	

for E . . .
see page 65

for H . . .
see page 71

for i-r
see page 247

In these words you can hear the vowel sound i as in pig

*

** **

** ** **

** ** ** ** [** **]

*

inert
infant
infect
infer(red)
infirm
inflame(d)
inflate
inflict
inform(ed)
ingot
inhale(d)
inject
injure(d)
inland
inlet
innate
inner
innings
input
inquest
inquire/enquire(d)
insane
inscribe(d)
insect
insert
*inshore (near the
  shore)
inside
*insight
  (understanding)
insist
inspect
inspire(d)
instal(led)
*instance (example)
instant
*instants (moments)
instead
instinct
instruct
insult
*insure(d) (protect
  against loss)
-see next page

for E ...
see page 65

for H ...
see page 71

* *

impromptu(s)
improper
improvement
improving
improvise(d)
      ze
impudence
impudent
impulsive

im- or em- ?

incessant
*incidence (rate of
  happening)
incident
*incidents (events)
incision
incisor
included
including
inclusion
inclusive
incoming
incomplete
incorrect
increasing
indented
indenture(d)
India
Indian
indicate
indifferent
indignant
indigo
indirect
indistinct
induction
inductive
indulgence
indulgent
industry(-ies)
inertia
infantry
infection
infectious
inference
inferring
infinite
inflation
influence(d)
-see next page

for i-r
see page 247

* * *

improper

* * * *

impractical
impregnable
impressionism
impressionist
impunity
impurity(-ies)

im- or em- ?

inability
inaccessible
inaccurate
inadequate
inappropriate
inattentive
inaugural
inauguration
incapable
incidental(ly)
inclination
incognito
incompatible
incomprehensible
incongruity(-ies)
incongruous
inconsistent
inconvenience
inconvenient
incorporate(d)
incubation
incubator
increasingly
incredible
incubator
incubation
incurable
indefinitely
independence
independent
indicated
indication
indicator
indifferent
indigestible
indigestion
indignation
indispensable
individuality
individual(ly)
indivisible
-see next page

73

In these words you can hear the vowel sound i as in pig

✻ ✻   ✻ ✻ ✻   ✻ ✻ ✻ ✻ [✻ ✻ ✻]

intact	informal(ly)	Indonesia
intake	informant	industrial(ly)
intend	infra-red	industrialisation
*intense (very strong)	infrequent	zation
intent	ingenious	industrialise(d)
*intents (purposes)	inhabit(ed)	ze
interest	inherent	industrious
into	inherit(ed)	inedible
intrigue(d)	inhuman	inefficiency
intrude	initial(led)	inefficient
invade	injection	inequality(-ies)
invent	injury(-ies)	inevitable
inverse	injustice	inexpensive
invert	innermost	inexperienced
invest	innkeeper	inferior
invite	*innocence (freedom	infinitesimal(ly)
invoice(d)	from guilt)	infinitive
involve(d)	innocent	infinity
inward	*innocents (people	infirmary(-ies)
	who have done	inflammable
in- or en- ?	no wrong)	inflammation
	inquiry/enquiry(-ies)	inflammatory
iq- or eq- ?	inscription	inflationary
	insisted	inflexible
Iran	insolence	influential(ly)
Iraq	insolent	influenza
	inspection	informally
ir- or er- ?	inspector	information
	installing	informative
Islam	instalment/	infuriate
isn't	installment	ingenious
issue(d)	instantly	ingenuity
isthmus	institute	ingredient
	instruction	inhabitant
is- or es- ?	instructor	inhabited
	instrument	inhabiting
itself	insulate	inheritance
	insulin	inherited
iv- or ev- ?	insulting	inheriting
	insurance	inhospitable
ix - or ex- ?	–see next page	initialling
		initiate
		initiative
		injurious
		innovation
		innumerable
		inoculate

for E . . .
see page 65

for H . . .
see page 71

for i-r
see page 247

inorganic(ally)
inquisition
inquisitive
–see next page

In these words you can hear the vowel sound i as in pig

✢ ✢ ✢   ✢ ✢ ✢ [✢ ✢]

integer   insanitary
integral   insanity
integrate   insecticide
intensive   insensitive
intention   insignificant
intercept   inspiration
interested   installation
interesting   intantaneous
interfere(d)   institution
interlock(ed)   insufficient
interlude   insulation
internal(ly)   insulator
interpret(ed)   integration
interrupt   integrity
intersect   intellectual(ly)
intersperse(d)   intelligence
interval   intelligent
intervene(d)   intensify(-ies)
interview(ed)   (intensified)
intestine   intensity(-ies)
intimate   intentional(ly)
intricate   interaction
intriguing   interception
introduce(d)   interchangeable
intruder   interested
intrusion   interesting
invaded   interference
invader   interior
invalid   intermission
invasion   intermittent
invention   internally
inventive   intermediate
inventor   international(ly)
inventory(-ies)   interpolate
inversion   interpretation
investment   interpreted
investor   interpreter
invited   interpreting
involvement   interrogate
                         interrogation
in- or en- ?   interrogative
                         interrupted
iq- or eq- ?   intersection
–see next page   intervention
                         intestinal(ly)
                         intolerable
                         intonation
                         intoxicate
                         intoxication
                         –see next page

for E ...
see page 65

for H ...
see page 71

In these words you can hear the vowel sound i as in pig

* * *

Iraqi
irrigate
irritate

ir- or er- ?

Islamic

is- or es- ?

Italian
italic
Italy

it- or et- ?

ix- or ex- ?

* * * * [* *]

intransitive
intravenous
introduction
introductory
invariably
inventory(-ies)
invertebrate
investigate
investigation
investigator
invisible
invitation
involuntary

in- or en- ?

iq- or eq- ?

Iranian
irrational(ly)
irregular
irregularity(-ies)
irresistible
irrigation
irritability
irritable
irritation

ir- or er- ?

is- or es- ?

italicise(d)
      ze

it- or et- ?

iv- or ev- ?

ix- or ex- ?

for E ...
see page 65

for H ...
see page 71

for i-r
see page 247

In these words you can hear the vowel sound i as in pig

J

*	* *	* * *	* * * * [* *]
gin	ginger(ed)	genetic(ally)	genetically
	gipsy/gypsy(-ies)		geographically
jib(bed)	giraffe	gibberish	geography(-ies)
jig(ged)		Gibraltar	geological(ly)
	gymnast	gingerbread	geology
	gymslip		geometrical(ly)
	gypsy/gipsy(-ies)	gymnastics	geometry(-ies)
		gymnosperm	geranium
	jibbing		
	jiffy		**gymnasium**
	jigging		
	jigsaw		
	jingle(d)		
	jingling		

In these words you can hear the vowel sound i as in pig

77

K

   *   * *   * * *   * * * *

kick(ed)	kidded	kidnapper	kilometre
kid(ded)	kidding	kidnapping	kindergarten
kids	kidnap(ped)	kilogram	
kill(ed)	kidney	kimono(s)	knickerbocker
kiln	killer		
kilt	killing		
kin	kindle(d)		
king	kindling		
kink(ed)	kingdom		
kiss(ed)	kinky(-ier,-iest)		
kit(ted)	kipper		
	kissing		
knit(ted)	kitchen		
[knit]	kitted		
	kitten		
	kitting		

knickers
knitted
knitting

for C . . .
see page 59

for Qu
see page 83

for i-r
see page 248

In these words you can hear the vowel sound i as in pig

L

*	* *	* * *	* * * * [*]
lick(ed)	liberal(ly)	liberal(ly)	legitimate
lid	lichen	liberate	
lift	licorice	liberty(-ies)	liberally
limb	lifted	licorice	liberation
limp(ed)	lifting	limited	limitation
link(ed)	lily(-ies)	limiting	linguistically
*links (connections /	limit(ed)	linear	linoleum
golf course)	limpet	linguistic(ally)	literally
lip	linen	liniment	literary
lisp(ed)	linger(ed)	liquorice	literacy
list	linking	literal(ly)	literature
lit	lintel	literate	
live(d)	lipstick	literature	lyrically
	liquid	lithium	
lynch(es)	liquor	liverish	
*lynx(es) (animal)	liquorice	livery(-ies)	
	listed		
	listen(ed)	lyrical(ly)	
	listless		
	litmus		
	litter(ed)		
	little		
	liver		
	livid		
	living		
	lizard		
	lyric(ally)		

In these words you can hear the vowel sound i as in pig

*   * *   * * *   * * * * [*]

*	**	***	**** [*]
midge	miaow	magician	manipulate
midst	mickey	malicious	
milk(ed)	midday	malignant	mechanical(ly)
mill(ed)	middle		melodically
*mince (cut into	midget	meander(ed)	melodious
small pieces)	midnight	mechanic(ally)	memorial
minced	midpoint	medallion	menagerie
mink	midway	melodic(ally)	meridian
mint	mildew(ed)	melodious	meticulous
*mints (more than	milkman	memento(es/s)	
one mint)	miller	meniscus(es/-i)	military
Miss	millet		millilitre
miss(es)	million	midsummer	millimetre
*miss(ed) (did miss)	mimic(ked)	militant	millionairess(es)
*mist (thin fog)	mineral	military	minority(-ies)
mitt	mingle(d)	militia	miraculous
mix(es)	mingling	milligram	miserable
mixed	minim	milliner	missionary(-ies)
	minnow	millionaire	misunderstand
myth	minstrel	mimicking	[misunderstood]
	minute	mimicry	
	mirage	mineral	mysterious
	mirror(ed)	miniature	mysticism
	mischief	minimal(ly)	mythology(-ies)
	misdeal	minimum	myxomatosis
	[misdealt]	minister(ed)	
	mislay	Minorca	
	[mislaid]	minuend	
	mislead	miracle	
	[misled]	mischievous	
	missile	miserable	
	missing	misery(-ies)	
	mission	misfortune	
	misspell(ed)	misgivings	
	[misspelt]	missionary(-ies)	
	misspend	mistaken	
	[misspent]	mistletoe	
	mistake		
	[mistook]	mnemonic	
	[mistaken]		
	mistress(es)	myriad	
	mistrust	mystery(-ies)	
	misuse(d)	mystical	
	mitten	mystify(-ies)	
	mixture	(mystified)	
		mythical	

Monsieur(Messieux)

Mr.
Mrs.

mystic(al)

for i-r
see page 249

In these words you can hear the vowel sound i as in pig

N

*	* *	* * *	* * * *

*

knit(ted)
[knit]

nib
nil
nip(ped)
*nit (egg of
    louse / nitwit)

nymph

* *

knickers
knitted
knitting

neglect

nibble(d)
nibbling
nickel
nickname
nimble
nipping
nipple
nitwit

* * *

mnemonic

negation
neglectful(ly)

* * * *

knickerbocker

nativity(-ies)

necessity(-ies)
neglectfully
negotiate

O

*	* *	* * *	* * * * [* *]

* *

omit(ted)

* * *

official(ly)

omission
omitted
omitting

opinion

* * * * [* *]

auxiliary(-ies)

obliterate
oblivion
oblivious
obsidian

officially

original(ly)
originality
originate

In these words you can hear the vowel sound i as in pig

81

*	* *	* * *	* * * * [* * *]
pick(ed)	permit	Pacific	particular
pig(ged)	persist	pavilion	particularly
pill			
pin(ned)	physics	peculiar	peculiar
pinch(es)	physique	permission	pedestrian
pinched		permitted	peninsula
pink(ed)	pianist	permitting	peninsular
pip(ped)	piano(s)	persistence	perimeter
pit(ted)	picket	persistent	permissible
pitch(es)	picking	petition(ed)	petroleum
pitched	pickle(d)		
pith	pickling	physical(ly)	phenomena
	pickup	physician	phenomenal(ly)
prick(ed)	picnic	physicist	phenomenon
*prince (son of king)	*picture (painting,		philatelist
print	drawing or	pianist	philosophical(ly)
*prints (more than	photograph)	piano(s)	philosophy(-ies)
one print)	picture(d)	piccolo(s)	physically
	*pidgin (mixture of	picturesque	physiological(ly)
	two languages)	pinafore	physiology
	*pigeon (bird)	pinnacle	
	pigging	piranha	pianoforte
	piglet	piteous	pituitary
	pigment	pivoted	
	pigtail	pivoting	political(ly)
	pilchard		
	pilgrim	position(ed)	precipitate
	pillar		precipitation
	pillow(ed)	precaution	predictable
	pimple(d)	preceded	predominantly
	pincers	preceding	preliminary(-ies)
	pinion	precisely	preoccupation
	pinning	precision	presentable
	pipping	precocious	presumably
	*pistil (part of	prediction	principally
	flower)	preferring	proficiency
	*pistol (small hand	preparing	prohibited
	gun)	prescription	prohibiting
	piston	presented	prohibitive
	pitchblende	presenting	proliferate
	*pitcher (container	pretended	proliferation
	for liquids)	prettier	prolifically
	pitching	prettiest	provisional(ly)
	piteous	prevention	
	pitting	preventive	publicity
	pity(-ies)	primitive	
	(pitied)	–see next page	
	pivot(ed)		
	pixie		
	pizza		
	–see next page		

In these words you can hear the vowel sound i as in pig

* *

precede
precise
predict
prefer(red)
prepare(d)
prescribe(d)
present
preserve(d)
preside
presume(d)
pretence
pretend
pretty(-ier,-iest)
prevail(ed)
prevent
prickle(d)
prickly
primrose
princess(es)
printed
printer
printing
prism
prison
prisoner

pygmy(-ies)

* * *

*principal (chief)
principally
*principle (rule of
    action)
principled
prisoner
privacy
privilege(d)
prodigious
proficient
prohibit(ed)
prolific(ally)
provincial
provision
provisions

pyjamas
Pyrenees
pyramid
pyrites

Q

*

quick
quid
quill
quilt
quin
quince
quip(ped)
quit(ted)
[quit]
quiz(zed)

* *

quibble(d)
quibbling
quickly
quintet
quipping
quitted
quitting
quiver(ed)

* * *

quicksilver
quintuplet

for i-r
see page 251

✻	✻ ✻	✻ ✻ ✻	✻ ✻ ✻ ✻ [✻ ✻]
*real (genuine)	react	reaction	rapidity
	really	reactor	
rib(bed)	rebel(led)	reagent	reactionary(-ies)
rich(es)	rebound	realise(d)	realism
rid(ded)	recall(ed)	ze	realistic(ally)
[rid]	receipt	rebelling	reality(-ies)
ridge(d)	receive(d)	rebellion	receptacle
rift	recess(es)	rebellious	reciprocal(ly)
rig(ged)	recessed	receding	reciprocate
rim(med)	recite	receiver	recovery(-ies)
*ring(ed) (circle)	reclaim(ed)	receiving	refinery(-ies)
*ring (sound)	recoil(ed)	reception	refrigerator
[rang]	record	receptive	regretfully
[rung]	recruit	recession	relationship
ringed	reduce(d)	recessive	reliability(-ies)
rinse(d)	refer(red)	recital	reliable
rip(ped)	refine(d)	recorded	reluctantly
risk(ed)	reflect	recorder	remarkable
	reform(ed)	recording	remembering
*wring (twist)	refract	recover(ed)	repetitive
[wrung]	refrain(ed)	reduction	republican
wrist	refresh(es)	referral	repudiate
	refreshed	referring	resentfully
	refund	reflected	respectable
	refuse(d)	reflection	respectfully
	regain(ed)	reflector	respectively
	regard	reflexive	responsibility(-ies)
	regret(ted)	refraction	responsible
	rehearse(d)	refreshment	resuscitate
	reject	refusal	resuscitation
	rejoice(d)	regarded	returnable
	rejoin(ed)	regardless	reverberate
	relate	regatta	reversible
	relax(es)	regretful(ly)	
	relaxed	regretted	rhythmically
	release(d)	regretting	
	relent	rehearsal	ridiculous
	relief	rejection	ritually
	relieve(d)	related	
	rely(-ies)	relation	
	(relied)	relentless	
	remain(ed)	reliance	
	remark(ed)	religion	
	remind	religious	
	remote	reluctant	
	remove(d)	remainder	
	renew(ed)	remaining	
	renown(ed)	-see next page	
	repaid		
	repair(ed)		
	repay		
	[repaid]		
	-see next page		

In these words you can hear the vowel sound i as in pig

* *

repeal(ed)
repeat
repel(led)
repent
replace(d)
reply(-ies)
    (replied)
report
repose(d)
reproach(es)
reproached
request
require(d)
research(es)
researched
*resent (feel
    angry at)
reserve(d)
resign(ed)
resist
resolve(d)
resort
resource(d)
respect
respire(d)
respond
response
restore(d)
restrain(ed)
restrict
result
resume(d)
retain(ed)
retard
retire(d)
retort
retreat
return(ed)
reveal(ed)
revenge(d)
reverse(d)
review(ed)
revise(d)
revive(d)
revolt
revolve(d)
reward

rhythm
rhythmic(ally)
-see next page

* * *

reminded
reminder
removal
removing
Renaissance
repeated
repeating
repellent
repelling
repentance
replacement
reported
reporter
republic
repulsive
requirement
researcher
resemblance
resemble(d)
resembling
resentful(ly)
resentment
resistance
resistor
resources
respectful(ly)
respective
resplendent
responsive
restriction
resultant
resulted
resulting
retarded
retention
retentive
retirement
returning
reversal
revision
revolver
rewritten

rhythmical(ly)

rickety
ridicule(d)
rigorous
ritual(ly)
riveted/rivetted
riveting/rivetting

In these words you can hear the vowel sound i as in pig

✻ ✻

ribbing
ribbon
ridded
ridden
ridding
riddle(d)
riddling
*rigger (person
  who rigs)
rigging
rigid
*rigor (rigid state)
*rigour (severe
  conditions)
rimming
ringing
ripping
ripple(d)
rippling
risen
ritual(ly)
river
rivet(ed/ted)

wriggle(d)
wriggling
wrinkle(d)
wrinkling
written

In these words you can hear the vowel sound i as in pig

✻	✻ ✻	✻ ✻ ✻	✻ ✻ ✻ ✻ [✻ ✻]
cinch(es)	cement	celestial	celestial
			certificate
schist	cigar	chivalrous	citizenship
scrimp	cirrus	chivalry	civilisation
scrip	cistern		zation
script	citrus	cigarette	
	city(-ies)	*cilia (more than one	cylindrical
shift	civic	cilium)	
shin(ned)	civil(ly)	cilium(-a)	salinity
ship(ped)		cinema	satirical(ly)
shrill		cinnamon	
shrimp	*cygnet (young swan)	citizen	schizophrenia
shrink	*cymbals (discs to clash)	civilian	schizophrenic(ally)
[shrank]		civilise(d)	
[shrunk/shrunken]	*Scilly (Isles)	ze	security(-ies)
	scissors		severity(-ies)
	scribble(d)	civilly	
sick	scripture		significant
sieve(d)		cylinder	similarity(-ies)
sift	seclude	Cypriot	similarly
sill	secrete		simplicity
silk	secure(d)	scriptural(ly)	simplification
silt	select		simulation
sin(ned)	settee	secession	simultaneous
since	severe	secluded	sincerity
sing		secretion	sister-in-law
[sang]	shilling	selected	situated
[sung]	shimmer(ed)	selecting	situation
sink	shingle	selection	
[sank]	shipment	selective	
[sunk/sunken]	shipping	selector	solicitor
sip(ped)	shipwreck(ed)	sequoia	sophisticated
sit	shiver(ed)	severely	
[sat]	shrivel(led)		specifically
six(th)			spiritually
		shipbuilding	
skid(ded)	sickness	shrivelling	statistically
skill(ed)	signal(led)	–see next page	stimulation
skim(med)	*signet (seal / ring)		
skimp(ed)	*silly(-ier,-iest)		subsidiary(-ies)
skin(ned)	(lacking sense)		sufficiently
skip(ped)	silver(ed)		–see next page
skit	simmer(ed)		
	simple		
slick	simpler		
slid	simply		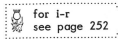 for i-r see page 252
slim(med)	–see next page		
sling			
[slung]			
slink			
[slunk]			
slip(ped)			
slit			
[slit]			
–see next page			

✻	✻ ✻	✻ ✻ ✻	✻ ✻ ✻ ✻ [✻ ✻]
smith	sincere	Sicily	syllabically
	sinew	signalling	symbolically
sniff(ed)	singer	signature	symbolism
snip(ped)	singing	signify(-ies)	symbiosis
	single(d)	(signified)	symbiotic(ally)
sphinx(es)	singly	silhouette	symmetrical(ly)
spill(ed)	sinning	silica	sympathetic(ally)
[spilt]	sipping	silicon	symphonically
spin	sissy(-ies)	*sillier (more silly)	synonymous
⌊span⌋	sister	silliest	synthesiser
⌊spun⌋	sitter	silverware	synthetically
spit	sitting	similar	systematic(ally)
[spat⌋	sixpence	simile	
[spit]	sixteen(th)	simplify(-ies)	
splint	sixty(-ies)	(simplified)	
split	sizzle(d)	simulate	
⌊split⌋	sizzling	sincerely	
sprig		Singapore	
spring	skidded	singular	
⌊sprang⌋	skidding	sinister	
[sprung⌋	skilful(ly)	sixtieth	
	skillet		
squib	skimming	skilfully	
squid	skinning		
squint	skinny(-ier,-iest)	slippery	
	skipper		
stick	skipping	snivelling	
[stuck]	skittle		
stiff		specific(ally)	
still(ed)	slimming	spiritual(ly)	
stilts	slipper(ed)		
sting	slippery	statistics	
[stung]	slipping	stimulant	
stink	slipstone	stimulate	
⌊stank⌋	slither(ed)	stimulus(-i)	
[stunk⌋	slitting	stinginess	
stint			
stitch(es)	smitten	submission	
stitched		submissive	
strict	sniffle(d)	submitted	
string	sniffling	submitting	
[strung]	snigger(ed)	subscription	
strip(ped)	snippet	sufficient	
-see next page	snivel(led)	suspicion	
	-see next page	suspicious	
		Switzerland	
		swivelling	
		-see next page	

-see next page

for i-r
see page 252

In these words you can hear the vowel sound i as in pig

*

swift
swig
swill(ed)
swim
[swam]
[swum]
swing
[swung]
swish(ed)
Swiss
switch(ed)

* *

spilling
spinach
spindle
spinning
spinster
spitting
splinter(ed)
splitting
spirit
springboard
springtime
sprinkle(d)
sprinkling

squirrel

sticking
sticky(-ier,-iest)
stigma
stingy(-ier,-iest)
stirrup
stitches
stitching
stricken
stridden
stringent
stripper
stripping
striven

submit(ted)

swiftly
swimmer
swimming
swindle(d)
swindling
swinging
swivel(led)

symbol
*symbols (signs)
symptom
syringe(d)
syrup
system

* * *

sycamore
syllabic(ally)
syllable
symbolic(ally)
symbolise(d)
        ze
symmetry(-ies)
sympathy(-ies)
symphonic(ally)
symphony(-ies)
synchromesh
synchronise(d)
        ze
syndicate
synonym
synthesis(syntheses)
synthetic(ally)
Syria

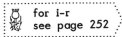
for i-r
see page 252

In these words you can hear the vowel sound i as in pig

89

*	* *	* * *	* * * * [* *]
thick	terrain	terrific(ally)	telegraphy
thin(ned)			telephonist
thing	thicket	timpani	terrestrial(ly)
think	thickness		terrifically
[thought]	thimble	tradition	
this	thinner	tremendous	theatrical(ly)
thrift	thinning	tributary(-ies)	theodolite
thrill(ed)	thistle	trickery	theological(ly)
	thither	Trinidad	theology(-ies)
tick(ed)	thrifty(-ier,-iest)		theoretical(ly)
till	thriven	typical(ly)	
tilt		tyrannise(d)	traditional(ly)
tin(ned)	ticket	ze	tributary(-ies)
tint	tickle(d)	tyranny(-ies)	trigonometric
tip(ped)	ticklish		trigonometry
tit	tiller		
	timber		typically
trick(ed)	timid		tyrannical(ly)
trim(med)	tinder		tyrannosaurus
trip(ped)	tingle(d)		
	tingling		
twig(ged)	tinkle(d)		
twin(ned)	tinkling		
twinge	tinning		
twist	tinsel		
twit	tipping		
twitch(es)	tiptoe(d)		
twitched	tissue		
	titter(ed)		
	tribute		
	trickle(d)		
	trickling		
	tricky(-ier,-iest)		
	trigger(ed)		
	trillion		
	trimming		
	trimmings		
	trinket		
	triple(d)		
	triplet		
	tripling		
	tripping		
	twiddle(d)		
	twiddling		
	twigging		
	twinkle(d)		
	twinkling		
	twinning		
	twisted		
	twisting		
	twitter(ed)		

for i-r
see page 253

In these words you can hear the vowel sound i as in pig

✻

✻ ✻

✻ ✻ ✻

✻ ✻ ✻ ✻

until

V

✻

✻ ✻

✻ ✻ ✻

✻ ✻ ✻ ✻ [✻]

vicar
vicious
victim
victor
victual
vigil
vigour
villa
village
*villain (wicked
    person)
*villein (free
    villager in
    medieval times)
vineyard
viscose
vision
visit(ed)
visual(ly)
vivid
vixen

vanilla

vermilion

vibrato
vicarage
victimise(d)
    ze
victory(-ies)
video
Vietnam
vigilance
vigilant
vigorous
villager
vinegar
viola
visible
visited
visiting
visitor
visual(ly)
visualise(d)
    ze
vitamin

validity

velocity(-ies)
vermiculite

vicinity
Victorian
victorious
Vietnamese
vigilante
visibility
visualise(d)
    ze
visually

for i-r
see page 254

*

whelk
*which (that /
    which one)
whiff(ed)
Whig
whim
whip(ped)
whisk(ed)
whiz(zed)

wick
width
wig(ged)
will(ed)
wilt
win
[won]
wince(d)
wind
wing(ed)
wink(ed)
wish(es)
wished
wisp
wit(ted)
*witch (woman said
    to use magic)
with

*wring (twist)
[wrung]
wrist
writ

* *

whimper(ed)
whinny(-ies)
    (whinnied)
whippet
whipping
whisker(ed)
whiskey
whisky(-ies)
whisper(ed)
whistle(d)
whistling
*whither (to which
    place)
Whitsun
whittle(d)
whittling
whizzing

wicked
wicker
wicket
widow(ed)
wigging
wiggle(d)
wiggling
wigwam
willing
willow
windmill
window
windpipe
windscreen
windward
windy(-ier,-iest)
winkle(d)
winkling
winner
winning
winter(ed)
wintry
wishing
wisdom
wistful(ly)
-see next page

* * *

whichever

wilderness(es)
window-sill
wintertime
wistfully
withdrawal

* * * *

witticism

for i-r
see page 255

In these words you can hear the vowel sound i as in pig

* *

witchcraft
withdraw
[withdrew]
withdrawal
withdrawn
*wither(ed) (become
    dry and shrivelled)
withhold
[withheld]
within
without
withstand
[withstood]
witness(ed)
witty(-ier,-iest)
wizened

women

wriggle(d)
wriggling
wrinkle(d)
wrinkling
written

for i-r
see page 255

Z

*

zinc
zip(ped)

* *

zigzag(ged)
zipper
zipping
zither

* * *

zigzagging
Zimbabwe

* * * *

*	* *	* * *	* * * * [* * * *]
*-all (every one) -alms	-abroad abscond	abolish(es) abolished	abdominal abominable abominate

*-awe (fear and
  wonder)
-awed
-awl (boring tool)
 	
-ought
	across
	
	adopt
	
	agog
		acknowledge(d)
		
		allotment
		allotted
		allotting
		-almighty
		alongside
		-already
		-alternate
		
		apostle
		-appalling
		
		astonish(es)
		astonished
		
		-audible
		-audience
		-auditory
		-aurally
		-aurora
		-Austria
		-authentic(ally)
		-authoress(es)
		-authorise(d)
		      ze
		-autograph(ed)
		
		-awfully
			accommodate
			accommodation
			acknowledgement/
			acknowledgment
			acknowledging
			
			-alternating
			-alternative
			-alternator
			-altogether
			
			anonymous
			
			apologetic(ally)
			apologise(d)
			      ze
			apology(-ies)
			apostrophe
			approximate
			approximately
			approximation
			
			astonishment
			astrology
			astronomer
			astronomy
			
			-auditory
			Australia
			-authentically
			-authority(-ies)
			-autobiography(-ies)
			-autobiographical(ly)
			-automatic(ally)
			-automation
			-automobile
			-autonomic
			-autonomous
			-auxiliary(-ies)

allot(ted)
almost
aloft
along
-alright
-also
*-altar (holy table)
*-alter(ed) (change)
-although
-always

anon

-appal(led)
-applaud
-applause

assault

-auburn
-auction(ed)
*-auger (tool)
*-augur (suggest for
  the future)
-August
-august
-aural(ly)
-austere
-author
-autumn

-awesome/awsome
-awful(ly)
-awkward

for H . . .
see page 102

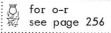

for o-r
see page 256

In these words you can hear the vowel sound o as in dog

*

*-bald (lacking hair)
-balk/baulk(ed)
*-ball (round object /
    dance)
*-balled (made into a
    ball)
*-balm (ointment)
-baulk/balk(ed)
*-bawl (yell)
*-bawled (did yell)

block(ed)
*blond (man with
    fair hair)
*blonde (woman with
    fair hair)
blot(ted)

bob(bed)
bog(ged)
*bomb (explosive
    device)
bombed
bond
boss(es)
bossed
-bought
box(es)
boxed

-brawl(ed)
-broad
bronze(d)
-brought
broth

* *

-balmy
-balsa
balsam
-Baltic
-ballroom
-basalt
-bauxite

because
-befall
[befell]
-[befallen]
belong(ed)
beyond

blancmange
blockade
blockboard
blossom(ed)
blotted
blotter
blotting

bobbing
body(-ies)
    (bodied)
boggy(-ier,-iest)
bombard
bomber
bonnet
bonny(-ier,-iest)
borrow(ed)
bossy(-ier,-iest)
bother(ed)
bottle(d)
bottling
bottom(ed)
boxer
boxing

-broadcast
-[broadcast]
-broadside
bronchial
bronco

* * *

-befallen
belonging

bodily
borrowing
botany

-broadcasting
broccoli
bronchitis

* * * *

barometer

binocular
binoculars

Bolivia
botanical

brontosaurus

In these words 'o' is a neutral vowel.
It sounds like the 'a' in 'astonish'.

Bolivia   botanical   brocade

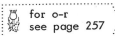

for o-r
see page 257

95

In these words you can hear the vowel sound o as in dog

C

SHORT
VOWEL (o)

-call(ed)
-calm(ed)
*-caught (got /
    trapped)
-caulk(ed)
-cause(d)
-caw(ed)

-chalk(ed)
chop(ped)

*-clause (words in
    sentence / part
    of written
    agreement)
-claw(ed)
*-claws (curved nails
    or limbs)

clock(ed)
clod
clot(ted)
cloth

cock(ed)
cod
cop(ped)
*cops (the police)
*copse (small wood)
cost
[cost]
cot
cough(ed)

-crawl(ed)
crock(ed)
croft
crop(ped)

cross(es)
crossed

for Qu ...
see page 109

-calling
-cauldron
-causing
-caustic(ally)
-caution(ed)
-cautious

chocolate
chopper
chopping
chopsticks
chronic(ally)

clockwise
clotted
clotting

cobbler
cobweb(bed)
cocker
cockerel
cockle
Cockney
cockpit
cockroach(es)
cocktail
codfish
coffee
coffin
*collage (picture
    made by sticking
    items to a board)
collar(ed)
colleague
collect
*college (educational
    establishment)
collie
collier
column(ed)
combat(ted)
combine
comet
comic
comma
comment
commerce
common
commune
-see next page

cauliflower
-caustically

chloroform(ed)
chlorophyll
chronically

cochlea
cockerel
colliery(-ies)
colonise(d)
    ze
colony(-ies)
colonist
colossal(ly)
combatted
combatting
comedy(-ies)
comical(ly)
commentary(-ies)
commonplace
commonwealth
communal(ly)
communist
compensate
competence
competent
*complement
    (something that
    completes)
complicate
*compliment
    (expression of
    praise or
    politeness)
composite
comprehend
compromise
concentrate
concentric
concoction
conference
confidence
confident
confiscate
congregate
congruent
conical
conifer
conjugate
connoisseur
conqueror
-see next page

-caustically

chronically
chronological(ly)

colossally
combination
comically
commentator
commodity(-ies)
communally
communism
commutative
commutator
comparable
compensation
competition
*complementary
    (making up a
    whole)
complication
*complimentary
    (expressing praise)
composition
compositor
comprehension
comprehensive
computation
concentration
concertina
condensation
confidential(ly)
confirmation
confrontation
conglomerate
conglomeration
congregation
conscientious
consecration
consequently
conservation
consolation
constellation
constitution
-see next page

for o-r
see page 258

In these words you can hear the vowel sound o as in dog

✳ ✳   ✳ ✳ ✳   ✳ ✳ ✳ ✳ [✳]

compact	consciousness	continental(ly)
complex(es)	consecrate	continuity(-ies)
compound	consequence	contraception
comrade	consequent	contraceptive
concave	consonant	contradiction
concept	constitute	contribution
concert	contemplate	controversial(ly)
concoct	continent	controversy(-ies)
concord	contradict	conversation
concrete	contrary	coronation
conduct	convalesce(d)	correlation
	correspond	*correspondence
conflict	corridor	(exchange of
congress	cosmetic(ally)	letters /
*conker (horse	cosmically	similarity)
chestnut)	cosmonaut	correspondent
conic	cottoning	*correspondents (those
*conquer(ed) (defeat)		sending letters or
conquest	crockery	reports)
conscience	crocodile	corresponding
conscious		cosmetically
conscript		cosmically
console		
constant		
contact		kilometer
content		
contents		
contest		
context		
contour(ed)		
contract		
contrast		
convent		
converse		
convert		
convex		
convict		
convoy		
copper		
copy(-ies)		
(copied)		
copping		
*coral (substance		
formed from bones		
of sea creatures)		
*corral (enclosure for		
horses and cattle)		
cosmic(ally)		
costly		
costume(d)		
cottage		
cotter(ed)		
cotton(ed)		
-see next page		

for Qu ...
see page 109

for o-r
see page 258

In these words you can hear the vowel sound o as in dog

* *

-crawling
cropping
crossbar
crossing
crossroads
crosswise
crossword
crotchet

for Qu ...
see page 109

for o-r
see page 258

In these words the first letter 'o' is a neutral vowel.
It... er.... er.... er.... sounds like the 'a' in 'astonish'.

'CORRECT' WORDS

cholesterol
chorale
cocoon(ed)
collapse(d)
collapsible
collect(ing)
collection
collective
collector
collide
collision
cologne
colonial(ly)
combat(ted)
combatting
combine(d)
combining
combustible
combustion
comedian
comedienne
command(er)
commandment
commemorate
commemoration
commence(d)
commercial(ly)
commission(ed)
commissioner
commit(ted)
commitment
committee
committing
commodity(-ies)
commotion
communal(ly)
commune(d)
communicate
communication
communion

community(-ies)
commutative
commute(r)
companion
compare(d)
comparing
comparison
compartment
compassion(ate)
compatible
compel(led)
compelling
compete
competitive
competitor
compile(d)
complain(ed)
complaint
complete(ly)
completion
complexion
component
compose(d)
composer
compress(es)
compressed
compression
compressor
comprise(d)
comprising
compulsory
compute(r)
computerise(d)
  ze
conceal(ed)
conceit(ed)
conceive(d)
concentric
conception
concern(ed)

concerning
concession
conclude
conclusion
concurrent
concuss(es)
concussed
concussing
concussion
condemn(ed)
condense(d)
condenser
condition(ed)
conditional(ly)
conduct(ion)
conductor
confectioner(y)
confer(red)
conferring
confess(es)
confessed
confession(al)
confessor
confetti
confide
confine(d)
confirm(ed)
conflict
conform(ed)
conformist
conformity
confront
confuse(d)
confusion
congenital(ly)
congratulate
congratulations
coniferous
conjecture(d)
conjunction

connect(ed)
connecting
connection
connector
conscription
consecutive
consensus
consent
conservative
conserve(d)
consider(ed)
considerable
considerate
consideration
consist(ing)
consistency(-ies)
consistent
console(d)
conspicuous
conspiracy(-ies)
conspire(d)
constabulary(-ies)
constituency(-ies)
constituent
construct(ed)
construction
constructive
consult
consume(d)
consumer
consumption
contagious
contain(ed)
container
contaminate
contamination
contemporary(-ies)
contempt(ible)
contemptuous
contend

content
contention
contest(ant)
contingency(-ies)
continual(ly)
continuation
continue(d)
continuous
continuum
contract(ion)
contractor
contralto(s)
contraption
contrary
contrast
contribute(d)
control(led)
controller
controlling
convenience
convenient
convention(ally)
converge(d)
convergent
converse(d)
conversion
convert(ible)
convey(ed)
conveyer
convict(ion)
convince(d)
convulse(d)
convulsion
convulsive
correct(ed)
correction
correctly
corrode
corrosion
corrupt(ion)

In these words you can hear the vowel sound o as in dog

✲

-daub(ed)
-dawn(ed)

dock(ed)
dodge(d)
dog(ged)
doll(ed)
don(ned)
dong(ed)
dot(ted)
✲-draw (pull /
    sketch)
[drew]
-[drawn]
✲-drawer (sliding
    container)
-drawl(ed)
drop(ped)

✲ ✲

-daughter
-dawdle
-dawdling

demobbed

dissolve(d)

doctor(ed)
doctrine
dodgem
dodger
dodging
dodgy(-ier,-iest)
dogging
doghouse
dollar
dolphin
donkey
donning
dotted
dotting

-drawbridge
-drawing
droplet
dropout
dropping

✲ ✲ ✲

demolish(es)
demolished
deposit(ed)
deposited

dishonest

doctrinal(ly)
document
doggedly
dominant
dominate
domino(es)

✲ ✲ ✲ ✲ [✲]

democracy(-ies)
denomination
denominator
deposited
depositing

disqualify(-ies)
    (disqualified)

doctrinally
dolphinarium
domination

dromedary(-ies)

> In these words 'o' is a neutral vowel.
> It sounds like the 'a' in 'astonish'.
>
> domain   domestic(ally)   domesticate

for o-r
see page 259

E

✲

✲ ✲

encore(d)

en- or in- ?

evolve(d)

exalt
-exhaust

✲ ✲ ✲

em- or im- ?

en- or in- ?

erotic(ally)

exalted
-exhausted
-exhaustion
exotic(ally)

✲ ✲ ✲ ✲ [✲]

ecology
economy(-ies)

el- or il- ?

em- or im- ?

en- or in- ?

equality

erotically

exotically

for I ...
see page 102

for o-r
see page 259

In these words you can hear the vowel sound o as in dog

F

✲

-fall
 [fell]
-[fallen]
 false
 fault

-fawn(ed)

-flaunt
-flaw(ed)
 flock(ed)
 flog(ged)
 flop(ped)

 fog
 fond
 font
-fought
 fox(es)
 foxed

-fraud
 frock
 frog
 from
 frond
 frost
 froth(ed)

> for th ...
> see page 133

✲ ✲

-falcon
-fallen
-falling
-fallout
 falter(ed)
 faulty

 flogging
 flopping
 floppy(-ier,-iest)
 floral
 florist

 fodder
 foggy(-ier,-iest)
 foghorn
 follow(ed)
 folly(-ies)
 fondle(d)
 fondling
 forage(d)
 forehead
 foreign
 forest
 forgone/foregone
 forgot
 fossil
 foster(ed)
 foxglove

 frogman
 frolic(ked)

 phosphate

✲ ✲ ✲

 foggiest

 follower
 following
 foreigner
 forestry
 forgotten

 frolicking

 phosphorus

✲ ✲ ✲ ✲ [✲]

 ferocity

 phenomena
 phenomenal(ly)
 phenomenon
 philosophy(-ies)
 photographer
 photography

> for o-r
> see page 260

In these words you can hear the vowel sound o ⁄ as in dog

✶	✶ ✶	✶ ✶ ✶	✶ ✶ ✶ ✶
-gaunt	-gaudy(-ier,-iest)	galoshes	geography(-ies)
-gauze			geology
	globule	Gibraltar	geometry(-ies)
gloss(es)	glossy(-ies)		
glossed		globular	
	gobble(d)	glockenspiel	
-gnaw(ed)	*gobbling (greedily	glossary(-ies)	
	eating)		
god	goblet	godparents	
God	*goblin (evil spirit)	golliwog	
golf(ed)	goddess(es)	*gorilla (ape)	
gone	goggles	gossiping	
gong	golly		
gosh	gosling	grovelling	
got	gospel		
	gossip(ed)		
	Gothic		
	grotto(es/s)		
	grotty(-ier,-iest)		
	grovel(led)		
	grovelling		

for o-r
see page 261

> In this word 'o' is a neutral vowel.
> It sounds like the 'a' in 'astonish'.
>
> gorilla

*

*-hall (large room /
      passage)
halt
*-haul(ed) (drag /
      amount gained)
-hauled
-haunt
-hawk(ed)

hob
hog(ged)
honk(ed)
hop(ped)
hot

* *

-halter
-haughty(-ier,-iest)
-haunches

hobble(d)
hobbling
hobby(-ies)
hockey
hogging
Holland
holler(ed)
hollow(ed)
holly
honest
Hongkong
honour(ed)
hopper
hopping
hopscotch
horrid
horror
hostage
*hostel (place to stay
    in)
*hostile (unfriendly)
hotch-potch
hotter
hottest
hovel
hover(ed)

* * *

-haughtily

historic(ally)

holiday
hollyhock
homonym
honesty
honestly
honourable
horizon
horoscope
horrible
horrify(-ies)
   (horrified)
hospital
hovercraft

hypnotic(ally)

* * * * [*]

historical(ly)

holography
honorary
honourable
horizontal(ly)
horrifying
hospitable
hospitality
hostility(-ies)

hypnotically

for o-r
see page 261

I

*

* *

-instal(led)
involve(d)

iv- or ev- ?

* * *

impromptu(s)
improper

-installing
-instalment/
installment
involvement

ir- or er- ?

ix- or ex- ?

for o-r
see page 262

* * * * [*]

ic- or ec- ?

illogical(ly)

impossible

-inaugural
inoculate

iq- or eq- ?

ir- or er- ?

ix- or ex- ?

for E ...
see page 99

In these words you can hear the vowel sound o as in dog

J

*	* *	* * *	* * * *
-jaunt	-jaunty(-ier,-iest)	-Gibraltar	geography(-ies)
-jaw			geology
	jobbing	jocular	geometry(-ies)
job(bed)	jockey(ed)		
jog(ged)	jodhpurs		
jolt	jogging		
jot(ted)	jolly(-ies)		
	(jollied)		
	jostle(d)		
	jostling		
	jotted		
	jotter		
	jotting		

for o-r
see page 262

K

*	* *	* * *	* * * *
knob	knocker		kilometre
knock(ed)	knotted		
*knot(ted) (tied	knotting		knowledgeable
fastening / hard	knotty(-ier,-iest)		
part of wood /	knowledge		
sea mile [per			
hour])			

for C ...
see page 96

In this word 'o' is a neutral vowel. It sounds like the 'a' in 'astonish'.

Korea(n)

for o-r
see page 262

for Qu ...
see page 109

In these words you can hear the vowel sound o as in dog

L

L

✻	✻ ✻	✻ ✻ ✻	✻ ✻ ✻ ✻ [✻ ✻]
-launch(es)	-launcher	laconic(ally)	laboratory(-ies)
-launched	-launder(ed)	-launderette	laconically
-law	-laundry(-ies)		
-lawn	laurel	logical(ly)	logarithm
	-lawyer	lollipop	logically
lob(bed)		longitude	longitudinal(ly)
*loch (Scottish word for 'lake')	lobbing		
*lock (fastening device)	lobby(-ies) (lobbied)		
locked	lobster		
lodge(d)	locker		
loft	locket		
log(ged)	lodger		
long(ed)	lodging		
lop(ped)	lofty(-ier,-iest)		
loss(es)	logging		
lost	logic(ally)		
lot	longer		
	longest		
	lopping		
	lorry(-ies)		
	lotto		
	lozenge		

for o-r
see page 263

In these words you can hear the vowel sound o as in dog

M

*

malt
-maul(ed)
-mauve

mob(bed)
mock(ed)
mop(ped)
mosque
moss(es)
moth

for o-r
see page 263

* *

Malta

mobbing
model(led)
modelling
moderate
modern
modest
module
mollusc
monarch
mongol
mongoose(s)
monsoon
monster
monstrous
mopping
*moral(ly) (concerning
    right and wrong)
*morale (confidence)
morrow
mossy(-ier,-iest)
mottled
motto(es/s)

* * *

melodic(ally)

mnemonic

moccasin
mockery(-ies)
modelling
moderate
modernise(d)
    ze
modesty
modify(-ies)
    (modified)
molasses
molecule
monastery(-ies)
monitor(ed)
monochrome
monotone
monoxide
monument
morally
moralise(d)
    ze
Morocco
mosquito(es)

* * * * [* * *]

mahogany
majority(-ies)

melodically

moderation
moderato
modification
modifier
molecular
monochromatic(ally)
monopolise(d)
    ze
monopoly(-ies)
monotonous
monumental(ly)
morality(-ies)

mythology(-ies)

In these words the
'o' may be neutral.

Mohammed   momentum
molasses   morale
molecular

N

*

-gnaw(ed)

knob
knock(ed)
*knot(ted) (tied fastening /
    hard part of wood /
    sea mile [per hour])

-naught/nought (zero)

nod(ded)
*not (used in
    denial, negation,
    refusal)
notch(es)
notched
-nought/naught (zero)

* *

knocker
knotted
knotting
knotty(-ier,-iest)
knowledge

-naughty(-ier,-iest)

nodding
nodule
nonsense
nostril
novel
novice
nozzle

* * *

mnemonic

-nautical(ly)
-naughtier
-naughtiest
-naughtiness

neurotic(ally)

nocturnal(ly)
nominal(ly)
nominate
novelty(-ies)

* * * *

knowledgeable

-nautically

neurotically

nocturnally
nominally
nonconformist
notwithstanding

for o-r
see page 263

In these words you can hear the vowel sound o as in dog

*

*-all (every one)
-alms

*-awe (fear and wonder)
-awed
*-awl (boring tool)

odd

of
off

on

-ought

ox(en)

* *

almost
-alright
also
*~altar (holy table)
*-alter(ed) (change)
-although
-always

-auburn
-auction(ed)
*-auger (tool)
*-augur (suggest for the
future)
-August
-august
-aural(ly)
-austere
-author
-autumn

-awesome/awsome
-awful(ly)
-awkward

honest
honour(ed)

object
oblique
oblong

o'clock
octane
octave

oddment

offer(ed)
offering
office
offset
offshore
offside
offspring
offstage
often

olive
-see next page

for H . . .
see page 102

* * *

-almighty
-already
-alternate

-audible
-audience
-auditory
-aurally
-aurora
-Austria
-authentic(ally)
-authoress(es)
-authorise(d)
ze
-autograph(ed)

-awfully

honesty
honourable

obsolete
obstacle
obvious

occupant
occupy(-ies)
(occupied)
octagon
October
octopus(es/-i)
oculist

oddity(-ies)

offering
offertory(-ies)
officer

ominous
omnibus

oncoming
onlooker
-see next page

* * * * [* * * *]

-alternating
-alternative
-alternator
-altogether

-auditory
Australia
-authentically
-authority(-ies)
-autobiography(-ies)
-autobiographical(ly)
-automatic(ally)
-automation
-automobile
-autonomic
-autonomous
-auxiliary(-ies)

honorary
honourable

obligation
observation
obsidian
obviously

occupation
occupier
octagonal

offertory(-ies)

operated
operatic(ally)
operating
operation
operator
opportunity(-ies)
opposition
optically
optimally
optimistic(ally)
-see next page

for o-r
see page 264

In these words you can hear the vowel sound **o** as in **dog**

✷   ✷ ✷   ✷ ✷ ✷   ✷ ✷ ✷ ✷ [✷ ✷]

omelette	opera	orienteering
	operate	
onset	opossum	oxidisation
onslaught	opposite	zation
onward	optical(ly)	oxyacetylene
	optician	
opera	optimal(ly)	
optic(ally)	optimist	
option	optional	
orange	orator	
	oratory	
osprey	origin	
ostrich(es)		
	osmium	
otter	osmosis	

┌─────────────────┐   ┌─────────────────┐
│ for H ...   │   oxen   oxidise(d)   │ for o-r   │
│ see page 102   │   oxide   ze   │ see page 264   │
└─────────────────┘   oxygen   └─────────────────┘

for H ... see page 102
for o-r see page 264

In these words the first letter 'o' is a neutral vowel.
It... er.... er.... er.... sounds like the 'a' in 'astonish'.

'ORIGINAL' WORDS

obedience	obscene	obsessive	offence	oppress(es)
obedient	obscure(d)	obstruct(ion)	offend	oppressed
obey(ed)	obscurity(-ies)	obstructive	offensive	oppression
object(ion)	observant	obtain(ed)	official(ly)	oppressive
objectionable	observatory(-ies)	obtuse	omission	oppressor
objective	observe(d)	occasion(al)	omit(ted)	original(ly)
oblige(d)	observer	occasionally	omitting	originality
oblique	observing	occur(red)	opinion	originate
obliterate	obsess(es)	occurrence	opossum	
oblivion	obsessed	occurring	opponent	
oblivious	obsessional(ly)	o'clock	oppose(d)	

✻	✻ ✻	✻ ✻ ✻	✻ ✻ ✻ ✻ [✻ ✻]
-palm(ed)	-palfrey	peroxide	pathology
*-pause (brief gap / hesitate)	phosphate	phosphorus	phenomena
-paused			phenomenal(ly)
*-paw (foot of animal)	plotted	podgier	phenomenon
-pawed	plotting	podgiest	philosophy(-ies)
-pawn(ed)		policy(-ies)	photographer
*-paws (feet of animal)	pocket	politics	photography
	podded	pollinate	
	podding	pollution	politician
plot(ted)	podgy(-ier,-iest)	poltergeist	pollination
	polish(es)	polygon	Polynesia
pod(ded)	polished	ponderous	polynomial
pomp	polka	*populace (common people)	polyphonic(ally)
pond	pollen	*populous (full of people)	polyphony
pop(ped)	ponder(ed)		polytechnic
pot(ted)	pontoon	popular	polyurethane
	popcorn	populate	popularity
	poplar	positive	pomegranate
-prawn	poplin	possible	population
prod(ded)	popping	possibly	possibility(-ies)
prompt	poppy(-ies)	postulate	
prong(ed)	porridge	pottery(-ies)	predominantly
prop(ped)	possum	poverty	probability(-ies)
	posture(d)		proclamation
-psalm	potted	-precaution	profitable
	potting	probable	propaganda
		probably	proposition
	problem	prodigal	prosecution
	prodded	prodigy(-ies)	prosperity
	prodding	profited	provocation
	produce	profiting	provocative
	product	progeny	
	*profit(ed) (gain)	projectile	
	project	promenade	
	prolong(ed)	prominent	
	promise(d)	promising	
	proper	propagate	
	*prophet (inspired religious leader)	propelling	
	propose(d)	propellor	
	propping	*prophecy(-ies) (statement about a future event)	
	prospect		
	prosper(ed)	*prophesy(-ies) (make a statement about the future) (prophesied)	
	prostate		
	prostrate		
	proverb		
	province	properly	
		property(-ies)	
		-see next page	

for o-r
see page 265

In these words you can hear the vowel sound o as in dog

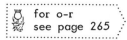

* * *

prosecute
prospective
prospector
prosperous
Protestant
prostitute
providence
provident

for o-r
see page 265

In these words the first letter 'o' is a neutral vowel.
It... er.... er.... er.... sounds like the 'a' in 'astonish'.

'PROFOUND' WORDS

phonetic(ally)	probation	professional(ly)	promote	prospectus(es)
photographer	procedure	professor	promotion	protect(ed)
photography	proceed(ing)	proficiency	pronounce(d)	protection
police(man)	procession	proficient	pronouncement	protective
polite(ly)	proclaim(ed)	profound	pronouncing	protector
political(ly)	procure(d)	profuse	pronunciation	protest
pollute	prodigious	profusion	propel(led)	protractor
pollution	produce(d)	progression	propelling	protrude
polyphony	producer	progressive	propeller	provide(d)
position(ed)	producing	prohibit(ed)	proportional(ly)	providing
possess(es)	production	prohibiting	proposal	provincial
possessed	productive	prohibitive	propose(d)	provision(s)
possession	profane	project(ion)	proprietor	provisional(ly)
possessive	profess(es)	projectile	propulsion	provocative
potato(es)	professed	projector	prospect(ive)	provoke(d)
potential(ly)	professing	prolific(ally)	prospector	

Q

*	* *	* * *	* * * * [*]
	quadrant	quadrangle	quadrilateral
	quarrel(led)	quadratic	qualification
	quarry(-ies)	quadruped	
	(quarried)	quadruple(d)	
		quadruplet	
		qualify(-ies)	
		(qualified)	
		quality(-ies)	
		quantity(-ies)	
		quarantine	
		quarrelling	

In these words you can hear the vowel sound o as in dog

R

☆   ☆ ☆   ☆ ☆ ☆   ☆ ☆ ☆ ☆ [☆ ☆]

-raw

rob(bed)
rock(ed)
rod(ded)
romp(ed)
rot(ted)

wrath
wrong(ed)

-recall(ed)
resolve(d)
respond
response
revolt
revolve(d)

rhombus

robber
robbing
robin
rocker
rocket
rocky(-ier,-iest)
rodded
rodding
*rollick (act with
    enjoyment)
*rollock/rowlock
    (pivot for oar)
rosin(ed)
roster
rotted
rotten
rotting
*rowlock/rollock
    (pivot for oar)

rendezvous
responsive
revolver

robbery(-ies)
rockery(-ies)
rollicking

responsibility(-ies)
responsible

for o-r
see page 266

> In these words 'o' is a neutral vowel.
> It sounds like the 'a' in 'astonish'.
>
>   romance
>   romantic(ally)

In these words you can hear the vowel sound o as in dog

✲	✲ ✲	✲ ✲ ✲	✲ ✲ ✲ ✲ [✲]
-psalm	-salty(-ier,-iest)	-saucily	solubility
	-saucer		
salt	-saucepan	scholarship	spontaneity
-sauce	-saucy(-ier,-iest)		spontaneous
-saw	-saunter(ed)	shopkeeper	
-saw(ed)	sausage		symbolically
-[sawn]		soldering	symphonically
	scholar	solenoid	synonymous
-scald	scoffing	solitary	
scoff(ed)	Scotland	solitude	
scone	Scottish	soluble	
scotch(ed)		solution	
Scotch	shoddy(-ier,-iest)	sombrero(s)	
-scrawl(ed)	shopper	sovereignty(-ies)	
	shopping	soviet	
-shawl	shotgun		
shock(ed)		-strawberry(-ies)	
shod	-slaughter(ed)		
shone	slogging	symbolic(ally)	
shop(ped)	slopping	symphonic(ally)	
shot	sloppy(-ier,-iest)		
	slotted		
slog(ged)	slotting		
slop(ped)			
slosh(es)	-smaller		
sloshed	-smallest		
slot(ted)	-smallpox		
	smocking		
-small			
smock(ed)	sobbing		
smog	soccer		
	socket		
sob(bed)	sodden		
sock(ed)	soften(ed)		
sod	softer		
soft	softly		
solve(d)	software		
song	soggy(-ier,-iest)		
-sought	solder(ed)		
	solemn		
-spawn(ed)	solid		
spot(ted)	solvent		
-sprawl(ed)	solving		
-see next page	sorrow(ed)		
	sorry(-ier,-iest)		
	sovereign		
	-see next page		

for o-r
see page 267

In these words you can hear the vowel sound o as in dog

111

✲   ✲ ✲

squad
squash(ed)
squat(ted)
-squawk(ed)

-stalk(ed)
-stall(ed)
-staunch(es)
-staunched
stock(ed)
stodge
stop(ped)
-straw
strong

swab(bed)
swamp(ed)
swan
swap(ped)
*swat (slap with a
    flat object)
*swot (study hard)

sponsor(ed)
spotlight
spotted
spotting
sprocket

squabble(d)
squabbling
squadron
squalid
squander(ed)
squatted
squatter
squatting

-stalling
-stalwart
stockade
stocking(ed)
stodgy(-ier,-iest)
stopping
-strawberry(-ies)
stronger
strongest
strongly

swabbing
swallow(ed)
swapping
*swatted   (see
*swatting 'swat')
*swotted   (see
*swotting 'swot')

for o-r
see page 267

In these words the first letter 'o'
is a neutral vowel. It.. er... er...
sounds like the 'a' in 'astonish'.

society(-ies)	Somalia
solicitor	sophisticated
solution	soprano(s)

In these words you can hear the vowel sound o as in dog

T

☆

-talk(ed)
-tall
*-taut (tight)
*-taught (instructed)
-taunt

-thaw(ed)
thongs
-thought
throb(bed)
throng(ed)

tongs
top(ped)
toss(ed)

trod
trot(ted)
trough(ed)

☆ ☆

-talking
-taller
-tallest

-thoughtful(ly)
throbbing
throttle(d)

toddle(d)
toffee
toggle
tomboy
tonic
tonsil
topic
topping
topple(d)
toppling
topsoil
torrent
toxic
toxin

trodden
trolley
trombone
tropic(ally)
trotted
trotting

☆ ☆ ☆

-talkative

-thoughtfully

toboggan
tolerance
tolerate
tomahawk
tommy-gun
tomorrow
topical

tropical(ly)

☆ ☆ ☆ ☆

theodolite
thermometer

tonsillitis
topography
topology
topsy-turvy

tropically

☙ for o-r
   see page 268

> In these words the first letter 'o'
> is a neutral vowel. It.. er... er...
> sounds like the 'a' in 'astonish'.
>
> tobacco(s)   topography(-ies)
> tobacconist   torrential(ly)
> tomato(es)

U

☆

☆ ☆

upon

☆ ☆ ☆

☆ ☆ ☆ ☆

V

*

*vault (gymnastic
   leap /
   underground room /
   arched roof)

*volt (unit of
   electrical force)

* *

volley(ed)
voltage
volume
vomit(ed)

* * *

volatile
volcano(es/s)
volcanic(ally)
voluntary
volunteer(ed)

* * * * [*]

velocity(-ies)

volcanically

> In this word 'o' is a neutral vowel.
> It sounds like the 'a' in 'astonish'.
>
> vocabulary(-ies)

W

*

waft
-walk(ed)
-wall(ed)
waltz(es)
waltzed
wand
want
was
*wash(es)
washed
wasp
watch(es)
watched
*watt (unit of
   electric power)
*watts (units of
   electric power)

*what (that or those
   which / which /
   how much / I do
   not understand)
*what's (what is)

wrath
wrong(ed)
-wrought

* *

wadding
waddle(d)
waddling
-walking
wallet
wallow(ed)
-walnut
-walrus
wander(ed)
wanted
wanting
warrant
warren
washer
*washers (people or
   machines that
   wash / insulating
   rings)
*washes (cleans with
   water)
washing
wasn't
watchdog
watchful(ly)
watching
watchman
watchword
-water(ed)

wobble(d)
wobbling
wobbly
wonky(-ier,-iest)

* * *

-wallpaper(ed)
warrior
washable
watchfully
-waterfall
-waterfowl
-watershed

whatever

* * * *

-walkie-talkie

> for o-r
> see page 269

114

In these words you can hear the vowel sound o as in dog

Y

*

yacht
-yawn(ed)

* *

yoghourt/
yoghurt/yogurt
yonder

* * *

* * * *

for o-r
see page 269

Z

*

* *

zombi/zombie

* * *

* * * *

zoology

In these words you can hear the vowel sound o as in dog

*

* *

above
abrupt

-adjourn(ed)
adjust
adult

-afoot
among
amongst

-assure(d)

-august

* * *

abundance
abundant

accomplish(es)
accomplished
accustom(ed)

adjuster
adjustment

another

assumption
-assurance

* * * * [*]

accompaniment
accompany(-ies)
  (accompanied)
accomplishment

for u-r (ur/ir)
see page 242

B

*

blood
bluff(ed)
blunt
blush(es)
blushed

-book(ed)

-brook(ed)
brush(es)
brushed

buck(ed)
bud(ded)
budge(d)
buff(ed)
bug(ged)
bulb
bulge(d)
bulk
-bull
-see next page

* *

-because
become
[became]
[become]
begun
beloved

bloodshed
bloody(-ier,-iest)
blubber(ed)
blunder(ed)

-bookcase
-booklet
-bookshelf(-ves)
borough
-bosom

brother
Brussels
-see next page

* * *

becoming
beloved

brotherhood

buccaneer(ed)
bucketing
bucketful
-Buddhism
budgerigar
budgeting
buffalo(es)
-bulletin
-bulldozer(ed)
bumblebee
bungalow
buttercup
butterfly(-ies)
buttermilk

* * * *

brother-in-law
budgerigar
Bulgaria

for u-r (ur/ir)
see page 243

- or oo as in woodpecker

In these words you can hear the sound U as in duck

*

* *

bump(ed)
bun
bunch(es)
bunched
bung(ed)
bunk(ed)
bus(es)
*bussed (carried
   by bus)
-bush(es)
-bushed
*bust (upper part
   of body /
   break / arrest)
*but (except /
   instead / yet)
*butt (large cask /
   person made fun
   of / thick end of
   tool or weapon /
   push with head)
buzz(es)
buzzed

bubble(d)
bubbling
bucket(ed)
buckle(d)
buckling
-Buddha
-Buddhist
budding
budget(ed)
budgie
budging
buffer(ed)
buffet
buffing
bugging
buggy(-ies)
bulbous
bulky(-ier,-iest)
-bulldog
-bullet
-bullfrog
-bullock
-bully(-ies)
- (bullied)
-bulrush(es)
bumper
bundle(d)
bundling
bungle(d)
bungling
bunion
bunker(ed)
bunny(-ies)
Bunsen
burrow(ed)
-bushel
bustle(d)
bustling
-butcher(ed)
butler
*butted (pushed
   with head)
*butter(ed) (spread
   with butter)
button(ed)
buttress(es)
buttressed
butty(-ies)
buzzard
buzzer

for u-r (ur/ir)
see page 243

- or oo as in woodpecker

In these words you can hear the sound u as in duck

117

C

*	* *	* * *	* * * * [*]
chuck(ed)	chuckle(d)	colander/cullender	circumference
chug(ged)	chuckling	colourful(ly)	
chum(med)	chugging	colourless	colourfully
chump	chumming	combustion	combustible
chunk(ed)	chutney	comfortable	compulsory
		company(-ies)	
club(bed)	clubhouse	concurrent	crustacean
cluck(ed)	clumsy(-ier,-iest)	concussing	
clump(ed)	cluster(ed)	concussion	culminate
clung	clutter(ed)	conduction	cultivation
clutch(ed)		conductor	culturally
	-colonel	conjunction	-curiosity(-ies)
come	colour(ed)	conjurer/or	customary
[came]	comfort	constable	
[come]	coming	constructed	
-cook(ed)	compass(es)	construction	
-could	concuss(es)	constructive	
	concussed	consumption	
-crook	conduct	convulsion	
crumb	confront	convulsive	
crunch(es)	conjure(d)	corruption	
crunched	construct	countrymen	
crush(es)	consult	countryside	
crushed	convulse(d)	coverage	
crust	-cooker	covering	
crutch(es)	-cooking		
	corrupt	crustacean	
cub	-couldn't		
cuff(ed)	country(-ies)	cul-de-sac	
cup(ped)	couple(d)	culminate	
-cure(d)	coupling	cultivate	
cut	courage	cultural(ly)	
[cut]	cousin	cumbersome	
	cover(ed)	-curator	
		-curio	
	-crooked	-curious	
	crumble(d)	currency(-ies)	
	crumbling	custody	
	crumpet	customary	
	crumple(d)	customer	
	crumpling		
	-see next page		

> for u-r (ur/ir) see page 244

- or oo as in woodpecker

In these words you can hear the sound U as in duck

✻ ✻

-cuckoo
cuddle(d)
cuddling
culprit
culture(d)
cunning
cupboard
cupping
-curate
*currant (fruit)
*current (flowing
   stream / present)
curry(-ies)
   (curried)
-cushion(ed)
custard
custom
customs
cutter
cutting

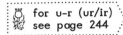
for u-r (ur/ir) see page 244

In this word the 'ou' is a neutral vowel.

courageous

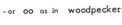
-or oo as in woodpecker

☆

does
done
*dost (old form of
    'do', used with
    'thou')
doth
dove

drug(ged)
drum(med)
drunk

duck
*ducked (did duck)
*duct (tube or pipe)
dug
dull(ed)
dumb
dump(ed)
dunce
dusk
*dust (particles of
    earth or waste
    matter)
Dutch

☆ ☆

*discuss(es) (debate)
*discussed (debated)
*disgust (strong
    dislike)
disrupt
distrust

doesn't
double(d)
doubling
dozen

drugging
drummer
drumming

duchess(es)
duckling
duffel/duffle
dugout
dummy(-ies)
dumpling
dungeon
-during
dustbin
duster
dusty(-ier,-iest)

☆ ☆ ☆

deduction
deductive
destruction
destructive

discomfort
discourage(d)
discover(ed)
discussing
discussion
disgusting
disruption
disruptive

dungarees

☆ ☆ ☆ ☆

discovery(-ies)

for u-r (ur/ir)
see page 245

E

☆

for I . . .
see page 123

☆ ☆

em- or im- ?

-endure(d)
engulf(ed)
enough
*-ensure(d) (make
    certain)
entrust

en- or in- ?

erupt

-Europe

☆ ☆ ☆

emulsion(ed)

em- or im- ?

encourage(d)
-endurance

en- or in- ?

erupted
eruption

☆ ☆ ☆ ☆

encouragement

en- or in- ?

-European

for u-r
see page 245

- or oo as in woodpecker

In these words you can hear the sound U as in duck

F

✲	✲ ✲	✲ ✲ ✲	✲ ✲ ✲ ✲ [✲]
flood	flourish(es)	fluctuate	fluctuation
fluff(ed)	flourished	-fluorescent	-fluorescent
flung	fluffy(-ier,-iest)		
flush(es)	-fluoride	frontier	functionally
flushed	-fluorine	frustrating	fundamental(ly)
flux(es)	flurry(-ies)	frustration	
	(flurried)		
-foot	fluster(ed)	-fulfilling	
	flutter(ed)	functional(ly)	
front		funnelling	
	-football	funnier	
fudge(d)	-foothill	funniest	
-full	-foothold	-furious	
fun	-footpath		
fund	-footstep		
fuss(es)	-forsook		
fussed			

frontier
frustrate

fudging
-fulcrum
-fulfil(led)
-fully
 fumble(d)
 function(ed)
 funfair
 fungi
*fungous (spongy or
  in other ways
  like a fungus)
*fungus (type of
  plant)
 funnel(led)
 funny(-ier,-iest)
 furrow(ed)
-fury(-ies)
 fuzzy(-ier,-iest)

for th . . .
see page 133

for ∪-r (ur/ir)
see page 246

-or oo as in woodpecker

In these words you can hear the sound ∪ as in duck

*

glove(d)
glum
glut

-good
-goods
-gourd

grub(bed)
grudge(d)
gruff
grunt

gulf
gull(ed)
gulp(ed)
gum(med)
gun(ned)
gush(es)
gushed
gust
gut(ted)
guts

* *

glutton

-goodbye
-goodness
-goodnight
-gooseberry(-ies)
govern(ed)

grubbing
grubby(-ier,-iest)
grudging
grumble(d)
grumbling
grumpy(-ier,-iest)

gudgeon
gullet
gulling
gulley/gully(-ies)
gumboil
gumming
gunner
gunning
guppy(-ies)
gusto
gusty(-ier,-iest)
gutter
gutting
guzzle(d)
guzzling

* * *

gluttony

-gooseberry(-ies)
governor
government

gunpowder
guttural(ly)
guttering

* * * *

gutturally

for u-r (ur/ir)
see page 246

- or oo as in woodpecker

In these words you can hear the sound U as in duck

*	* *	* * *	* * * *
-hood	honey(ed)	honeybee	Hungarian
-hook(ed)		honeycomb	
	hubbub	honeydew	
hub	huddle(d)	honeymoon	
hug(ged)	huddling		
hum(med)	hugging	hummingbird	
hump(ed)	hullo	Hungary	
hunch(es)	humble(d)	hungrier	
hunched	humbling	hurricane	
hung	humming	hurrying	
hunt	hundred		
hush(es)	hundredth		
hushed	hunger(ed)		
husk	hungry(-ier,-iest)		
hut	hunted		
hutch(es)	hunter		
	hunting		
	-hurrah!		
	-hurray!		
	hurry(-ies)		
	(hurried)		
	husband		
	husky(-ies)		
	hustle(d)		
	hustling		

for u-r
see page 247

I

*	* *	* * *	* * * * [* * * *]
	indulge(d)	impulsive	illustrious
	instruct		
	insult	im- or em- ?	-incurable
	*-insure(d) (protect		industrial(ly)
	against loss)	induction	industrialisation
		inductive	zation
	in- or en- ?	indulgence	industrialise(d)
		indulgent	ze
		injustice	industrious
		instruction	-infuriate
		instructor	-injurious
		insulting	
		-insurance	in- or en- ?
		in- or en- ?	

for E ...
see page 120

for u-r
see page 247

- or oo as in woodpecker

In these words you can hear the sound u as in duck

123

J

SHORT VOWEL U   SHORT VOWEL

*

judge(d)
jug(ged)
jump(ed)
junk
just
jut(ted)

* *

judgement/judgment
judging
juggle(d)
juggler
juggling
jumble(d)
jumbling
jumper
jumping
junction
jungle
-juror
-jury(-ies)
justice
jutting

* * *

justify(-ies)
(justified)

* * * * [*]

-jurisdiction
-jurisprudence
justification

K

*

* *

knuckle(d)
knuckling

* * *

* * * *

for C ...
see page 118

 for u-r (ur/ir)
see page 248

- or oo as in woodpecker

In these words you can hear the sound u as in duck

L

✻ | ✻ ✻ | ✻ ✻ ✻ | ✻ ✻ ✻ ✻

-look(ed)
love(d)

luck
lug(ged)
lugs
lull(ed)
lump(ed)
lunch(es)
lunched
lung
lunge(d)
-lure(d)
lush
lust

London
-lookout
lover
lovely(-ier,-iest)

lucky(-ier,-iest)
luggage
lugging
*lumbar (lower back)
*lumber (junk /
   timber / move
   awkwardly)
lumbered
luncheon(ed)
luscious
lustre
lusty(-ier,-iest)

lovable
loveliest
luckier
luckiest
luckily
lullaby(-ies)
lumbago
lumberjack
Luxembourg/Luxemburg
luxury(-ies)

luxuriant
luxurious

 for u-r
see page 248

-or oo as in woodpecker

In these words you can hear the sound U as in duck

✻	✻ ✻	✻ ✻ ✻	✻ ✻ ✻ ✻ [✻]
monk	-manure(d)	mulberry(-ies)	-maturity
month	-mature(d)	multiple	mother-in-law
-moor(ed)		multiply(-ies)	mother-of-pearl
	-mistook	multiplied	multiplicand
much	mistrust	multitude	multiplication
muck(ed)		muscatel	multiplicative
muff(ed)	Monday	muscular	multiplier
musk	money(ed)		
mud	mongrel		
mug(ged)	monkey(ed)		
mum	-mooring		
mumps	-Moslem		
munch(es)	mother(ed)		
munched			
mung	muddle(d)		
mush	muddling		
must	muddy(-ier,iest)		
	mudguard		
	*muffin (teacake)		
	*muffing (missing a shot or catch)		
	muffle(d)		
	muffling		
	muggy		
	mulberry(-ies)		
	mumble(d)		
	mumbling		
	mummy(-ies)		
	*muscat (wine / grape)		
	*muscle (body tissue)		
	muscled		
	muscling		
	mushroom(ed)		
	*musket (gun)		
	-Muslim		
	*muslin (fine thin cotton)		
	*mussel (shellfish)		
	mustang		
	*mustard (plant with hot-tasting seeds)		
	muster		
	*mustered (called together)		
	mustn't		
	musty(-ier,-iest)		
	mutter(ed)		
	mutton		
	muzzle(d)		
	*muzzling (putting a muzzle on)		

In this word the 'ou' is a neutral vowel.

moustache

for u-r (ur/ir) see page 249

- or oo as in woodpecker

In these words you can hear the sound U as in duck

N

*

*none (not one)
-nook

nudge(d)
null
numb(ed)
*nun (woman in
    convent)
nut

* *

knuckle(d)
knuckling

nothing

nudging
nugget
number(ed)
nutmeg
nutty(-ier,-iest)
nuzzle(d)
nuzzling

* * *

nonetheless

for u-r
see page 249

⓪

*

once
*one (1)

for H ...
see page 123

* *

august

-obscure(d)
    obstruct

oneself
onion

other

oven

* * *

obstruction
obstructive

occurrence

otherwise

* * * *

-obscurity(-ies)

for u-r
see page 249

- or **oo** as in woodpecker

In these words you can hear the sound **u** as in duck

※

pluck(ed)
plug(ged)
*plum (fruit)
*plumb (lead weight
    on a cord / do
    work of plumber)
plumbed
plump(ed)
plunge(d)
plus(es)
plush

-poor

pub
puff(ed)
pug
-pull(ed)
pulp(ed)
pulse(d)
pump(ed)
pun(ned)
punch(es)
punched
punt
pup
-pure
-push(es)
-pushed
*-puss(es) (cat)
*pus (liquid from
    poisoned place)
*-put (place)
-[put]
*putt (hit golf
    ball gently /
    throw weight)

※ ※

plover
plugging
plumber
plumbing
plunder(ed)
plunging
-plural(ly)

-poorly

-procure(d)

public(ly)
publish(es)
published
-pudding
puddle(d)
puddling
puffin
-pulley
-pulpit
pulsar
pumice
pumpkin
pungent
punctual(ly)
puncture(d)
punish(es)
punished
punning
puppet
puppy(-ies)
-purely
-pushchair
-pussy(-ies)
putted
*-putting (placing)
*putting (doing
    putts)
putty(-ies)
    (puttied)
puzzle(d)
puzzling

※ ※ ※

percussion
percussive

-plurally

production
productive
propulsion

publicly
publican
publisher
-pullover
punctually
punctuate
punishment
-purify(-ies)
-    (purified)
-purity

※ ※ ※ ※ [※]

pronunciation

publication
publicity
pulmonary
punctually
punctuation
-purification

for u-r
see page 250

-or oo as in woodpecker

In these words you can hear the sound U as in duck

R

✻	✻ ✻	✻ ✻ ✻	✻ ✻ ✻ ✻ [✻]
-rook	refund	recover(ed)	recovery(-ies)
-room	result	reduction	reluctantly
*rough (uneven /		reluctant	republican
harsh / crude)	roughage	republic	resuscitate
roughed	roughen(ed)	repulsive	resuscitation
	roughly	resultant	
rub(bed)		resulted	-Romania/Roumania/
ruck	rubber	resulting	Rumania
*ruff (collar)	rubbing		
rug	rubbish	-rookery(-ies)	
rum	rubble		
rump	rucksack	ruffian	
run	rudder		
[ran]	ruddy		
[run]	ruffle(d)		
*rung (step of	ruffling		
ladder / sounded)	Rugby		
runt	rugged		
rush(es)	rugger		
rushed	rumble(d)		
rust	rumbling		
rut(ted)	rumpus(es)		
	runner		
*wrung (twisted)	running		
	runny(-ier,-iest)		
	runway		
	rupture(d)		
	rushing		
	Russia		
	Russian		
	rustic		
	rustle(d)		
	rustling		
	rusty(-ier,-iest)		
	rutted		
	rutting		

for u-r
see page 251

-or oo as in woodpecker

*

scrub(bed)
scruff
*scull(ed) (row)
scrum
scum

-shook
-should
shove(d)
shrub
shrug(ged)
shrunk
shunt
shush(es)
shushed
shut
[shut]

*skull (bone of
   the head)
skunk

sludge
slug
slum(med)
slump(ed)
slunk
slush

smudge(d)
smug
smut

snuff(ed)
snug

*some (a certain
   number or amount)
*son (male child)
-soot

sponge(d)
spun
sprung
-see next page

* *

scrubbing
scuffle(d)
scuffling
sculptor
sculptress(es)
sculpture
scurry(-ies)
   (scurried)
scuttle(d)
scuttling

-secure(d)

-shouldn't
shovel(led)
shrugging
shudder(ed)
shuffle(d)
shuffling
shutter(ed)
shutting
shuttle(d)
shuttling

sluggish
slumber(ed)
slumming
slurry

smother(ed)
smudging
smuggle(d)
smuggler
smuggling

snuffing
snuffle(d)
snuffling

somehow
someone
something
sometime
sometimes
somewhat
somewhere
southern

splutter(ed)
spongy(-ier,-iest)
-sputnik
-see next page

* * *

scullery(-ies)

shrubbery(-ies)
shuttlecock

slovenly

somebody
somersault

structural(ly)
studying

submarine
subsequent
substitute
subtrahend
suddenly
suffering
suffocate
sulphuric
sultana
summarise(d)
       ze
*summary(-ies)
   (brief account)
summertime
*summery (like
   summer)
sumptuous
supplement

* * * * [*]

circumference

-security(-ies)

structurally

substitution
supplementary(-ies)

for ur (ur/ir)
see page 252

- or oo as in woodpecker

In these words you can hear the sound u as in duck

*

* *

-stood
struck
strung
strut(ted)
stub(bed)
stuck
stud(ded)
stuff(ed)
stump(ed)
stun(ned)
stung
stunk
stunt
strut(ted)

such
suck(ed)
suds
sulk(ed)
*sum(med) (total /
   exercise with
   numbers)
*sun (source of
   sunlight)
sunned
sung
sunk
-sure

swung

stomach(ed)
structure
struggle(d)
struggling
strutting
stubbing
stubble
stubborn
stubby(-ier,-iest)
studding
study(-ies)
   (studied)
stuffing
stumble(d)
stumbling
stunning
stutter(ed)

subject
subset
substance
subtle
suburb
subway
*succour (help)
*sucker (person or
   thing that sucks /
   shoot from stem or
   root / person who
   is easily tricked)
suckle(d)
suckling
suction
sudden
suffer(ed)
suffix(es)
-sugar(ed)
sulky(-ier,-iest)
sullen
sulphate
sulphur
sultan
summer
summing
summit
summon(ed)
sumptuous
-see next page

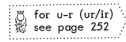

for u-r (ur/ir)
see page 252

- or oo as in woodpecker

In these words you can hear the sound u as in duck

131

✢ ✢

sunbathe(d)
sunburn(ed/t)
*sundae (sweet dish)
*Sunday (day)
sunflower
sunken
sunlight
sunlit
sunning
sunny(-ier,-iest)
sunrise
sunset
sunshine
suntan(ned)
supper
supple
-surely
suspect

for u-r (ur/ir)
see page 252

In these words the first 'u'
sounds like 'a' in 'astonish'.

'SUCCESSFUL' WORDS

subdue(d)	suburban	supporting
subject(ion)	succeed	suppose(d)
submerge(d)	success(es)	supposedly
submission	successful(ly)	surrender(ed)
submissive	succession	surround(ed)
submit(ted)	successive	surroundings
submitting	successor	susceptible
subordinate	sufficient(ly)	suspect(ed)
subscribe(d)	suggest(ed)	suspend
subscription	suggestible	suspense
subside	suggesting	suspension
subsidiary(-ies)	suggestion	suspicion
substantial(ly)	supply(-ies)	suspicious
subtend	(supplied)	sustain(ed)
subtract(ing)	support(ed)	
subtraction	supporter	

- or oo as in woodpecker

In these words you can hear the sound u as in duck

T

*

thrush(es)
thrust
[thrust]

thud(ded)
thug
thumb(ed)
thump(ed)
thus

*ton (measure of
    weight)
tongue(d)
*tonne (1000 kilos)
-took
touch(es)
touched
tough
-tour(ed)

truck
trudge(d)
trunk
truss
*trussed (tied up
    firmly)
*trust (faith)

tub
tuck(ed)
tuft
tug(ged)
*tun (large barrel)
tusk

* *

thorough
thudded
thudding
thunder(ed)

touchdown
touching
touchy(-ier,-iest)
toughen(ed)
-tourist

trouble(d)
troubling
trudging
trumpet(ed)
truncheon
trundle(d)
trundling
trussing
trustee

tubby(-ier,-iest)
tugging
tumble(d)
tumbling
tummy(-ies)
tundra
tungsten
tunnel(led)
turret
tussle(d)
tussling

* * *

thoroughbred
thoroughly
thunderous
thunderstorm

-tournament

troublesome
trumpeted
trumpeting
trustworthy

tunnelling

* * * *

 for u-r (ur/ir)
see page 253

-or oo as in woodpecker

In these words you can hear the sound u as in duck

✷	✷ ✷	✷ ✷ ✷	✷ ✷ ✷ ✷ [✷ ✷]
up(ped)	onion	otherwise	ultimately
	other		ultrasonic(ally)
us	oven	ugliest	ultraviolet
	udder	ultimate	unbearable
			unbelievable
	ugly(-ier,-iest)	umbrella	uncannier
			uncanniest
	Ulster	unable	uncertainty(-ies)
		unabridged	uncomfortable
	umpire(d)	unaided	unconsciously
		unaware	unconventional(ly)
	unbend	unbeaten	uncooperative
	[unbent]	unbroken	undecided
	unbind	unbuckle(d)	undercurrent
	[unbound]	unbutton(ed)	underdeveloped
	unbolt	uncanny(-ier,-iest)	undergraduate
	uncle	uncertain	underlying
	unclean	uncommon	understanding
	under	unconscious	understudy(-ies)
	undo	uncover(ed)	(understudied)
	[undid]	undamaged	undertaken
	[undone]	undaunted	undertaker
	undress(es)	undefined	underwater
	undressed	underclothes	underwritten
	unearth(ed)	underfoot	undesirable
	unfair	undergo	undoubtedly
	unfit(ted)	[underwent]	uneasiness
	unfold	[undergone]	unemployment
	unharmed	underground	unexpected
	unheard	undergrowth	unfamiliar
	unhurt	underline(d)	unfortunately
	unjust	underneath	ungratefully
	unkind	underscore(d)	unhappily
	unknown	undersell	-see next page
	unlatch(es)	[undersold]	
	unlatched	understand	
	unless	[understood]	
	unlike	undertake	
	unload	[undertook]	
	unlock(ed)	[undertaken]	
	unpack(ed)	underwear	
	unroll(ed)	underworld	
	unsafe	underwrite	
	unscrew(ed)	[underwrote]	
	unseen	[underwritten]	
	unsolved	undisturbed	
	-see next page	undoing	
		unduly	
		-see next page	

for H ...
see page 123

 for u-r
see page 254

- or oo as in woodpecker

In these words you can hear the sound U as in duck

✳ ✳   ✳ ✳ ✳   ✳ ✳ ✳ ✳ [✳ ✳]

untie(d)	uneasy(-ier,-iest)	unimportant
until	unending	uninhabited
unto	unequal(led)	unlimited
untold	uneven	unmistakable
untouched	unexplored	unnecessarily
untrained	unfasten(ed)	unnecessary
untrue	unfinished	unpopular
unused	unfitting	unpredictable
unveil(ed)	unfriendly(-ier,-iest)	unprotected
unwell	unfurnished	unquestionably
unwind	ungrateful(ly)	unravelling
[unwound]	unguarded	unreasonable
unwise	unhappy(-ier,-iest)	unrelated
unwrap(ped)	unhealthy	unreliable
	uninjured	unsanitary
uphill	unlikely	unsociable
upkeep	unlucky(-ier,-iest)	unsuccessful(ly)
upland	unnatural	unsuitable
upon	unnoticed	unusually
upper	unpainted	
upright	unpleasant	upholstery
uproar	unravel(led)	
uproot	unravelling	
upset	unscramble(d)	
[upset]	unscrambling	
upside	unselfish	
upstairs	unsettled	
upstream	unstable	
upturn(ed)	unsteady	
upward	untangle(d)	
	untangling	
usher(ed)	untidy(-ier,-iest)	
	untying	
utmost	unwanted	
utter(ed)	unwelcome	
	unwilling	
	unworthy	
	unwrapping	
	unusual(ly)	

upbringing
upheaval
upholster(ed)
uprising
upsetting
upside down

usherette
utterance

utterly

In these words the 'u' may be pronounced as a neutral vowel.

unless   until   upon

 for u-r see page 254

- or oo as in woodpecker

for H ... see page 123

In these words you can hear the sound U as in duck

V

*

* *

vulgar
vulture

* * *

vulnerable

* * * * [* *]

vulgarity(-ies)
vulnerable
vulnerability

for u-r
see page 254

W

*

once
*one (1)

-wolf(wolves)
-wolfed
*-won (gained)
*-wood (timber / area
    with many trees)
-wool
*-would (was willing
    to / used to /
    was going to)

*wrung (twisted)

* *

oneself

-woman
 wonder(ed)
 wondrous
-wooden
-woodland
-woodwork
-woollen
-woolly
 worry(-ies)
    (worried)
-worsted
-wouldn't

* * *

wonderful(ly)
wondering
-woodcutter
-woodpecker

* * * *

wonderfully

for u-r
see page 254

Y

*

young
*-your (belonging
    to you)
*-you're (you are)
-yours

* *

youngster
-yourself
-yourselves

_ * * *

* * * *

- or oo as in woodpecker

In these words you can hear the sound U as in duck

*

ace(d)
ache(d)

age(d)

*aid (help)
*aide (helper)
*ail(ed) grow weak
aim(ed)
ain't

*ale (beer)

ape(d)

*ate (did eat)

eh

*eight (8)
eighth

for H ...
see page 144

* *

abate
ablaze
able
abstain

acclaim(ed)
acorn
acre
acquaint

afraid

again
against
aged
agent
ageing/aging

ailment

amaze(d)
amen

ancient
angel
anus

apex
April
apron

arrange(d)
array(ed)

ashamed
Asia
Asian
astray

attain(ed)

avail(ed)

awake(d)
[awoke]
[awoken]
await
away

eighteen(th)
eighty(-ies)

élite

* * *

abeyance
abrasive

acquaintance
acreage

adjacent

agency(-ies)

alien

amazement
amazing
amiable

apricot

arrangement

attainment

awaken(ed)

eightieth

* * * * [* *]

alienation

amiable

Arabia
Australia

availability
available
aviation
aviator

for ae-r
see page 236

In these words you can hear the vowel sound ae as in snail

137

*	**	***	****
babe	baby(-ies)	bakery(-ies)	babysitting
bake(d)	babied	basically	basically
*bail (bar on	bacon	bayonet(ed/ted)	bayonet(t)ed
cricket stumps /	baker		
payment for	baking	behaviour	
release / bail	baseball		
out)	basement	bravery	
bailed	basic(ally)	brazier	
bait	basin		
*baize (cloth)	basis		
*bale (bundle /	bathing		
bale out)			
baled	became		
*base (foot / central	behave(d)		
establishment /	betray(ed)		
worthless)			
*based (established)	blazer		
*bass (low sound)			
*baste (cover with	bracelet		
melted fat /	braces		
tack together)	brazen		
bathe(d)	brazier		
bay(ed)	breakdown		
*bays (more than	breakers		
one bay)	breaking		
	breakthrough		
beige	brigade		
	brocade		
blade			
blame(d)			
blaze(d)			
brace(d)			
*braid (plait /			
edging cloth)			
braille			
brain(ed)			
*braise/braize (fish)			
*brake (means of			
slowing or			
stopping)			
brave(d)			
bray			
*brayed (did bray)			
*braze(d) (join with			
hard solder)			
*break (smash in			
pieces /			
interrupt /			
suddenly change)			
[broke]			
[broken]			

for ae-r
see page 236

In these words you can hear the vowel sound ae as in snail

C

✳	✳ ✳	✳ ✳ ✳	✳ ✳ ✳ ✳ [✳]
cage(d)	cable(d)	capable	Canadian
cake(d)	cabling		capability(-ies)
came	canine	changeable	
cane(d)	casing	chaotic(ally)	chaotically
cape			
case(d)	chamber	contagious	
cave(d)	changing	container	
	chaos	conveyer	
chain(ed)	chasing	courageous	
change(d)			
chase	complain(ed)	crayoning	
*chased (did chase)	complaint	craziest	
*chaste (pure)	contain(ed)	crazily	
	convey(ed)	created	
claim(ed)		creating	
clay	cradle(d)	creation	
	cradling	creative	
crane(d)	crater(ed)	cremation	
crate	crayon(ed)	crustacean	
crave(d)	crazy(-ier,-iest)		
craze(d)	create		
	cremate		

for Qu ...
see page 148

for ae-r
see page 236

In these words you can hear the vowel sound ae as in snail

*

dale
dame
Dane
date
day
*days (more than
   one day)
*daze (state of not
   thinking clearly)
dazed

deign

drain(ed)
drake
drape(d)

**

dahlia
daily
dainty(-ier,-iest)
daisy(-ies)
danger
Danish
data
daybreak
daydream(ed)
daylight
daytime

debate
debris
début/debut
*decade (ten years)
decay(ed)
*decayed (did decay)
deflate
delay(ed)
derail(ed)
detain(ed)

dictate
disgrace(d)
dismay(ed)
displace(d)
display(ed)

domain

drainage
draper

***

dahlia
daintily
dangerous

deflation

dictation
dictator
disable(d)
disabling
disgraceful(ly)
displacement

drapery(-ies)

****

disablement
disgracefully

> for ae-r
> see page 237

In these words you can hear the vowel sound ae as in snail

E

*

eh

eight
eighth

* *

éclair

eighteen(th)
eighty(-ies)

élite

embrace(d)

encase(d)
engage(d)
engrave(d)
enrage(d)
enslave(d)

en- or in- ?

equate

erase(d)

escape(d)
estate
estrange(d)

evade

exchange(d)
exclaim(ed)
exhale(d)
explain(ed)

* * *

eightieth

em- or im- ?

enable(d)
enabling
endanger(ed)
engagement
engraving

en- or in- ?

equation
equator

eraser

evasion

explaining

* * * *

en- or in- ?

er- or ir- ?

for H ...
see page 144

for I ...
see page 144

for ae-r
see page 237

In these words you can hear the vowel sound ae as in snail

* ** *** ****

face(d)
fade
fail(ed)
*faint (weak)
faith
fake(d)
fame(d)
*fate (destiny)

feign(ed)
*feint (mock attack)
*fete (festival)

flake(d)
flame(d)

frail
frame(d)
fray(ed)
freight

phase(d)
phrase(d)

fable(d)
faded
failure
faithful(ly)
famous
fatal(ly)
favour(ed)
favourite

flavour(ed)

forgave
forsake
[forsook]
[forsaken]

fragrance
fragrant
framework
freighter
frustrate

faithfully
fallacious
fatally
favourable
favourite

filtration

formation
forsaken

frustrating
frustration

favourable
favourably

for th ...
see page 151

for ae-r
see page 238

In these words you can hear the vowel sound ae as in snail

※

gain(ed)
*gait (way of
  walking)
gale
game
gaol/jail
gaoled/jailed
gape(d)
*gate (entrance)
gauge(d)
gave
gay
gaze(d)

glaze(d)

grace(d)
*grade (standard)
grain(ed)
grape
*grate (grid / rub
  hard)
grave
gray/grey
graze(d)
*great (big /
  important)
grey/gray
*greyed (turned
  grey)

※ ※

gaily
gaoler/jailer
gaseous
gateway

glacial

graceful(ly)
gracious
gradient
grapefruit
grateful(ly)
*grater (gadget for
  grating)
grating
graveyard
gravy(-ies)
*greater (more great)
greatest
greatly
grenade
greyhound

※ ※ ※

gaiety(-ies)

*glacier (mass of
  slow-moving ice)
*glazier (workman
  who fits glass
  in windows)

gracefully
gradation
gradient
gratefully

※ ※ ※ ※

geranium

gymnasium

for ae-r
see page 238

In these words you can hear the vowel sound ae as in snail

※

*hail (hard frozen
   rain / call name
   or greetings /
   come from)
hailed
*hale (very healthy)
haste
hate
*hay (dried grass)
haze

*hey! (ho!)

※ ※

halo(ed)
hasten(ed)
hasty(-ier,-iest)
hated
hatred
haven
haystack
hazel
hazy(-ier,-iest)

hurray!

※ ※ ※

halfpenny(-ies)
hastily

herbaceous

for ae-r
see page 238

I

※

for E ...
see page 141

※ ※

ic- or ec- ?

el- or el- ?

em- or im- ?

inflame(d)
inflate
inhale(d)
innate
insane
invade

in- or en- ?

ir- or er- ?

is- or es- ?

ix- or ex- ?

※ ※ ※

impatience
impatient

inflation
invaded
invader
invasion

in- or en- ?

iq- or eq- ?

ir- or er- ?

iv- or ev- ?

ix- or ex- ?

※ ※ ※ ※ [※]

incapable
inflationary

Iranian

for ae-r
see page 239

In these words you can hear the vowel sound ae   as in snail

J

LONG
VOWEL ae

*

jade
jail/gaol
jailed/gaoled
jay

* *

jaded
jailer/gaoler

* * *

Jamaica

* * * *

geranium

gymnasium

K

*

*knave (rascal)

* *

* * *

* * * *

for C ...
see page 139

for Qu ...
see page 148

L

*

lace(d)
laid
*lain (rested)
lake
lame(d)
*lane (narrow road)
late
lathe
lay
[laid]
*lays (poems)
*laze (take it easy)

* *

label(led)
labour(ed)
ladies
ladle(d)
ladling
lady(-ies)
Laos
*laser (apparatus
    making light beams
    that can cut)
lately
later
latest
latex
lay-by
*layer (thickness of
    laid material /
    one that lays)
laying
layout
lazy(-ier,-iest)

* * *

labelling
labourer
ladybird
*lazier (more lazy)
laziest
laziness

lumbago

for ae-r
see page 239

In these words you can hear the vowel sound ae as in snail

145

M

*

mace
*made (formed)
*maid (girl)
*mail (post /
    armour)
mailed
maim(ed)
*main (chief /
    strength)
*maize (corn)
make
[made]
*male (masculine)
*mane (hair, as on
    neck of horse or
    lion)
mate
may
*maze (puzzle with
    many paths)

**

maiden
mainland
mainly
mainsail
maintain(ed)
maker
make-up
makeshift
making
major
manger
mania
maple
mason
matron
maybe

mislay
[mislaid]
mistake
[mistook]
[mistaken]

***

maintenance
majorette
Malaya
mania
maniac
masonry
mayonnaise

mistaken

****

Malaysia

for ae-r
see page 239

N

*

*knave (rascal)

nail(ed)
name(d)
*nave (part of
    church)
*nay (no)

*née (born with
    the name:-)
*neigh (noise made
    by horses)
neighed

**

naked
naming
narrate
nasal(ly)
nation
native
nature
*naval (concerning
    warships)
*navel (tummy-button)
navy(-ies)

neighbour

***

narration
narrator
nationwide
nasally

negation
neighbourhood
neighbouring
neighbourly

****

In these words you can hear the vowel sound ae as in snail

*

* *

obey(ed)
obtain(ed)

* * *

occasion

* * * * [*]

Australia

occasional(ly)

P

*

pace
*paced (did pace)
page(d)
paid
*pail (bucket)
*pain (suffering)
paint
*pale (whitish)
*pane (sheet of
    glass)
*paste (mixture of
    powder and liquid)
pave(d)
pay
[paid]

phase(d)
phrase(d)

*place(d) (position)
plague(d)
*plaice (fish)
*plain (area of
    level land /
    simple)
*plane (aeroplane /
    flat surface /
    smoothing tool)
plate
play(ed)

*praise(d)
    (glorify /
    high approval)
*pray (ask for help)
*prays (asks for
    help)
*prey (victim)

* *

pagan
painful(ly)
painted
painter
painting
papal
paper(ed)
parade
pastry(-ies)
patent
*patience (ability to
    wait for results)
patient
*patients (people under
    medical treatment)
patron
pavement
paying
payload
payment

persuade

phrasing

placement
placing
*plaintiff (person who
    takes legal action)
*plaintive (sad-sounding)
player
playful(ly)
playing
playground
playmate
playtime
playwright

portray(ed)

prevail(ed)
proclaim(ed)
profane

* * *

painfully
painstaking
palatial(ly)
patiently
patriot

persuasion
persuasive

playfully

potato(es)

probation

* * * * [* *]

palatially
palaeontologist/
paleontologist
patriotic(ally)

for ae-r
see page 239

In these words you can hear the vowel sound ae as in snail

*

quail(ed)
quaint
quake(d)

* *

Quaker
quaver(ed)

R

*

race(d)
rage(d)
raid
rail(ed)
*rain (water falling
    from clouds)
rained
*raise(d) (lift up)
rake(d)
range(d)
rate
rave(d)
ray
*rays (beams)

*reign (rule)
*rein (strap to
    control an animal)

* *

rabies
racial(ly)
racing
racist
*radar (radio
    detection)
*raider (person who
    raids)
railing
railway
rainbow
raincoat
raindrop
rainfall
raining
rainy(-ier,-iest)
raises
raisin
raising
raven
rayon
razor

reclaim(ed)
refrain(ed)
regain(ed)
regime
reindeer
relate
remain(ed)
repay
[repaid]
replace(d)
restrain(ed)
retain(ed)

* * *

racially
radial(ly)
radiant
radiate
radio(ed)
radium
radius(-ii)
rainier
rainiest
rapier
racism
rateable
ratio(s)

reagent
related
relation
remainder
remaining
Renaissance
replacement

rotation

* * * * [*]

radially
radiation
radiator
radioactive

relationship

Romania/Roumania/
Rumania

for ae-r
see page 240

In these words you can hear the vowel sound ae as in snail

∻

safe
sage
*sail (travel by
    boat / sheet fixed
    to mast)
sailed
saint
sake
*sale (selling)
same
sane
save(d)
say
[said]

scale(d)
scrape(d)

shade
*shake (move quickly
    in different
    directions)
[shook]
[shaken]
shale
shame(d)
shape(d)
shave(d)
*sheik (Arab ruler)

skate
skein

slain
slate
slave(d)
*slay (kill)
[slew]
[slain]
*sleigh (sledge)

snake
snail

space(d)
*spade (tool)
Spain
*spayed (operated
    on to remove
    ovaries)
sprain(ed)
spray(ed)
-see next page

∻ ∻

sable
sabre
sacred
safeguard
safely
safer
safety
sago
sailing
sailor
salesman
saline
Satan
*saver (person or
    thing that saves)
saving
savings
saviour
*savour (enjoy a
    taste or smell)
saying

scalene
scaly
scraper

séance

shaded
shaker
shaking
shameful(ly)
shaver
shaving

skateboard
skater
skating

spacecraft
spaceship
spacesuit
spacious
-see next page

∻ ∻ ∻

savoury(-ies)

shakily
shamefully

slavery

stabilise(d)
    ze
stadium
*stationary (still)
*stationery (writing
    materials)
stratosphere

∻ ∻ ∻ ∻

stabiliser
    zer
*stationary (still)
*stationery (writing
    materials)

for ae-r
see page 240

In these words you can hear the vowel sound a̅e̅ as in snail

*

* *

stage(d)
*staid (serious and
   dull)
stain(ed)
*stake (stick /
   bet / prize)
staked
stale
state
stave(d)
[stove]
stay
*stayed (did stay)
*steak (meat)
*straight (without
   curves)
strain(ed)
*strait (channel)
straits
strange
stray(ed)

*suede/suède (soft
   undressed leather)

sway
*swayed (did sway)

stable(d)
stabling
stagecoach
stainless
stamen
staple(d)
stapling
stated
statement
statesman
station(ed)
status
staying
straighten(ed)
strangely
stranger
stratus

survey(ed)
sustain(ed)

 for ae-r
see page 240

In these words you can hear the vowel sound ae as in snail

T

*

*tail (part at the
   back)
tailed
take
[took]
[taken]
*tale (story)
tame(d)
tape(d)
taste

they
they'd
they'll
they've

trace(d)
trade
trail(ed)
train(ed)
*trait
   (characteristic)
*tray (board with
   raised edges, for
   carrying things)

* *

table(d)
tabling
taken
taking
takings
tailor(ed)
*taper(ed) (become
   thinner towards
   one end / waxed
   spill or wick)
*tapir (animal)
tasted
tasteful(ly)
tasty(-ier,-iest)

terrain

today

tracing
traded
trademark
trader
trading
trailer
trainer
training
traitor

* * *

tablecloth
tablespoon
takeaway
tastefully

for ae-r
see page 241

V

*

vague
*vain (conceited)
*vale (valley)
*vane (blade)
vaned

*veil(ed) (cover)
*vein (blood vessel /
   mood / streak)

* *

vacate
vacant
vapour

* * *

*vacation (holiday /
   process of leaving)
*vocation (calling /
   occupation)

* * * * [*]

vocational(ly)

for ae-r
see page 241

In these words you can hear the vowel sound ae as in snail

*   * *   * * *   * * * *

*wade (walk in water)
wage(d)
waif
*wail(ed) (cry)
*waist (narrow part
   of body)
*wait (stay)
*waive (no longer
   enforce)
wake(d)
[woke]
[woken]
Wales
wane(d)
*waste (rubbish)
*wave (hand signal /
   surge)
waved
*way (path)

*weigh (find the
   weight of)
*weighed (found the
   weight of)
*weight (heaviness /
   value)

*whale (sea-mammal)
*whey (watery part
   of sour milk)

wafer
wager(ed)
waistcoat
*waited (did wait)
waiter
waiting
waitress(es)
waken(ed)
wasted
wasteland
wavelength
waver(ed)
waving
wavy(-ier,-iest)
waylay
[waylaid]

weighbridge
weighing
*weighted (having
   added weight)
weightless

weightlessness

for ae-r
see page 241

Y

*   * *   * * *   * * * *

yea

In these words you can hear the vowel sound ae as in snail

✼	✼ ✼	✼ ✼ ✼	✼ ✼ ✼ ✼ [✼]
	achieve(d)	achievement	abbreviation
	adhere(d)	adhesive	aesthetically
	agree(d)	Aegean aesthetic(ally)	agreeable
	anneal(ed)	agreement	amenable
	appeal(ed) appear(ed)	allegiance	anaemia/anemia anaesthetist/ anesthetist
	asleep	amino amoeba	appreciate
	austere	anaemic/anemic	
		appearance	
		arena	

*   * *   * * *   * * * *

*be (to be / exist)
*beach(es) (shore)
beached
bead
beak(ed)
beam(ed)
*bean (vegetable)
beard
beast
*beat (batter /
   defeat)
[beat]
[beaten]
*bee (insect)
*beech (tree)
beef(ed)
*been (from 'to be')
*beer (drink)
*beet (plant with
   sweet root)

*bier (frame to bear
   coffin)

bleach(es)
bleached
bleak
bleat
bleed
[bled]
bleep(ed)

*breach(es) (gap /
   act of breaking)
breached
breathe(d)
*breech(es) (bottom
   part of gun)
breed
[bred]
breeze(d)
brief(ed)

beacon
beagle
beagling
beaker
beanstalk
beaten
*beater (person or
   thing that beats)
beating
beaver(ed)
beehive
beeswax
beetle
beetroot
being
belief
believe(d)
beneath
bereave(d)
[bereft]
beseech(es)
beseeched
[besought]
besiege(d)
*beta (Greek letter b)
between

breathing
briefcase
briefly

In these words the first letter 'e'
is pronounced like the 'i' in 'pig'.

'BENEVOLENT' WORDS

became	beginning	beseech(es)
because	behalf	beseeched
become	behave(d)	[besought]
[became]	behaviour	beset(ting)
[become]	behead	[beset]
becoming	beheld	besides
befall	behind	bestow(ed)
[befell]	behold	betray(ed)
[befallen]	[beheld]	betwixt
before(hand)	belong(ed)	beware
befriend	belonging	bewilder(ed)
begin	beloved	bewitch(es)
[began]	below	bewitched
[begun]	benevolent	beyond
beginner	bereft	

In these words you can hear the vowel sound ee as in eagle

C

*

cease(d)
*cede (give up)

*cheap (at low cost)
cheat
cheek(ed)
*cheep (chirp)
cheeped
cheer(ed)
cheese(d)
chief

clean(ed)
clear(ed)
cleat
cleave(d)
[cleft]
[clove]
[cloven]

*creak (noise)
creaked
cream(ed)
crease(d)
creed
*creek (inlet / stream)
creep
[crept]

keel(ed)
keen
keep
[kept]
*key (lever for lock or other mechanism / important / musical scale)
keyed

*quay (wharf)

for Qu ...
see page 167

* *

career(ed)

cedar
*ceiling (inner roof of room)

ce- or ci- ?

cheaper
*cheater (person who cheats)
cheeky(-ier,-iest)
cheerful(ly)
*cheetah (animal)
chiefly
chieftain

cleaner
cleaning
clearance
clearing
clearly
cleavage

compete
complete
conceal(ed)
conceit
conceive(d)

creature
creeper

keeper
keeping
keyhole
Kenya

kiosk

* * *

cathedral

*cereal (food from grain / plant producing grain)

ce- or ci- ?

cheerfully

completion
completely
conceited

creosote

Korea
Korean

* * * *

chameleon

comedian
comedienne
convenience
convenient

In these words the first letter 'e' is pronounced like the 'i' in 'pig'.

'CREATIVE' WORDS

celestial	creative
cement	cremate
create(d)	cremation
creating	crescendo(s)
creation	crevasse

155

In these words you can hear the vowel sound ee as in eagle

*

* *

* * *

* * * * [* *]

deal
[dealt]
*dean (presiding
    officer)
*dear (beloved /
    expensive)
deed
deem(ed)
*dene (small valley)
deep
*deer(deer) (animal)

dream(ed)
[dreamt]

dealer
decease(d)
deceit
deceive(d)
decent
decode
decrease(d)
decree(d)
deepen(ed)
deeper
deeply
defeat
defect
deflate
degree
delete
demon
detail(ed)
detour

de- or di- ?

diesel
disease(d)
*discreet (careful
    not to embarrass)
*discrete (separate)
displease(d)

dreaming
dreary(-ier,-iest)

decoding
defeated
deflation
deletion
deviate

decompression
depreciate
depreciation
deteriorate
deterioration
deviation

**In these words the first letter 'e'
is pronounced like the 'i' in 'pig'.**

'DELIGHTFUL' WORDS

debate
decamp(ed)
decay(ed)
December
deception
deceptive
decide
deciduous
decipher(ed)
decision
decisive
declare(d)
decline(d)
decry(-ies)
    (decried)
deduce(d)
deduction
deductive
defect(or)
defective
defence
defend(ant)
defender
defensive
defiance
defiant
deficiency(-ies)
deficient
define(d)
deflation
deflect(ion)
deform(ed)
defy(-ies)
    (defied)
delay(ed)
deliberate(ly)
delicious
delight(ed)
delightful(ly)
delirious
deliver(ed)
deliverance

delivery(-ies)
demand(ed)
demobbed
democracy(-ies)
demolish(es)
demolished
denial
denomination
denominator
denote
denounce(d)
deny(-ies)
    (denied)
depart(ure)
department
depend(ed)
dependable
dependant
dependants
dependence
dependency(-ies)
dependent
deport
deposit(ed)
depositing
depress(es)
depressed
depression
depressive
deprive(d)
derail(ed)
derivative
derive(d)
descend(ed)
descendant
descent
describe(d)
describing
description
descriptive
desert(ed)
deserve(d)

design(ed)
designer
desirable
desire(d)
despair(ed)
despatch(es)
despatched
despise(d)
despite
dessert
destroy(ed)
destroyer
destruction
destructive
detach(es)
detached
detain(ed)
detect(ion)
detective
detector
detention
deter(red)
detergent
determination
determine(d)
determining
deterrence
deterrent
deterring
detest
detract
develop(ed)
developer
developing
development
device
devise(d)
devote(d)
devotion
devour(ed)

In these words you can hear the vowel sound ee as in eagle

E

∗

each
ear
ease(d)
east
eat
[ate]
[eaten]
eaves

eel

eke(d)

eve

for H ...
see page 160

for I ...
see page 161

See also E
on page 65

See also I
on page 72

∗ ∗

eager
eagle
eardrum
earmark(ed)
earring
earshot
easel
Easter
eastern
eastward
easy(-ier,-iest)
eaten
eating

∗eerie (weird)

Egypt

either

equal(led)

era

even
evening
evil(ly)

exceed
extreme

∗eyrie/y(-ies) (nest of bird of prey)

∗ ∗ ∗

aesthetic(ally)

eagerly
easier
easiest
easily

em- or im- ?

endearment

en- or in- ?

equalise(d)
      ze
equalling
equally

evenly

excretion
extremely

oedipal
Oedipus

∗ ∗ ∗ ∗ [∗ ∗ ∗]

aesthetically

easygoing

ecclesiastical(ly)
ecological(ly)
economical(ly)
economics
economy(-ies)
ecumenical(ly)

em- or im- ?

en- or in- ?

equatorial
equiangular
equidistant
equilateral
equilibrium

Ethiopia

evolution

exceedingly
experience(d)
exterior

In these words the first 'e' sounds like 'i'.

'EFFECTIVE' WORDS

ecclesiastical(ly)
eclipse(d)
ecology
edition
effect(ive)
effectively
efficient
Egyptian
eject(ion)
ejector
elaborate
elaboration
elastic(ally)
elasticity
elect(ion)

elector(ate)
electoral(ly)
electrical(ly)
electricity
electrocute
electrode
electrolysis
electrolyte
electrolytic(ally)
electromagnetic(ally)
electron
electronic(ally)
eleven(th)
elicit(ed)
eliciting

eliminate
elimination
Elizabethan
ellipse
elliptical(ly)
elope(d)
elusive
emancipation
emerge(d)
emergence
emergency(-ies)
emission
emit(ted)
emitter
emitting
emotional(ly)
emotive
emulsion(ed)
enable(d)
enabling
enact
enamel(led)
enamelling
enamour(ed)
endear(ed)

endearment
enormous
enough
enumerate
equality
equation
equator
equip(ped)
equipment
equipping
equivalence
equivalent
erase(d)
eraser
erect(ion)
erode
erosion
erotic(ally)
erratic(ally)
erupt(ed)
eruption
escape(d)
escarpment
especially
essential(ly)

establish(es)
established
establishment
estate
estrange(d)
eternal(ly)
evacuate
evacuation
evacuee
evade
evaluate
evaluation
evaporate
evaporation
evasion
event
eventual(ly)
evict
evolve(d)
exceed(ingly)
experience(d)
exterior
extreme(ly)

In these words you can hear the vowel sound **ee** as in **eagle**

157

F

*

fear(ed)
feast
*feat (act)
fee
feed
[fed]
feel
[felt]
*feet (more than
    one foot)

field
fiend
fierce
fiord/fjord

*flea (insect)
*flee (run away)
[fled]
fleece(d)
fleet

free(d)
*freeze (chill /
    change from
    liquid to solid /
    hold steady)
[froze]
[frozen]
*frieze (decorated
    band / type of
    cloth)

for th ...
see page 172

* *

faeces
fatigue(d)

fearful(ly)
feature(d)
feeble
feeding
feeler
feeling
female
fever(ed)

fielder
fiercely
fiord/fjord

fleecy(-ier,-iest)

foresee
[foresaw]
[foreseen]
freedom
freely
freestyle
freezer
freezing
frequent

* * *

fearfully

fiesta

frequency(-ies)
frequently

* * * *

In these words the first letter 'e'
is pronounced like the 'i' in 'pig'.

ferocious   ferocity

158

In these words you can hear the vowel sound ee as in eagle

G

✻	✻ ✻	✻ ✻ ✻	✻ ✻ ✻ ✻

*jeans (trousers)
jeep
jeer(ed)

gear(ed)
geese
gene
*genes (more than
    one gene)

gleam(ed)
glee

*grease (oily
    substance)
greased
*Greece (country)
greed
Greek
green
greet
grief
grieve(d)

Jesus

genie
geyser

greasy(-ier,-iest)
greedy(-ier,-iest)
greenhouse
Greenland
greeted
greeting
grievance

galena

genius(es)

graffiti
greedily
Greenlander

In these words the first letter 'e'
is pronounced like the 'i' in 'pig'.

genetic(ally)   geology
geographical(ly)   geometrical(ly)
geography(-ies)   geometry(-ies)
geological(ly)   geranium

In these words you can hear the vowel sound ee as in eagle

*

he
*heal(ed) (cure /
    get better)
heap(ed)
*hear (receive by
    ear)
[heard]
*hears (does hear)
heat
heath
heave
[hove]
heaved
*he'd (he had / he
    would)
*heed (notice /
    take seriously)
*heel (part of
    foot / shoe)
heeled
*he'll (he will)
*here (in this
    place)
*here's (here is)
he's

* *

hearing
heated
heathen
heating
Hebrew
hero(es)

* * *

haematite/hematite

helium
heretofore

* * * *

In this word the letter 'e'
sounds like the 'i' in 'pig'.

heroic(ally)

In these words you can hear the vowel sound ee as in eagle

*

ic- or ec- ?

if- or ef- ?

ij- or ej- ?

il- or el- ?

im- _or em- ?

increase(d)
indeed
intrigue(d)

in- or en- ?

iq- or eq- ?

ir- or er- ?

is- or es- ?

iv- or ev- ?

ix- or ex- ?

* *

ic- or ec- ?

id- or ed- ?

if- or ef- ?

ig- or eg- ?

ij- or ej- ?

illegal(ly)

il- or el- ?

immediate
impeachment

im- or em- ?

increasing
infrequent
ingenious
intriguing

in- or en- ?

iq- or eq- ?

ir- or er- ?

is- or es- ?

it- or ev- ?

ix- or ex- ?

* * *

ic- or ec- ?

illegally

il- or el- ?

immediate
immedictely
imperial(ly)

im- or em- ?

increasingly
inferior
ingenious
ingredient
interior

in- or en- ?

iq- or eq- ?

is- or es- ?

iv- or ev- ?

ix- or ex- ?

* * * * [*]

for E ...
see page 157

See also E
on page 65

See also I
on page 72

In these words you can hear the vowel sound ee as in eagle

*

** **

*** *** ***

**** **** **** ****

gene
*genes (more than one
   gene)

genie

Jesus

genius(es)

*jeans (trousers)
jeep
jeer(ed)

K

*

** **

*** *** ***

**** **** **** ****

keel(ed)
keen
keep
[kept]
*key (lever for lock
   or other
   mechanism /
   important /
   musical scale)
keyed

*knead (press with
   hands)
knee
kneel(ed)
[knelt]

*quay (wharf)

keeper
keeping
Kenya
keyboard
keyhole

kiosk

Korea
Korean

for C ...
see page 155

for Qu ...
see page 167

In these words you can hear the vowel sound ee as in eagle

✻   ✻ ✻   ✻ ✻ ✻   ✻ ✻ ✻ ✻

*lea (meadow)
*lead (show the way
    by going first /
    leash)
 [led]
 leaf
 league
*leak (unwanted
    escape)
 leaked
 lean(ed)
 [leant]
 leap(ed)
 [leapt]
 lease
*leased (rented)
 leash(es)
 leashed
*least (smallest
    amount)
 leave
 [left]
 leaves
*lee (shelter /
    sheltered side)
*leek (vegetable)
 leer(ed)

*lied (German song)

*leader (leading
    person or thing)
 leading
 leaflet
 leaning
*leaver (person
    who leaves)
 leaving
 leeward
 legion
 legal(ly)
*lever (tool)
 levered

*lieder (German
    songs)
 litre

leadership
legally
lenient
leverage

Lima-bean

> In these words the first letter 'e'
> is pronounced like the 'i' in 'pig'.
>
> legality   legitimate

*

me
meal
*mean (intend /
    miserly / poor)
[meant]
*meat (flesh of
    animal)
meek
*meet (be in
    contact /
    encounter)
[met]
mere

*mien (bearing /
    look of person)

* *

machine(d)
marine

meagre
mealtime
meaning
meantime
meanwhile
measles
merely
meeting
*meter (measuring
    machine)
metered
methane
*metre (unit of
    length / verse
    rhythm)

misdeal
[misdealt]
mislead
[misled]

* * *

machinist

meaningful(ly)
media
median
mediate
medium
meteor
meteorite

* * * * [* * * *]

machinery
material(ly)

meaningfully
mediation
mediator
meteorite
meteorological(ly)
meteorology

mysterious

In these words the first letter 'e'
is pronounced like the 'i' in 'pig'.

meander(ed)   memorial
mechanic(ally)   meniscus(es/-i)
melodic(ally)   meridian
melodious   meticulous
memento(es/s)   mnemonic

In these words you can hear the vowel sound ee as in eagle

✻   ✻ ✻   ✻ ✻ ✻   ✻ ✻ ✻ ✻ [✻]

*knead (press with hands)   nearby   Neapolitan
knee   nearer
kneel(ed)   nearest
[knelt]   nearly
                            neatly
                            needed
near(ed)   needle(d)
neat   needling
*need (require)   negro(es)
                            neon
niche   neither
niece

> In these words the first letter 'e'
> is pronounced like the 'i' in 'pig'.
>
> necessity(-ies)   neglectful(ly)
> negation   negotiate

O

✻   ✻ ✻   ✻ ✻ ✻   ✻ ✻ ✻ ✻

                           austere   oedipal   obedience
                                                     Oedipus   obedient

                           oblique
                           obscene

In these words you can hear the vowel sound ee as in eagle

*
* *
* * *
* * * * [* *]

*pea (vegetable)
*peace (period
   without war)
 peach(es)
*peak (highest
   point)
 peak(ed)
*peal (ringing)
*pealed (rang)
 peat
*pee (urinate)
*peel (rind / skin)
*peeled (removed
   the rind or skin)
 peen(ed)
 peep(ed)
*peer(ed) (look
   hard / person of
   equal rank / lord)

*piece (part)
 pieced
*pier (upright
   support /
   structure
   extending into
   the sea)
 pierce(d)
*pique (hurt pride)

 plea
 plead
*pleas (requests)
*please (used when
   asking / give
   pleasure)
 pleased
 pleat

 police(d)

 preach(es)
 preached
 preen(ed)
 priest

peaceful(ly)
peacetime
peacock
peahen
peanuts
penis(es)
people(d)
perceive(d)

pianist
piano(s)
pierrot

pleasing

police(d)
policeman

preacher
precede
precinct
prefect
prefix(es)
prefixed
preview
priestess(es)
proceed

peaceable
peacefully
period

policeman

preceded
preceding
premature
premium
previous
procedure
proceeding

periodic
periodical(ly)

pianoforte

predecessor
prehistoric(ally)
previously

In these words the first letter 'e'
is pronounced like the 'i' in 'pig'.

'PHENOMENAL' WORDS
peculiar
pedestrian
peninsula
peninsular
perimeter
petition(ed)
petroleum
phenomena
phenomenal(ly)
phenomenon
precaution
precipitate
precipitation
precise(ly)
precision
precocious
predict(ion)
predictable
predominantly

prefer(red)
preferring
preliminary(-ies)
prepare(d)
preparing
prescribe(d)
prescription
present(ed)
presentable
presenting
preserve(d)
preside
presumably
presume(d)
pretence
pretend(ed)
prevail(ed)
prevent(ion)
preventive

In these words you can hear the vowel sound ee as in eagle

*	**	***	****
*quay (wharf)	queasy(-ier,-iest)		
queen(ed)	query(-ies)		
queer			

R

*	**	***	**** [** **]
reach(es)	ravine	reaction	reactionary(-ies)
reached		reactor	realism
*read (look at and	reaches	reagent	realistic(ally)
understand)	reaching	realise(d)	reality(-ies)
[read]	react	ze	reasonable
*real (genuine)	reader	reappear(ed)	rechargeable
ream(ed)	reading	rearrange(d)	reconstitute
reap(ed)	really	reasoning	regionally
rear(ed)	reamer	reassure(d)	rehabilitation
*reed (plant /	rearm(ed)	receding	reinforcement
vibrating strip)	reason(ed)	receiver	relaxation
reef(ed)	rebate	receiving	reproduction
*reek(ed) (stink)	rebound	recently	reunion
*reel(ed) (spool /	rebuild	reconstruct	
wind / stagger)	[rebuilt]	regional(ly)	
	receipt	regrouping	
*wreak(ed) (bring about)	receive(d)	reinforce(d)	
wreath(ed)	*recent (not long	renaming	
	past)	repeated	
	recess(es)	repeating	
	recessed	replacement	
	reclaim(ed)	reproduce(d)	
	recoil(ed)	reunion	
	redo	rewritten	
	[redid]		
	[redone]	rheostat	
	refill(ed)		
	reflex(es)		
	refund		
	regain(ed)		
	region		
	regroup(ed)		
	-see next page		

-see next page

In these words you can hear the vowel sound ee as in eagle

* *

reject
*relaid (laid again)
relay
[relaid]
*relayed (sent on as
    received)
release(d)
relief
relieve(d)
remake
[remade]
rename(d)
repay
[repaid]
repeal(ed)
repeat
replace(d)
research(es)
researched
reset
[reset]
retail(ed)
retell
[retold]
retreat
reveal(ed)
rewrite
[rewrote]
[rewritten]

In these words the first letter 'e' is pronounced like the 'i' in 'pig'.

'REFRESHING' WORDS

react(ion)	regret(ted)	requirement
reactionary(-ies)	regretful(ly)	research(es)
reactor	regretting	researched
reagent	rehearsal	researcher
real	rehearse(d)	resemblance
realise(d)	reject(ion)	resemble(d)
ze	rejoice(d)	resembling
realism	rejoin(ed)	resent
realistic(ally)	relate(d)	resentful(ly)
reality(-ies)	relation(ship)	resentment
really	relax(es)	reserve(d)
rearm(ed)	relaxed	resign(ed)
rebel(led)	relent(less)	resist(ance)
rebelling	reliable	resistor
rebellion	reliability(-ies)	resolve(d)
rebellious	reliance	resort
rebound	religion	resource(d)
recall(ed)	religious	resources
receptacle	reluctant(ly)	respect(able)
reception	rely(-ies)	respectful(ly)
receptive	(relied)	respective(ly)
recess(es)	remain(ed)	respire(d)
recessed	remainder	respond
recession	remaining	response
recessive	remark(ed)	responsibility(-ies)
reciprocal(ly)	remarkable	responsible
reciprocate	remember(ed)	responsive
recital	remembering	restore(d)
recite	remembrance	restrain(ed)
reclaim(ed)	remind(ed)	restrict(ion)
recoil(ed)	reminder	result(ed)
record(ed)	remote	resultant
recorder	removal	resulting
recording	remove(d)	resume(d)
recover(ed)	removing	resuscitate
recovery(-ies)	Renaissance	resuscitation
recruit	renew(ed)	retain(ed)
reduce(d)	renown(ed)	retard(ed)
reduction	repair(ed)	retire(d)
refer(red)	repay	retirement
referral	[repaid]	retort
referring	repeal(ed)	retreat
refine(d)	repeater	return(ed)
refinery(-ies)	repel(led)	returnable
reflect(ed)	repellent	returning
reflection	repelling	reveal(ed)
reflector	repentance	revenge(d)
reflexive	repetitive	reverberate
reform(ed)	replace(d)	reverse(d)
refract(ion)	replacement	reversal
refrain(ed)	reply(-ies)	reversible
refresh(es)	(replied)	review(ed)
refreshed	report(ed)	revise(d)
refreshment	reporter	revision
refrigerator	repose(d)	revive(d)
refund	reproach(es)	revolt
refuse(d)	reproached	revolve(d)
refusal	republic(an)	revolver
regain(ed)	repudiate	revue
regard(ed)	repulsive	reward
regardless	request	
regatta	require(d)	

In these words you can hear the vowel sound ee as in eagle

✳   ✳ ✳   ✳ ✳ ✳   ✳ ✳ ✳ ✳ [✳]

cease(d)
*cede (give up)

*scene (part of
    play / display /
    place / view)
scheme(d)
scream(ed)
screech(es)
screeched
screen(ed)

*sea (ocean)
*seas (oceans)
seal(ed)
*seam(ed) (join)
seat
*see (register by
    eye / understand)
[saw]
[seen]
*seed (part of a
    plant from which
    a new one can
    grow / selected
    player in a
    tournament draw)
seek
[sought]
*seem(ed) (appear)
*seen (registered by
    eye / understood)
seep(ed)
seer
*sees (does see)
seethe(d)
*seize (grab)
seize(d)
-see next page

cedar
*ceiling (inner roof of room)

scenic(ally)

*sealing (fastening)
sealskin
*seaman (sailor)
*seamen (sailors)
seaport
seashore
seaside
season(ed)
seated
seaweed
*secret (kept hidden)
*secrete (produce
    liquid in body /
    hide)
seedling
seeing
seeking
seesaw
seething
seizure
*semen (sperm-
    carrying liquid)
sepal
sequence
sequel
sequin(ned)
series
settee
severe

sheepskin

*Signor (Italian for
    'Mr.')
sincere

skier
skiing

sleeper
sleeping

speaker
speaking
species
-see next page

*cereal (food from grain /
    plant producing grain)

scenery
scenically

seasoning
secrecy
secretion
*senior (older / more
    important)
*serial(ly) (parts in
    order)
serious
severely

Signora
sincerely

sleepily

strategic(ally)

scenically

seniority(-ies)
serially
seriously

Signorina

speedometer

strategically

In these words you can hear the vowel sound ee as in eagle

*

* *

she
sheaf(-ves)
*shear(ed) (cut off
    wool or hair)
[shorn]
shears
sheath(ed)
she'd
sheen
sheep(sheep)
*sheer (pure / very
    steep / very
    thin / go off at
    an angle)
sheered
sheet
she'll
she's
shield
shriek(ed)

siege

ski(ed)

sleek
sleep
[slept]
sleet
sleeve(d)

smear(ed)

sneak(ed)
sneer(ed)
sneeze(d)

speak
[spoke]
[spoken]
spear(ed)
speech(es)
speed
[sped]
sphere
spree
-see next page

steamer
steeple
steering
streaky(-ier,-iest)
streamer
streamlined

succeed

sweeper
sweeping
sweetheart
Sweden

In these words you can hear the vowel sound ee as in eagle

✼

squeak(ed)
squeal(ed)
squeeze(d)

*steal (thieve /
    move quietly)
[stole]
[stolen]
steam(ed)
steed
*steel (metal)
steeled
steep
steer(ed)
streak(ed)
stream(ed)
street

*suite (pieces that
    go together)

Swede
swede
sweep
[swept]
*sweet (of sugary
    taste / nice)

In these words the first letter
'e' sounds like the 'i' in 'pig'.

'SELECTED' WORDS

secession   selecting
seclude(d)   selection
secrete   selective
secretion   selector
secure(d)   sequoia
security(-ies)   severity(-ies)
select(ed)   specific(ally)

In these words you can hear the vowel sound ee as in eagle

*

**

***

**** [* *]

*tea (drink / meal)
teach(es)
[taught]
teak
*team (working
group/ playing
side)
teamed
*tear (sign of
distress)
*teas (drinks /
meals)
*tease(d) (mock in
fun / comb)
teat
*tee (support for
golf ball)
*teem (swarm)
teemed
teens
teeth

thee
theme
these
thief
three

*tier (one of a
number of levels)
tiered

treat
tree

tweed
tweet

teacher
teaching
teamwork
teapot
teaspoon
teeming
teepee/tepee
teething

theatre
theorem
theory(-ies)
thesis(-es)

trapeze
treacle
treason
treatment
treaty(-ies)
treetops
trio

tweezers

tedious
tedium
teenager

trachea

theatrical(ly)
theodolite
theological(ly)
theology(-ies)
theoretical(ly)

trapezium

In these words the first letter
'e' sounds like the 'i' in 'pig'.

'TERRIFIC' WORDS

telegraphy   theodolite
telephonist   theological(ly)
tepee   theology(-ies)
terrestrial(ly)   theoretical(ly)
terrific(ally)   tremendous
theatrical(ly)

In these words you can hear the vowel sound ee as in eagle

V

*	**	***	****
veal	vehicle	vehement	
	veneer(ed)	vehicle	
via	Venus		
	veto(es)	viola	
	vetoed		
	via		

> In this word the letter 'e'
> sounds like the 'i' in 'pig'.
>
> velocity(-ies)

*   * *   * * *   * * * *

*	* *	* * *	* * * *
*we (people speaking)	weakling	wearily	
*weak (feeble)	weakness(es)	weariness	
*weal (mark left on skin by whip)	weary(-ier,-iest) weasel	wheelbarrow	
*weald (open or wooded country)	weaver weaving		
*weave (interlace threads)	weekend		
[wove]	weekly		
[woven]	weevil		
*we'd (we had / we would)	wheelie		
*wee (small / pass water)			
*weed (passed water)			
*weed (unwanted wild plant)			
*week (seven days)			
weep			
[wept]			
*weir (dam across river)			
weird			
*we'll (we will)			
*we're (we are)			
*we've (we have)			
wheat			
*wheel (round rotating frame or disc)			
*wheeled (did wheel)			
wheeze(d)			
*wield (have and use)			
*wreak(ed) (bring about)			
wreath(ed)			

In these words you can hear the vowel sound ee as in eagle

Y

*

ye
year
yeast

yield

* *

yielding

* * *

* * * *

Z

*

zeal

* *

zebra
zero(es/s)

* * *

* * * *

In these words you can hear the vowel sound ee as in eagle

175

*	* *	* * *	* * * *
*aisle (part of church / gangway)	abide [abode]	abided	advisable advisory
		adviser	
*aye (yes)	acquire(d)		annihilate
		alignment	
	admire(d)	alliance	
	advice	almighty	
	advise(d)		
		appliance	
	alight		
	alike	arrival	
	alive		
	ally(-ies)	assignment	
	(allied)	asylum	
	apply(-ies)		
	(applied)		
	arise		
	[arose]		
	[arisen]		
	arrive(d)		
	aside		
	assign(ed)		

for H . . .
see page 182

awhile
awry

In these words you can hear the vowel sound ie as in lion

bide(d)
[bode]
bike(d)
bile
bind
[bound]
*bite (tear with
  teeth)
[bit]
[bitten]

blight
blind

bribe
bride
bright
brine

*buy (purchase)
[bought]
*buyer (purchaser)

*by (beside / not
  after / past /
  through / etc.)
*byre (cow-house)
*byte (unit of
  information)

behind
beside
besides

bias(ed/sed)
bible
biceps
binding
biped
bisect
bison

blindfold

*bridal (of the bride)
bridegroom
bridesmaid
*bridle (gear for
  controlling a
  horse)
bridled
bridling
brighten(ed)
brighter
brightest
brightly

buyer
buying

bye-bye
bypass(ed)
byway

biasing/biassing
bicycle(d)
binary

bribery

by-product

biennial(ly)
bifurcated
bilateral(ly)
binomial
biographical(ly)
biography(-ies)
biological(ly)
biology

chide(d)
[chid/chidden]
child
chime(d)
*choir (singing
    group / part of
    church)
Christ

*cite (give as
    example / quote)

climb(ed)

cried
cries
crime
cry(-ies)
    (cried)

kind
kite

childhood
china
China
Chinese

cider
cipher(ed)

client
climate
climax(es)
climaxed
climber
climbing

collide
combine(d)
compile(d)
comprise(d)
confide
confine(d)
conspire(d)

crisis(-es)
crying

cycle(d)
cyclist
cyclone
cypress(es)

Cyprus

kindly
kindness

climatic

combining
comprising

criterion(-ia)

cytoplasm

kaleidoscope

for Qu ...
see page 189

D

*   * *   * * *   * * * *

dial(led)
dice
-see next page

decide
decline(d)
decry(-ies)
    (decried)
-see next page

decipher(ed)
decisive
defiance
defiant
-see next page

delightfully
desirable
-see next page

In these words you can hear the vowel sound **ie** as in **lion**

*

*die (cease living /
    small cube / tool
    for stamping or
    shaping)
died
dike/dyke
*dine (have dinner)
dined
*dire (desperate)
dive(d)

dried
drive
[drove]
[driven]
dry(-ies)
    (dried)

*dye(d) (stain)
*dyer (person using
    dyes)
dyke/dike
*dyne (unit of force)

* *

define(d)
defy(-ies)
    (defied)
delight
deny(-ies)
    (denied)
deprive(d)
derive(d)
describe(d)
design(ed)
desire(d)
despise(d)
despite
*device (gadget /
    plan)
*devise(d) (invent /
    work out)

dial(led)
dialling
diamond
diary(-ies)
diecast
diet
digest
dilute
dining
direct
disguise(d)
dislike(d)
diver
diverge(d)
diverse
divert
divide
divine(d)
diving

*drier (more dry)
driest
drily/dryly
driver
driveway
driving
*dryer/drier (person,
    substance or
    machine that dries)
drying
dryly/drily

*dyeing (using dye)
*dying (ceasing to
    live)

* * *

delighted
delightful(ly)
denial
describing
designer

diagnose(d)
diagram
dialect
dialling
dialogue
diamond
diaphragm
diarrhoea
diatom
digestion
dilemma
diluted
dimension
dinosaur
dioxide
directed
direction
directive
directly
director
disciple
diversion
divided
dividers
dividing
divisor

dynamic(ally)
dynamite
dynamo(s)

* * * * [* * *]

diabetes
diagnosis(-es)
diagonal(ly)
diagrammatic(ally)
dialectical(ly)
diameter
digestible
dimensional
directory(-ies)
diversity

dynamically
dynamometer

In these words you can hear the vowel sound ie as in lion

*

*eye (visual organ)
*eyed (looked at
    with interest)

* *

eider
either

enquire/inquire(d)
entire

en- or in- ?

esquire

excite

eyeball
eyebrow
eyeing
eyelash(es)
*eyelet (small hole)
eyelid
eyesight

* * *

eisteddfod

enlighten(ed)
enquiry/inquiry(-ies)
entirely
entitle(d)

en- or in- ?

excited
excitement
exciting

* * * * [* *]

encyclopedia
environment
environmental(ly)

excitedly

en- or in- ?

for H . . .
see page 182

for I . . .
see page 183

In these words you can hear the vowel sound ie   as in lion

‹›

fight
[fought]
*file (tool /
    information
    system / line of
    people)
filed
*find (discover)
[found]
fine
*fined (made to pay
    a fine)
fire(d)
five

flies
flight
fly(-ies)
[flew]
[flown]

*friar (religious
    man who lived by
    begging)
fried
*frier (person who
    fries)
fright
fry(-ies)
    (fried)

*phial (small vessel or
    bottle)

for th . . .
see page 192

‹› ‹›

fibre
fibrous
fiery
fighter
fighting
final
finance(d)
finding
finest
finite
firearm
firefly(-ies)
firelight
fireman
fireplace
firewood
firework
firing
fiver

flier
flying
flywheel

*friar (religious
    man who lived by
    begging)
*frier (person who
    fries)
Friday
frighten(ed)
frightening
frightful(ly)

‹› ‹› ‹›

fibreglass
finally
financial(ly)
fire-engine

frightening
frightfully

‹› ‹› ‹› ‹›

financially

G

*

jive(d)

*gibe/jibe (taunt)

glide

*gneiss (rock)

grime
grind
[ground]

*guide (show the
  way)
*guise (appearance)
guy
*guyed (ridiculed)
*guys (more than one
  guy / does guy)
*gybe/gibe/jibe
  (alter course by
  swinging sail)

* *

jiving

Geiger

giant

glider

goodbye
goodnight

grimy(-ier,-iest)

guidance

gyrate

* * *

gigantic

Guyana

gyroscope

H

*

height

*hi (!)
hide
[hid]
[hidden]
*high (tall / great)
*higher (taller /
  greater)
hike(d)
hind
*hire(d) (grant use
  if paid / employ)
hive(d)

* *

haiku

hiding
hi-fi
higher
highest
highlands
highlight
highly
Highness
highway

hybrid
hygiene
hyphen

* * *

hibernate
highwayman

horizon

hyacinth
hydraulic(ally)
hydrofoil
hydrogen
hygienic(ally)
hyphenate

* * * * [* * *]

hibernation
hieroglyphics

hydraulically
hydrocarbon
hydrochloric
hydroelectric(ally)
hydrometer
hygienically
*hyperbola (form of
  curve)
*hyperbole
  (exaggeration)
hyphenated
hypotenuse
hypothesis(-es)
hypothetical(ly)

In these words you can hear the vowel sound ie as in lion

*

*aisle (part of church / gangway)

*aye (yes)

*eye (visual organ)
*eyed (looked at with interest)

*I (the person speaking)

*I'd (I would / I had)

*I'll (I will)

 I'm

*ion (charged particle)

*iron (metal)
 ironed

*isle (island)

 I've

for E ...
see page 180

* *

eider
either

*eyelet (small hole)

iceberg
ice-cream
ice-floe
Iceland
icing
icon
icy(-ier,-iest)

idea
ideal(ly)
*idle (lazy)
*idol (image for worship)

 ignite

imply(-ies)
 (implied)

*incite (urge)
incline(d)
inquire/enquire(d)
inscribe(d)
inside
*insight (understanding)
inspire(d)
invite

in- or en- ?

*ion (charged particle)

Ireland
iris(es)
Irish
*iron (metal)
ironed
ironing

island
*islet (small island)

item

ivy

ix- or ex- ?

* * *

eisteddfod

icicle

idea
ideal(ly)
idolise(d)
 ze

incisor
inquiry/enquiry(-ies)
invited

in- or en- ?

iodine

Irishman
ironic(ally)
ironmonger

isolate
isotope

ivory(-ies)

ix- or ex- ?

* * * * [* * *]

ideally
identical(ly)
identification
identified
identify(-ies)
 (identified)
identity(-ies)
ideological(ly)

in- or en- ?

ironical(ly)
ironmonger

isometric(ally)
isomorphic
isosceles
isotopic
isolation

itinerant
itinerary(-ies)

In these words you can hear the vowel sound ie as in lion

J

*

*gybe/gibe/jibe (alter course by swinging sail)

*jibe/gibe (taunt)
jive(d)

* *

giant

gyrate

jiving

* * *

gigantic

gyroscope

* * * *

K

*

kind
kite

knife(-ves)
knifed
*knight (Sir --- / chess piece)

* *

kindly
kindness

* * *

* * * *

kaleidoscope

.·˙ for C ... ˙·.
.· see page 178 ·.

·˙ for Qu ... ˙·.
: see page 189 ·˙

184

In these words you can hear the vowel sound **i͡e** as in **lion**

*

*liar (person who
      tells lies)
lice
lie(d)
lie
[lay]
[lain]
life(-ves)
light
[lit]
like(d)
lime(d)
line(d)
lion

*lyre (musical
      instrument)

* *

*liar (person who
      tells lies)
*licence (official
      permission)
*license(d) (give
      official
      permission)
*lichen (plant)
lido
lighted
lighter
lighthouse
lighting
*lightning (electric
      flash in the sky)
lightweight
likely
*liken(ed) (thought of
      as similar)
likewise
lilac
limelight
limestone
liner
lining
lino
lion
lively(-ier,-iest)
livestock

lying

* * *

liable
library(-ies)
*lightening (making
      lighter)
likelihood
livelihood

* * * *

librarian

In these words you can hear the vowel sound **ie** as in **lion**

*	* *	* * *	* * * * [*]
mice	mica	microchip	microcomputer
*might (would perhaps / power)	microbe	microphone	micrometer
	mighty	microscope	microprocessor
mild	migrate	microwave	microscopic
mile	mileage	migration	minority(-ies)
mime(d)	milestone		
*mind (system of thought and feeling / look after / watch / object)	*miner (worker in mine)		
	mining		
	*minor (less important)		
mine	minus		
*mined (did mine)	miser		
*mite (tiny thing)	missile		
	minute		
my	mitre(d)		
	myself		

In these words you can hear the vowel sound ie as in lion

*	* *	* * *	* * * *
*gneiss (rock)	neither	nightingale	Nigeria
		ninetieth	
knife(-ves)	nightdress(es)	nitrogen	
knifed	nightfall		
*knight (Sir --- / chess	nightie		
piece)	nightmare		
	nighttime		
*nice (pleasant)	nineteen(th)		
nigh	ninety(-ies)		
*night (hours of	nitrate		
darkness)	nitric		
nine			
ninth	nylon		

O

*	* *	* * *	* * * *
	alright	almighty	
	oblige(d)		

In these words you can hear the vowel sound ie as in lion

*phial (small vessel
    or bottle)

*pi (3.142 / Greek
    letter)
*pie (meat or fruit
    baked in pastry)
pike
pile(d)
pine(d)
pint
pipe(d)

pliers
plight
ply(-ies)
    (plied)

price(d)
*pride (high opinion
    of oneself)
*pried (did pry)
*pries (does pry or
    prise)
prime(d)
prior
*prise/prize (lever
    with a metal bar)
*prised (did prise)
*prize (reward /
    value / prise)
*prized (did prize)
*pry(-ies) (inquire
    into private
    matters / lever
    with a metal bar)
    (pried)

pyre

perspire(d)

pilot
pious
pipeline
piper
piping
pirate

pliers
plywood

polite

precise
prescribe(d)
preside
prior
private
provide

psychic(ally)

pylon
python

piety
pineapple
pioneer

politely

precisely
primary(-ies)
primeval
privacy
provided
providing

psychical(ly)
psychosis(-es)
psychotic(ally)

pyrites

primarily
priority(-ies)
proprietor

psychiatric(ally)
psychiatrist
psychiatry
psychically
psychoanalyse(d)
psychoanalysis
psychoanalyst
psychological(ly)
psychologist
psychology(-ies)
psychotherapist
psychotherapy
psychotically

In these words you can hear the vowel sound **ie** as in **lion**

Q

*

*choir (singing group /
    part of church)

quiet
*quire (24 sheets of
    writing paper)
quite

* *

quiet

* * *

quietly

R

*

*rhyme/rime (to
    end with the
    same sound)
rhymed

rice
ride
[rode]
[ridden]
*right (correct /
    direction)
*rime (hoar-frost)
rind
ripe
rise
[rose]
[risen]
*rite (ceremony)

*rye (grain)

*write (set down on paper)
[wrote]
[written]
writhe(d)
*wry (twisted)

* *

recite
refine(d)
rely(-ies)
    (relied)
remind
reply(-ies)
    (replied)
require(d)
resign(ed)
respire(d)
retire(d)
revise(d)
revive(d)
rewrite
[rewrote]
[rewritten]

rider
riding
rifle(d)
rightful(ly)
riot(ed)
ripen(ed)
rising
rival(led)

writer
writing
wryly

* * *

recital
reliance
reminded
reminder
requirement
retirement

rightfully
rioted
rioting
rivalling

* * * * [* *]

refinery(-ies)
reliability(-ies)
reliable

rhinoceros(es/-i)

riboflavin

In these words you can hear the vowel sound **ie** as in **lion**

✲	✲ ✲	✲ ✲ ✲	✲ ✲ ✲ ✲ [✲ ✲]
*cite (quote)	cider	psychical(ly)	cytoplasm
	cipher(ed)	psychosis(-es)	
scythe(d)		psychotic(ally)	psychiatric(ally)
scribe	cycle(d)		psychiatrist
	cycling	saliva	psychiatry
shine	cyclist		psychically
[shone]	cypress(es)	scientist	psychoanalyse(d)
*shire (county)			psychoanalysis
shrine	psychic(ally)	Siamese	psychoanalyst
shy(-ies)		silently	psychological(ly)
(shied)	science	sizable/sizeable	psychologist
*shyer (more shy)	scientist		psychology(-ies)
	scriber	skyscraper	psychotherapist
*side (edge /	scribing		psychotherapy
surface /		society(-ies)	psychotically
aspect / team)	shining		
sigh	shiny(-ier,-iest)	spiralling	scientific(ally)
*sighed (did sigh)	shyer	spirally	
*sighs (more than	shyly/shily		seismology
one sigh)		surprising	
*sight (vision)	Siam	survival	Siberia
*sign(ed) (mark with	sideboard	survivor	
a meaning)	sidelight		society(-ies)
*sine (function of	sideline		
an angle)	siding		
sire(d)	signing		
*site (place)	signpost		
*size (spatial	silence(d)		
extent / a weak	silent		
glue)	siphon		
sized	siren		
	sisal		
sky(-ies)			
	skyline		
*sleight (quickness)			
slice(d)	slightly		
slide	slimy(-ier,-iest)		
[slid]	slyly/slily		
*slight (small /			
thin and	smiling		
delicate / treat			
without respect)	spicy(-ier,-iest)		
slime	spider		
sly	spinal		
	spiral(led)		
smile(d)	spiral(ly)		
smite	sprightly(-ier,-iest)		
[smote]	-see next page		
[smitten]			
-see next page			

In these words you can hear the vowel sound **ie** as in lion

*   * *

snipe(d)   stifle(d)
                      stifling
spice(d)   stipend
spike(d)   striking
spine   stylus(es/-i)
spire
spite   subscribe(d)
spline(d)   subside
spy(-ies)   supply(-ies)
   (spied)   (supplied)
                      surprise(d)
squire   survive(d)

*stile (barrier
   with steps)
 stride
 [strode]
 [stridden]
 strife
 strike
 [struck]
 [stricken]
 stripe(d)
 strive
 [strove]
 [striven]
 sty(-ies)
*style (manner)
 styled

 swipe(d)

*	* *	* * *	* * * * [*]
*thigh (upper part of leg)	Taiwan	thiamine	titanium
thine	Thailand	timetable(d)	triangular
thrice	thyroid	tinier	triangulation
thrive(d)		tiniest	triceratops
[throve]	tidal		triumphally
[thriven]	tidings	trialling	
*thy (your)	tidy(-ier,-iest)	triangle	
*thyme (herb)	tiger	triumphal(ly)	
	tighten(ed)	triumphant	
*tide (ebb and flow)	tightly		
tie	tiling	typewriter	
*tied (fastened with knot)	timing		
tight	tiny(-ier,-iest)		
tights	tiresome		
tile(d)	title(d)		
*time (period)			
timed	tonight		
*tire (make weary / ring fitted to wheel)	trial(led)		
tired	trialling		
	tribesman		
trial(led)	trifle(d)		
tribe	tripod		
tripe	triumph(ed)		
try(-ies) (tried)	trying		
	twilight		
twice			
twine(d)	tying		
	typhoon		
type(d)	typist		
*tyre (ring fitted to wheel)	tyrant		

In these words you can hear the vowel sound **ie** as in **lion**

V

*

via
*vial (small vessel
   or bottle)
vice
vie(d)
*vile (disgusting)
vine
*viol (stringed
   instrument)

* *

via
*vial (small vessel
   or bottle)
vibrate
Viking
*viol (stringed
   instrument)
violence
violent
violet
viper
virus
viscount
visor
vital(ly)

* * *

viaduct
vibrating
vibration
violate
violence
violent
violet
violin
vitally
vitamin

* * * *

variety(-ies)

vice-versa
violation
vitality
vivarium

W

*

*while (time / during
   the time that)
*whiled (did while)
whilst
*whine(d) (complain)
white
why

wide
wife(-ves)
*wild (untamed)
*wile (trick)
*wind(ed) (move by
   turning)
[wound]
*wine (drink)
*wined (supplied
   with wine)
wipe(d)
wire(d)
wise

*write (set down on
   paper)
[wrote]
[written]
writhe(d)
*wry (twisted)

* *

whitewash(es)
whitewashed
whiting
whitish

widely
widen(ed)
wider
widespread
wildlife
wildly
wily(-ier,-iest)
winding
wiper
wireless(es)
wiry(-ier,-iest)

writer
writing
wryly

* * *

* * * *

In these words you can hear the vowel sound ie as in lion

X

LONG
VOWEL ie

*   * *   * * *   * * * *

xylophone

Z

*   * *   * * *   * * * *

xylophone

In these words you can hear the vowel sound **ie** as in **lion**

✻   ✻ ✻   ✻ ✻ ✻   ✻ ✻ ✻ ✻ [✻]

	abode	approaching	ammonia
	afloat		ammonium
		aroma	
	ago		appropriate
		atonement	
	alone	atrocious	associate
			association
	approach(es)	awoken	associative
	approached		
	arose		
	atone(d)		
	awoke		

> for oe-r
> see page 256

B

✻   ✻ ✻   ✻ ✻ ✻   ✻ ✻ ✻ ✻

*beau (dandy)	behold	
	[beheld]	
blow	below	
[blew]	bestow(ed)	
[blown]		
	blowing	
boat	blowlamp	
boast		
*bode (did bide)	boatman	
*bold (brave)	bolster(ed)	
*bole (tree-trunk)	bonus(es)	
bolt	boulder	
bone(d)	bouquet	
both	bowler	
*bow (wood and		
string / knot /	brocade	
bend)	broken	
*bowed (curved like	broker	
a bow)		
*bowl (container /		
send a ball)		
*bowled (rolled /		
bowled out)		
bowls		
*broach(es) (open up)		
broached		
broke		
*brooch(es) (ornament)		

> In these words 'o' is a neutral vowel.
> It sounds like the 'a' in 'astonish'.
>
> Bolivia   botanical   brocade

> for oe-r
> see page 257

*	* *	* * *	* * * * [*]
choke(d)	chauffeur(ed)	chromium	coagulate
chose		chromosome	coefficient
chrome(d)	-choral		coincidence
	-chorus(es)	coconut	collinear
cloak(ed)	-chorused	coincide	colonial(ly)
close	chosen	commotion	cooperate
closed		component	cooperation
*clothe(d) (provide	cloakroom	composer	cooperative
with clothes)	closing	controller	coordinate
*clothes (garments)	clothesline	controlling	coordination
*clove (spice / did	closure	corrosion	
cleave)	clothing	cotangent	
*cloves (spice)	cloven		
	clover	kimono(s)	
coach(es)			
coached	coastal		
coal	coastline		
coast	coating		
coat	cobalt		
coax(es)	cobra		
coaxed	cocoa		
code	colder		
coke(d)	coleslaw		
cold	cologne		
colt	colon		
comb(ed)	compose(d)		
cone	console(d)		
cope(d)	control(led)		
cove	corrode		
	cosine		
croak(ed)	cosy/cozy(-ier,-iest)		
crow(ed)	crochet(ed)	for Qu ...	for oe-r
[crew]	crocus(es/-i)	see page 206	see page 258
[crown]	croquet		
	crowbar		

In these words the first letter 'o' is a neutral vowel.
It... er.... er.... er.... sounds like the 'a' in 'astonish'.

'COMMUNICATING' WORDS

cholesterol	collector	commandment	commitment	communion
chorale	collide	commemorate	committee	community(-ies)
cocoon(ed)	collision	commemoration	committing	commutative
collapse(d)	cologne	commence(d)	commotion	commuter
collapsible	colonial(ly)	commercial(ly)	communal(ly)	corrode
collect(ing)	comedian	commission(ed)	commune(d)	corrosion
collection	comedienne	commissioner	communicate	corrupt(ion)
collective	commander	commit(ted)	communication	

In these words you can hear the vowel sound **oe** as in goat

D

*

*doe (female deer)
dole(d)
dome(d)
don't
dose(d)
*dough (flour and
    water)
doze(d)

droll
drone(d)
drove

* *

decode
denote
devote

disclose(d)
disown(ed)
dispose(d)

docile
domain
donor
doughnut

* * *

decoding
devoted
devotion

diploma
disposal

domestic(ally)
donated
donation

* * * * [*]

diplomacy

domestically
domesticate

> for oe-r
> see page 259

> In these words the letter
> 'o' may be a neutral vowel.
>
> domain   domestic(ally)   domesticate

E

*

> for H . . .
> see page 200

> for I . . .
> see page 201

* *

elope(d)

em- or im- ?

enclose(d)
enfold
enrol(led)

erode

explode
expose(d)

* * *

emotion
emotive

em- or im- ?

enclosure
enrolling
enrolment

erosion

explosion
explosive
exponent
exposure

* * * * [*]

eau-de-cologne

emotional(ly)

> for oe-r
> see page 259

*   * *   * * *   * * * * [*]

float
*floe (floating ice-
    sheet)
*flow(ed) (run)

foal
*foaled (given birth
    to a foal)
foam(ed)
foe
*fold (bend double /
    crease / sheep
    enclosure)
folk

fro
froze

phone(d)

floated
floating
flowchart
flowing

focal
focus(es)/foci
focus(es/ses)
focused/focussed
folded
folding
folklore
foretold
forgo/forego
[forwent/forewent]
[forgone/foregone]

frozen

phobic
phoneme
photo

ferocious

focusing/focussing
foliage
folio

phobia
photograph(ed)

photocopier
photocopy(-ies)
  (photocopied)
photo-electric
photofinish
photographic(ally)
photosynthesis

for th ...
see page 208

for oe-r
see page 260

In these words you can hear the vowel sound **oe** as in **goat**

G

*   * *   * * *   * * * *

ghost

gloat
globe
glow(ed)

gnome

go
[went]
[gone]
goal
goat
goes
gold
*groan (deep moan)
groaned
grope(d)
gross(ed)
grove
grow
[grew]
*[grown] (developed)
growth

global(ly)
glowing

goatskin
going
golden
goldfish
gopher

*grocer (shopkeeper
   selling food and
   other goods)
*grosser (fatter /
   more disgusting)
grotesque
growing
grownup

globally

grocery(-ies)

for oe-r
see page 261

In these words you can hear the vowel sound oe as in goat

H

*

hoax(es)
hoaxed
hoe(d)
*hoes (more than
    one hoe)
*hold (grip /
    support /
    continue)
[held]
*hole (opening)
*holed (hit ball
    into hole)
home(d)
hope(d)
*hose (flexible
    water-pipe /
    stockings)
hosed
host
hove

*whole (total / complete)

* *

holding
*holy(-ier,-iest)
    (sacred / full of
    holes)
homeland
homesick
homeward
homework
hopeful(ly)
hopeless
hoping
hosepipe
hostess(es)
hotel

wholemeal
wholesale
wholesome
*wholly (totally /
    completely)

* * *

heroic(ally)

hopefully

hypnosis

* * * * [* * *]

heroically

homeopathic(ally)
homosexual(ly)

for oe-r
see page 261

I

*

for E ...
see page 197

* *

il- or el- ?

impose(d)

in- or en- ?

ir- or er- ?

ix- or ex- ?

* * *

immobile

im- or em-?

in- or en- ?

ir- or er- ?

ix- or ex- ?

* * * *

im- or em- ?

for oe-r
see page 262

In these words you can hear the vowel sound oe as in goat

J

✲
joke(d)

✲ ✲
joker

✲ ✲ ✲
jovial(ly)

✲ ✲ ✲ ✲
jovially

K

✲
knoll
*know (understand)
  [knew]
  [known]
*knows (does know)

✲ ✲
knowing

kosher

✲ ✲ ✲
kimono(s)

koala

✲ ✲ ✲ ✲

for C ...
see page 196

for Qu ...
see page 206

In this word 'o' is a neutral vowel.
It sounds like the 'a' in 'astonish'.

Korea(n)

L

✲
*lo (behold)
*load (amount carried)
loaf(-ves)
loafed
loam
*loan(ed) (lend /
    amount lent)
loathe(d)
*lode (vein of metal
    ore / ditch)
*lone (single)
*low (not high / moo)
*lowed (mooed)

✲ ✲
loaded
local(ly)
locate
locust
lodestone
logo(s)
lonely
lonesome
lotion
lower(ed)
lowest
lowlands
lowly

✲ ✲ ✲
locally
located
location
loneliness

✲ ✲ ✲ ✲
locality(-ies)
locomotion
locomotive
loganberry(-ies)

for oe-r
see page 263

201

In these words you can hear the vowel sound oe as in goat

*

mauve

*moan(ed) (complain)
moat
*mode (way /
    fashion)
mole
mope(d)
most
mould
moult
mow
*[mowed] (cut)
*[mown] (cut)

* *

mobile
molten
moment
mostly
motel
*motif/motive (theme /
    figure)
motion(ed)
*motive (cause of
    action)
motor(ed)
mouldy(-ier,-iest)
mower

* * *

Mohammed
molasses
momentary
momentum
mosaic
motionless
motorbike
motorist
motorway

* * * * [*]

melodious

mobility
molecular
momentarily
momentary
motorcycle

for oe-r
see page 263

> In these words the letter
> 'o' may be a neutral vowel.
>
> Mohammed   molecular   morale
> molasses   momentum

N

*

gnome

knoll
*know (understand)
[knew]
[known]
*knows (does know)

*no (not any)
node
*nose (part of face)
nosed
note

* *

noble
nomad
no-one
nosy(-ier,-iest)
notebook
noted
notice(d)
notion
nowhere
nova

* * *

neurosis(-es)

noblemen
nobody
nomadic
notable
notation
notify(-ies)
    (notified)
November

* * * * [*]

negotiate

nobility
noticeable
notification
notoriety
notorious

> In these words the letter
> 'o' may be a neutral vowel.
>
> nobility   notation
> nomadic   November

In these words you can hear the vowel sound oe as in goat

O

LONG VOWEL O e

*

oak
oath
oats

*ode (long poem)

*oh (!)

old

*owe (must pay)
*owed (did owe)
own(ed)

* *

although

oatmeal

obey(ed)
oblique
oboe

ocean
ochre

odour

ogre
ogress(es)

older
oldest

omen
omit(ted)

only

opal
opaque
open(ed)
opening
oppose(d)

-oral(ly)

osier

*ova (eggs)
oval
*over (above)
ovum(-a)

owing
owner

ozone

* * *

oasis(-es)

odious

omission
omitted
omitting

opening
opium
opponent

-orally

osier

ovary(-ies)
overalls
overboard
overcast
[overcast]
overcoat
overcome
[overcame]
[overcome]
overdo
[overdid]
[overdone]
overeat
[overate]
[overeaten]
overfeed
[overfed]
overflow(ed)
overgrow
[overgrew]
[overgrown]
overhang
[overhung]
overhead
overhear
[overheard]
overjoyed
overlap(ped)
overlay
[overlaid]
overload
overlook(ed)
-see next page

* * * * [*]

eau-de-cologne

obedience
obedient

oceanography

overlapping
overlooking
overwhelming

for H ...
see page 200

for oe-r
see page 264

In these words you can hear the vowel sound **oe** as in **goat**

203

* * *

overpower(ed)
override
[overrode]
[overridden]
overrun
[overran]
[overrun]
overseas
oversee
[oversaw]
[overseen]
overshoot
[overshot]
oversize
oversleep
[overslept]
overtake
[overtook]
[overtaken]
overthrow
[overthrew]
[overthrown]
overtime
overtone
overture
overturn(ed)
overwhelm(ed)
overwork(ed)

ownership

for oe-r
see page 264

In these words the first letter 'o'
is a neutral vowel. It.. er... er...
sounds like the 'a' in 'astonish'.

'OBLIGING' WORDS

obedience	offensive
obedient	official(ly)
obey(ed)	omission
oblige(d)	omit(ted)
oblique	omitting
obliterate	opinion
oblivion	opossum
oblivious	opponent
occasion(al)	oppose(d)
occasionally	oppression
occurr(ed)	oppressive
occurrence	oppressor
occurring	original(ly)
o'clock	originality
offence	originate
offend	

P

*

phone(d)

poach(es)
poached
poke(d)
*pole (long rod)
*poll (number of
   voters / head /
   cut off top)
polled
pope
pose(d)

probe(d)
prose

* *

patrol(led)

phobic
phoneme
photo(s)
-see next page

for oe-r
see page 265

* * *

patrolling

phobia
photograph(ed)

poetic(ally)
poetry
polio
postmaster
potency
potential(ly)
-see next page

* * * * [* *]

petroleum

photocopier
photocopy(-ies)
   (photocopied)
photographic(ally)
photosynthesis
-see next page

In these words you can hear the vowel sound oe as in goat

✳ ✳   ✳ ✳ ✳   ✳ ✳ ✳ ✳ [✳]

poacher	precocious	poetically
poem	probation	potentially
poet	procedure	
poetry	proceeding	prohibited
poker	programmer	prohibiting
Poland	programming	prohibitive
polar	progression	prolifically
Polish	progressive	protoplasm
polo	prohibit(ed)	protozoa
pony(-ies)	projectile	
postage	projection	
postal	projector	
poster	prolific(ally)	
postman	promotion	
postpone(d)	proposal	
posy(-ies)	prototype	
potent		
potion		
poultice(d)		
poultry		

for oe-r
see page 265

proceed
process(es)
processed
proclaim(ed)
profile(d)
profuse
*program (instructions for computer)
programmed
*programme (plan of performance / broadcast)
progress(es)
progressed
project
prologue
prolong(ed)
promote
pronoun
propose(d)
protein
protest
proton
proven
provoke(d)

> In these words the first letter 'o' is a neutral vowel. It.. er... er... sounds like the 'a' in 'astonish'.
>
> 'PROGRESSIVE' WORDS
>
> | | | |
> |---|---|---|
> | phonetic(ally) | profane | pronouncing |
> | photographer | profess(es) | pronunciation |
> | photography | professed | propel(led) |
> | police(man) | professing | propelling |
> | polite(ly) | professional(ly) | propeller |
> | political(ly) | professor | proportional(ly) |
> | pollute | proficiency | proposal |
> | pollution | proficient | propose(d) |
> | position(ed) | profound | proprietor |
> | possess(es) | profuse | propulsion |
> | possessed | profusion | prospect(ive) |
> | possession | progression | prospector |
> | possessive | progressive | prospectus(es) |
> | potato(es) | prohibit(ed) | protect(ed) |
> | potential(ly) | prohibiting | protection |
> | probation | prohibitive | protective |
> | procedure | project(ion) | protector |
> | proceed(ing) | projectile | protest |
> | procession | projector | protractor |
> | proclaim(ed) | proliferate | protrude |
> | procure(d) | proliferation | provide(d) |
> | prodigious | prolific(ally) | providing |
> | produce(d) | prolong(ed) | provincial |
> | producer | promote | provision(s) |
> | producing | promotion | provisional(ly) |
> | production | pronounce(d) | provocative |
> | productive | pronouncement | |

Q

*

quote
quoth

* *

quota
quotient

* * *

quotation

R

*

roach(roach)
*road (track)
*roam(ed) (wander)
roan
roast
robe(d)
*rode (travelled
    on/by)
*roe (fish eggs or
    sperm / small
    deer)
rogue
*role (actor's part)
*roll(ed) (turn over
    and over)
*Rome (city)
rope(d)
*rose (flower / did
    rise)
*rote (repetition)
rove
*row (line / move
    with oars)
*rowed (moved with
    oars)
*rows (lines / moves
    with oars)

*wrote (set down on paper)

* *

remote
repose(d)
reproach(es)
reproached
rewrote

robot
robust
rodent
roller
rolling
Roman
romance(d)
rosette
rotate
rotor
roving

* * *

rodeo
rolling-pin
romantic(ally)
rotary
rotation

* * * * [*]

rhododendron

romantically

In these words the first 'o' may be
pronounced like the 'a' in 'astonish'.

romance   rosette
romantic(ally)   rotation

 for oe-r
see page 266

In these words you can hear the vowel sound oe as in goat

S

‡

scold
scone
scope
scroll(ed)

*sew(ed) (stitch)
 [sewn]

shoal
show(ed)
 [shown]

*sloe (blackthorn
   fruit or bush)
 slope(d)
*slow (at a low
   speed)
 slowed

 smoke(d)
 smote

 snow(ed)

*so (therefore / to
   such a degree /
   in that way)
 soak(ed)
 soap(ed)
*sold (given for
   money)
*sole (only / part
   of foot and
   shoe / fish)
*soled (fitted with
   new sole)
*soul (spirit)
*sow(ed) (plant)
 [sown]

 spoke

 stoat
 stoke(d)
 stole
 stone(d)
 stove
 stow(ed)
 strobe
 strode
 stroke(d)
 stroll(ed)
 strove

‡ ‡

chauffeur

scrolling

sewing

shoulder(ed)

slogan
slower
slowly

smoking
smoky(-ier,-iest)
smoulder(ed)

snowball(ed)
snowdrop
snowfall
snowflake
snowman
snowshoes
snowstorm

sober(ed)
social(ly)
soda
sofa
solar
solder(ed)
soldier(ed)
solely
solo(s)
sonar

spoken
spokeshave
spokesman

stolen
stony(-ier,-iest)
-storey (floor)
-story(-ies) (tale)

suppose(d)

swollen

‡ ‡ ‡

chauvinist

samosa

sociable
socialist
socially
sodium
soldering
soprano(s)
soviet

stowaway

‡ ‡ ‡ ‡ [‡]

sociology
socialism
Somalia

supposedly

In these words the first 'o' is neutral.

society(-ies)	sophisticated
solicitor	soprano(s)
solution	

---

for oe-r
see page 267

In these words you can hear the vowel sound oe as in goat

T

*

those
though
throat
*throe (sharp pain)
*throne (state chair)
throned
throve
*throw (hurl)
[threw]
*[thrown] (hurled)

*toad (animal)
toast
*toe (part of foot)
*toed (placed toes
   against / fitted
   with a toe)
*told (did tell)
toll
*tolled (did toll)
tone(d)
tote
*tow (pull behind)
*towed (pulled
   behind)

troll

* *

throwing

toadstool
toasted
toastie
token
tonal(ly)
topaz
-Tory(-ies)
total(led)
totem

trophy(-ies)

* * *

tonally
totalling
totally

In these words the first 'o' is neutral.
It sounds like the 'a' in 'astonish'.

tobacco(s)	tomato(es)	topology
tobacconist	topography	torrential(ly)

* * * *

for oe-r
see page 268

V

*

vole
*volt (unit of
   electrical force)
vote

* *

vocal(ly)
voltage
voted

* * *

viola

vocally
vocation
voltmeter

* * * * [*]

vocabulary(-ies)
vocational(ly)

In these words the first 'o' may be
pronounced like the 'a' in 'astonish'.

vocabulary(-ies)   vocation(ally)

In these words you can hear the vowel sound **oe** as in **goat**

W

*	* *	* * *	* * * *
*whoa! (stop!)	wholemeal	woefully	
*whole (total / complete)	wholesale		
	wholesome		
*woe (distress)	*wholly (totally / completely)		
woke			
won't	woeful(ly)		
wove	woken		
	woven		for oe-r see page 269
*wrote (set down on paper)			

Y

*	* *	* * *	* * * *
*yoke (neck-piece)	yoga		
yoked	yoghourt/		
*yolk (yellow part of egg)	yoghurt/yogurt		for oe-r see page 269
	yogi		
	yokel		

Z

*	* *	* * *	* * * * [* *]
zone(d)		zodiac	zoological(ly)
			zoology

* | ** | *** | **** [*]

-about
abuse(d)

accrue(d)
accuse(d)
acute

adieu

-afoot

aloof

amuse(d)

approve(d)

assume(d)
assure(d)

amusement

assurance

accumulate
accumulation
accumulator

alluvial
alluvium

for H . . .
see page 215

In these words you can hear oo as in goose or ue as in newt

*

balloon(ed)

*blew (puffed)
bloom(ed)
*blue (colour)

-book(ed)
boom(ed)
-boor
boost
boot
booth

brew
*brewed (fermented)
*brews (does brew)
*brood (offspring)
-brook(ed)
broom
*bruise (injury)
bruised
brute

-bull
-bush(es)
-bushed

* *

baboon
balloon(ed)

beauty(-ies)

bluebell
bluetit

booby(-ies)
-bookcase
-booklet
-bookshelf(-ves)
booster
-bosom

brewer
brunette
brutal(ly)

-Buddha
-Buddhist
bugle
-bulldog
-bullet
-bullfrog
-bullock
-bully(-ies)
- (bullied)
bureau
-bushel
-butcher(ed)

* * *

bazooka

beautiful(ly)
Bermuda

boulevard

brewery(-ies)
brutally

-Buddhism
-bulletin
-bulldozer(ed)

* * * *

beautifully

*	* *	* * *	* * * * [*]
chew(ed)	canoe(d)	communal(ly)	communally
*chews (does chew)	cashew	communion	communicate
*choose (select)		commuter	communication
[chose]	chewing	computer	communion
[chosen]	choosing	conclusion	community(-ies)
*chute (slope for		confusion	commutative
things to slide	cocoon(ed)	consumer	computerise(d)
down)	commute		ze
	compute	crucially	
clue(d)	conclude	crucible	crucifixion
	confuse(d)	crucifix(es)	
-cook(ed)	consume(d)	cruciform	cumulative
cool(ed)	-cooker	crucify(-ies)	curiosity(-ies)
*coop (cage)	-cooking	(crucified)	
-could	cooler	cruelly	
*coup (stroke /	-couldn't	cruelty(-ies)	
successful	coupe		
action)	coupon	cubicle	
-course(d)		cucumber	
-court	-crooked	cumulus	
	crucial(ly)	curator	
crew	cruel(ly)	curio(s)	
crewed (acted as a	cruelty(-ies)	curious	
crew member)	cruet		
*crews (more than	cruiser	Kuwait	
one crew)	crusade		
-crook			
croon(ed)	cubic		
*crude (untreated /	cuboid		
done without	-cuckoo		
skill)	curate		
cruel(ly)	-cushion(ed)		
*cruise (voyage)			
cruised			
cube(d)			
*cue (rod / signal)			
cued			
cure(d)			
cute			

*queue (waiting line)
queued

> for Qu ...
> see page 219

In these words you can hear **oo** as in **goose** or **ue** as in **newt**

D

*	* *	* * *	* * * *
*dew (moisture)	deduce(d)	diffusion	dutifully
		disproven	
do	diffuse(d)		
[did]	disprove(d)	duelling	
[done]	dispute	duplicate	
*doer (active person)	disused	dutiful(ly)	
doom(ed)			
*dour (unsmiling)	doer		
	doing		
drew	doodle(d)		
droop(ed)	doodling		
*due (owing)	*dual (double)		
duke	ducal		
dune	*duel(led) (fight)		
	duelling		
	duet		
	duly		
	during		
	duty(-ies)		

E

*	* *	* * *	* * * * [* * *]
*ewe (female sheep)	em- or im- ?	*elusive (hard to find)	enthusiasm
*ewes (more than			enthusiastic(ally)
one ewe)	endure(d)	el- or il- ?	
	*ensure(d) (make		eucalyptus(es)
	certain)	em- or im- ?	euphonium
			European
	en- or in- ?	endurance	euthanasia
	Europe	en- or in- ?	exclusively
			exuberance
	exclude	eureka!	exuberant
	excuse(d)		

for H ...
see page 215

for I ...
see page 215

exclusion
exclusive
extrusion

In these words you can hear **oo** as in **goose** or **ue** as in **newt**

F

*

feud
*few (not many)

*flew (passed in
   flight)
*'flu (influenza)
*flue (pipe)
fluke
flute

food
fool(ed)
-foot
-fourth

fruit

fuel
-full
fume(d)
fuse(d)

*phew/whew (!)

for th ...
see page 222

* *

feudal(ly)
fewer

fluent
fluid
fluoride
fluorine

foodstuff
foolish
-football
-foothill
-foothold
-footpath
-footstep
-forsook

fuel(led)
fuelling
-fulcrum
-fulfil(led)
-fully
fury(-ies)
fusion
futile
future

* * *

feudally

fluorescent

foolhardy

fruiterer

fuelling
fugitive
-fulfilling
fumigate
funeral
furious
fuselage

* * * *

fluorescent

foolhardiness

G

*

gloom
glue(d)

*gnu (animal)

-good
-goods
goose(geese)
gourd

grew
groom(ed)
group(ed)
groove(d)

* *

gloomy(-ier,-iest)
glucose

-goodbye
-goodness
-goodnight
-gooseberry(-ies)
grouping
gruelling

* * *

-gooseberry(-ies)

gruelling

* * * *

In these words you can hear oo as in goose   or ue as in newt

H

*

*hew(ed) (cut down)
  [hewn]

-hood
 hoof(-ves)
 hoofed
-hook(ed)
*hoop (large ring or
   band)
 hoop(ed)
 hoot
 hooves
-house

*hue (colour)
 huge

who
whom
*whoop(ed) (cry out with joy)
whose

* *

hoover(ed)

hula
human
humid
humour(ed)
humus
-hurrah!
-hurray!

* * *

hooligan

*humerus (bone in
   upper arm)
*humorous (funny)

whoever
whooping-cough

* * * * [* *]

humanitarian
humanities
humanity
humidity
humiliate
humiliation

I

*

* *

immune
improve(d)
impure

include
induce(d)
*insure(d) (protect
   against loss)
intrude

in- or en- ?

ix- or ex- ?

* * *

illusion
*illusive (deceptive)

improvement
improving

included
including
inclusion
inclusive
inhuman
insurance
intruder
intrusion

in- or en- ?

* * * * [*]

illuminate
illumination

immovable
immunity
impunity
impurity(-ies)

incurable
infuriate
injurious
innumerable

in- or en-?

for E ...
see page 213

215

In these words you can hear **oo** as in **goose**   or **ue** as in **newt**

J

*

Jew
jewel(led)

juice
June

* *

jewel(led)
jeweller
jewellry/jewelry
Jewess(es)
Jewish

judo
juicy(-ier,-iest)
July
juror
jury(-ies)

* * *

Jacuzzi

jeweller
jewellry/jewelry

jubilant
jubilee
judicial(ly)
juicier
juiciest
junior
Jupiter
juvenile

* * * *

jubilation
judicially
jurisdiction
jurisprudence

K

*

*knew (understood)

....
: for C ...   :
: see page 212   :
....

* *

Kuwait

....
: for Qu ...   :
: see page 219   :
....

* * *

* * * *

L

*

*lieu (place)

*loo (toilet)
*loos (toilets)
-look(ed)
loom
loop(ed)
loose(d)
*loot (stolen goods)
*lose (have no
    longer / fail to
    win)
[lost]

lure(d)
*lute (musical
    instrument)

* *

lagoon

-lookout
loosely
loosen(ed)
loser
losing

ludo
lukewarm
lunar
lupin

* * *

lubricant
lubricate
luminous

* * * *

lubrication

In these words you can hear oo as in goose   or ue as in newt

*	* *	* * *	* * * * [*]
mew(ed)	manure(d)	manoeuvre(d)	maturity
*mewl(ed) (mew)	maroon(ed)		
*mews (houses converted from stables)	mature(d)	movable/moveable	municipal(ly)
			musically
	-mistook	museum	
	misuse(d)	musical(ly)	
moo		musician	
*mooed (went 'moo')	moonlight	mutation	
*mood (state of feeling)	mooring	mutiny(-ies) (mutinied)	
moon(ed)	-Moslem	mutineer	
moor(ed)	-mournful	mutually	
*moose (animal)	-mourning		
-mourn(ed)	movement		
move(d)	movie		
*-mouse (animal)	moving		
*mousse (sweet dish)			
	*mucous (of/covered with mucus)		
*mule (animal)	*mucus (slimy liquid)		
*muse (think deeply)	muesli		
mute	mural		
	music(ally)		
	-Muslim		
	mutual(ly)		

*

**

***

**** [*]

*gnu (animal)

*knew (understood)

*new (unused)
news
newt

-nook
noon
noose
-now

nude

neuron
neutral(ly)
neutron
newly
newton

nougat

nuisance

neurosis(-es)
neurotic(ally)
neutralise(d)
  ze
neutrally
newcomer
newsagent
newspaper
New Zealand

nuclear
nucleus(nuclei)
nudity
numeral
numerous
nutrient
nutrition
nutritious

pneumatic

neurotically
neutrality

numeration
numerator
numerical(ly)

pneumonia

O

*

**

***

****

ooze(d)

-out

obscure(d)
obtuse

obscurity(-ies)

for H ...
see page 215

In these words you can hear oo as in goose   or ue as in newt

*

pew
*phew/whew (!)

plume(d)

pool(ed)
*poor (badly off)
-pour(ed) (flow out)

proof
prove(d)
[proven]
prune(d)

-pull(ed)
*pure (unmixed)
-push(es)
-pushed
-puss(es)
-put
-[put]

* *

perfume(d)
Peru
pewter

plumage
plural(ly)
Pluto

pollute
poodle
poorly
-pouring

presume(d)
procure(d)
produce(d)
proofread
profuse
protrude
proven
prudence
prudent
pruning

-pudding
-pulley
-pulpit
puma
puny(-ier,-iest)
pupa(e)
pupil
purely
pursue(d)
pursuit
-pushchair
-pussy(-ies)
putrid
-putting

* * *

peculiar

plurally

pneumatic

pollution

producer
producing
profusion

-pullover
purify(-ies)
   (purified)
purity
pursuant
pursuer
putrify(-ies)
   (putrified)

* * * * [*]

peculiar

pneumonia

presumably

purification

Q

*

*queue (waiting
   line)
queued

* *

* * *

quintuplet

* * * *

In these words you can hear **oo** as in **goose**   or **ue** as in **newt**

R

✳	✳ ✳	✳ ✳ ✳	✳ ✳ ✳ ✳
*rood (crucifix / ½ of an acre)	racoon	refusal	repudiate
roof(ed)		removal	reunion
-rook	recruit	removing	
room(ed)	reduce(d)	-resources	rheumatism
roost	refuse(d)	reunion	
*root (part of plant / origin)	remove(d)		-Romania/Roumania/ Rumania
rouge	renew(ed)	rheumatic	
*route (way)	-resource(d)		
	resume(d)	-rookery(-ies)	
ruche(d)	*review (survey)		
*rude (impolite)	reviewed	ruinous	
rule(d)	*revue (theatrical entertainment)	rurally	
rue(d)			
*rued (regretted)	rhubarb		
	rooftops		
	roommate		
	rooster		
	routine		
	ruby(-ies)		
	ruin(ed)		
	ruler		
	rumour(ed)		
	rural(ly)		
	ruthless		

In these words you can hear **oo** as in **goose** or **ue** as in **newt**

S

*

*chute (slope for things
  to slide down)

school(ed)
scoop(ed)
screw(ed)

*shoe (footwear)
 [shod]
*shoo(ed) (scare
   away)
-shook
*shoot (fire / hit
   with bullet /
   move very fast /
   new growth from
   plant)
 [shot]
-should
 shrewd

skew(ed)

sleuth(ed)
slew
sluice

smooth(ed)

soon
-soot
 soothe(d)
 soup

spool(ed)
spoon(ed)
spruce

stew(ed)
-stood
 stool
*stoop (bend down)
 stooped
*stoup (basin for
   holy water)
 strew(ed)
 [strewn]

suit
sure

swoop(ed)

* *

saloon
salute

schoolboy
schoolgirl
schooner
scooter
scuba

seclude
secure(d)
sewage
sewer

shooting
-shouldn't

skewer(ed)

smoothly

snooker(ed)

sooner

spoonful
-sputnik

steward
Stuart
student
stupid

subdue(d)
Sudan
suet
-sugar(ed)
suitcase
suited
suitor
super
superb
supreme
surely

* * *

schoolteacher
screwdriver

secluded

solution
souvenir

stewardess(es)
studio
studious
stupendous
stupify(-ies)
  (stupified)

Sudanese
suicide
suitable
supervise(d)

* * * * [* *]

security(-ies)

stupidity(-ies)

suicidal(ly)
superconductor
superficial
superimpose(d)
superintendent
superior
superlative
supermarket
supernatural(ly)
supersonic(ally)
superstition
superstitious
supervision
supervisor
supremacy

221

In these words you can hear oo as in goose   or ue as in newt

T

*	* *	* * *	* * * * [*]
*threw (hurled)	tattoo(ed)	together	tubercular
*through (by way of / because of)	throughout	tomorrow	tuberculin
		tournament	tuberculosis
			tumultuous
*to (towards)	today	truthfully	
tomb	tonight		
*too (also)	toothbrush(es)	tubular	
-took	toothcomb	tuition	
tool(ed)	toothpaste		
toot	toothpick		
tooth(ed)	tourist		
tour(ed)	toward		
	towards		
*troop(ed) (move as a group)	trousseau		
*troupe (group of entertainers)	truly		
truce	truthful(ly)		
true(d)			
truth	tuba		
	Tuesday		
	Tudor		
tube(d)	tulip		
tune(d)	tumour		
	tumult		
*two (2)	*tuna (fish)		
	*tuner (person who tunes)		
	tunic		
	tuning		
	tutor(ed)		

In these words you can hear **oo** as in **goose** or **ue** as in **newt**

U

*	* *	* * *	* * * * [*]
*ewe (female sheep)	Europe	eureka!	eucalyptus
*ewes (more than one ewe)			euphonium
	union	uniform(ed)	European
*use (employ)	unique	unify(-ies)	euthanasia
used	unit	(unified)	
	unite	union	ubiquitous
		unison	
	urine	united	unicycle
		unity	unilateral(ly)
	usage	universe	universal(ly)
	useful(ly)		university(-ies)
	user	Uranus	
	using	urethane	uranium
	useless	urinate	
	usual(ly)	Uruguay	utility(-ies)
	usurp(ed)		utopia
		usable	
		usefully	
		usefulness	
		usually	
		utensil	
		uterus(es/-i)	
		utile	

for H ...
see page 215

for Y ...
see page 224

V

*	* *	* * *	* * * *
view(ed)	viewpoint		

W

*	* *	* * *	* * * *
*whew/phew (!)	-woman	whoever	
who	-wooden	whooping-cough	
whom	-woodland	-woodcutter	
*whoop(ed) (cry out with joy)	-woodwork	-woodpecker	
whose	-woollen		
	-woolly		
-wolf(-ves)	-wouldn't		
-wolfed	wounded		
*-wood (timber / area with many trees)			
-wool			
*-would (was willing to / used to / was going to)			
wound			

In these words you can hear **oo** as in **goose**   or **ue** as in **newt**

Y

*

*ewe (female sheep)
*ewes (more than one ewe)

*yew (tree)
*yews (yew trees)

*you (person / people)
 you'd
 you'll
*your (belonging to you)
*you're (you are)
 yours
 youth
 you've

 yule

> for U ...
> see page 223

* *

Europe

yourself
yourselves
youthful(ly)

* * *

eureka!

youthfully

* * * * [*]

eucalyptus
euphonium
European
euthanasia

Yugoslavia

Z

*

zoo
zoom(ed)

* *

* * *

* * * * [* *]

zoological(ly)
zoology

In these words you can hear **oo** as in **goose** or **ue** as in **newt**

A

✻	✻ ✻	✻ ✻ ✻	✻ ✻ ✻ ✻ [✻ ✻]
aft	aardvark	advancement	arbitrarily
		advancing	arbitrary
ah	advance(d)	advantage(d)	arbitration
			archeological
*alms (gifts to the	afar	afternoon	archeologist
poor)	after	afterwards	archeology
			architecture
*arc (curve)	aghast	answering	Argentina
arch(es)			argumentative
arched	alarm(ed)	apartheid	armadillo(s)
are	almond	apartment	arterial
*aren't (are not)			artesian
*ark (Noah's)	amen	arbitrate	articulate
arm(ed)		archaic	artificial(ly)
*arms (more than one	answer(ed)	architect	artillery
arm / weapons of		argument	
war)	apart	armada	
art		armament	
	*arbor (shaft)	armature	
ask(ed)	*arbour (garden or	armistice	
	part shaded by	armoury(-ies)	
*aunt (relative)	trees)	arsenal	
	arcade	arsenic	
	archer	artery(-ies)	
	arctic	arthropod	
	ardent	article	
	argon		
	argue(d)		
	armour(ed)		
	army(-ies)		
	artist		

for H . . .
see page 230

asking

Auntie/Aunty

In these words you can hear the vowel sound **ar** as in **shark**

✢	✢ ✢	✢ ✢ ✢	✢ ✢ ✢ ✢
*baa (lamb's cry)	*balmy (sweet- smelling, mad)	Bahamas	barbarian
balm	barbel	banana	
*bar(red) (prevent / barrier / rod)	barber	Barbados	
barb(ed)	bargain(ed)	barbecue(d)	
*bard (poet)	barley	barnacle	
barge(d)	barking	basketball	
bark(ed)	*barmy/balmy (mad)		
barn	barring		
*barred (prevented / fixed with bars)	barter(ed)		
bask(ed)	basket		
bath(ed)	basking		
	bastard		
	bathroom		
blast	*bazaar (Eastern market)		
bra			
branch(es)	behalf		
branched			
brass(es)	*bizarre (peculiar)		

In these words you can hear the vowel sound **ar** as in **shark**

✲   ✲ ✲   ✲ ✲ ✲   ✲ ✲ ✲ ✲

calf(-ves)   carbon   cacao   carbohydrate
*calve(d) (produce   carcass(es)   carbonate   carburetter
   a calf)   cardboard   cardigan   or
calm(ed)   cargo(es)   cardinal   carnivorous
can't   carmine   carnation
car   carpet   carnival
card   carton   carnivore
carp(ed)   cartoon   carpenter
cart   cartridge   carpentry
*carve(d) (cut)   carving   cartilage
cask   *caster/castor   castaway
*cast (throw /   (powdered sugar /
   mould / decide   swivelling wheel)   chancellor
   parts in a play /   casting   chapati
   squint)   castle
[cast]   *castor (oil)   commander
*caste (social   catarrh   commandment
   class)   compartment
                       chandler
*chance (lucky   charade   karate
   event / risk)   charcoal
chanced   charging
chant   charter(ed)
*chants (does   charming
   chant / more than   charring
   one chant)   *chorale (hymn tune)
charge(d)
charm(ed)   cigar
char(red)
chart   classmate
                       classroom
clasp(ed)
class(es)   command
classed   contrast
clerk   *corral (enclosure
                          for cattle and
craft   horses)

czar/tsar   craftsman

                       khaki

                       Koran

*

daft
dance(d)
dark
darn(ed)
dart

*draft (rough plan /
    selected group)
*draught (current of
    air / depth of
    ship in water /
    piece in game)
draughts

* *

dancer
dancing
darker
darkness
darling
data

demand
depart

disarm(ed)
discard
discharge(d)

drama
drastic(ally)
draughty(-ier,-iest)

* * *

demanded
department
departure

disaster
disastrous
dishearten(ed)

drastically

* * * *

disarmament

drastically

E

*

for H ...
see page 230

for I ...
see page 230

* *

embark(ed)

enchant
enlarge(d)
entrance(d)

er- or ir- ?

es- or is- ?

* * *

enchanting
entrancing

er- or ir- ?

escarpment

example

* * * *

em- or im- ?

In these words you can hear the vowel sound **ar** as in **shark**

F

✧	✧ ✧	✧ ✧ ✧	✧ ✧ ✧ ✧ [✧]
far	farmer	faraway	father-in-law
farm(ed)	farmhouse	fastener	
fast	farming		pharmaceutical
	farmyard	*fiancé (man engaged	
flask	*farther (greater	to be married)	
	distance)	*fiancée (woman	
France	farthered	engaged to be	
	farthest	married)	
	fasten(ed)		
	faster	pharmacist	
	fastest	pharmacy(-ies)	
	*father (male parent)		
	fathered		

G

✧	✧ ✧	✧ ✧ ✧	✧ ✧ ✧ ✧
gasp(ed)	garage(d)	gardener	
	garbage		
glance(d)	garden(ed)	Ghanaian	
glass(es)	gardener		
	gargle(d)	grasshopper	
gnarled	gargling		
	garland	guardian	
grant	garlic		
graph(ed)	garment	gymkhana	
grasp(ed)	garnet		
grass(es)	garter(ed)		
grassed			
	Ghana		
guard	ghastly(-ier,-iest)		
	giraffe		
	glasses		
	granted		
	grasslands		
	guitar		

H

*

half(-ves)
halve(d)
hard
hark(ed)
harm(ed)
harp(ed)
harsh
*hart (male deer)

*heart (organ that
    pumps blood /
    centre / inmost
    feelings)
hearth

* *

harbour(ed)
hardboard
harden(ed)
harder
hardest
hardly
hardship
hardware
hardwood
hardy(-ier,-iest)
harmful(ly)
harmless
harness(es)
harnessed
harpoon(ed)
harvest

hurrah!

* * *

harlequin
harmfully
harmonise(d)
        ze
harmonic(ally)
harmony(-ies)
harpsichord
Hawaii
Hawaiian

* * * * [*]

harmonica
harmonically
harmonium

I

*

for E ...
see page 228

* *

im- or em- ?

in- or en- ?

Iran
Iraq

Islam

* * *

in- or en- ?

Iraqi

is- or es- ?

ix- or ex- ?

* * * *

impassable

J

*

jar(red)

* *

giraffe

jarring

* * *

gymkhana

* * * *

In these words you can hear the vowel sound ar as in shark

K

☆

☆ ☆

khaki

Koran

☆ ☆ ☆

karate

☆ ☆ ☆ ☆

for C ...
see page 227

L

☆

lance(d)
larch(es)
lard
large
lark(ed)
last
laugh(ed)

☆ ☆

lager
larder
larger
largest
largely
largo
lasted
lather(ed)
laughter
*lava (melted rock
    from volcano)
*larva(e) (insect
    grub)

llama

☆ ☆ ☆

lasagne

☆ ☆ ☆ ☆

In these words you can hear the vowel sound **ar** as in shark

M

*

March
march(es)
marched
mark
marsh(es)
mask(ed)
mast

* *

mama
marble(d)
marching
margin
market(ed)
marking
*marshal (officer)
marshalled
*martial (warlike)
*marten (animal)
*martin (bird)
martyr(ed)
marvel(led)
massage(d)
master(ed)

morale
moustache(d)

* * *

macabre
margarine
marginal(ly)
marketed
marmalade
marshalling
marshmallow
marvelling
marvellous
masterpiece
mastery

* * * *

marginally
marsupial

N

*

gnarled

* *

nasty(-ier,-iest)

* * *

narcissus(es/-i)
narcotic
nastier
nastiest

* * * *

In these words you can hear the vowel sound **ar** as in **shark**

P

*	* *	* * *	* * * * [*]
palm(ed)	papa	Pakistan	Pakistani
par	parcel(led)	parcelling	parliamentary
parch(es)	pardon(ed)	parliament	participant
parched	parka	partialling	participate
park(ed)	parking	partially	participation
part	parlour	particle	pastorally
pass(es)	parsley	partisan	
*passed (went by)	parson	partition(ed)	pharmaceutical
*past (time that has	partake	partnership	
passed / beyond)	[partook]	passers-by	pianoforte
path	[partaken]	pasteurise(d)	
	partial(led)	ze	
plant	partly	pastoral(ly)	
	partner(ed)		
prance(d)	partridge	pharmacist	
	party(-ies)	pharmacy(-ies)	
psalm	passing		
	passport		
	password	pianist	
	pasture(d)	piano(s)	
		piranha	
	pianist		
	piano(s)	plantation	
	planted	ptarmigan	
	planting		
	plaster(ed)	pyjamas	
	plaza		

> In this word 'ar' is a neutral vowel.
>
> particular(ly)

R

*	* *	* * *	* * * *
raft	rafter	rascally	rechargeable
ranch(es)	rascal(ly)	raspberry(-ies)	remarkable
rasp(ed)	raspberry		
	rather	regarded	
		regardless	
	rearm(ed)	retarded	
	regard		
	remark(ed)		
	retard		

In these words you can hear the vowel sound ar as in shark

233

S

* | * * | * * * | * * * * [*]

psalm

scar(red)
scarf(-ves)

shaft
shark
sharp

slant

smart

snarl(ed)

spar(red)
spark(ed)
sparse

staff(ed)
stance
star(red)
starch(es)
starched
stark
start
starve(d)

charade

cigar

sample(d)
sampler
sampling
sardine

scarlet
scarring

sergeant

sharpen(ed)
sharpening
sharply

sparkle(d)
sparkling
sparring

starboard
starfish
starlight
starling
starring
starry
started
starting
startle(d)
startling
starving
stratum(strata)

surpass(ed)

safari
Sahara
salami
sarcasm
sarcastic(ally)

sharpening

soprano(s)

staccato
starvation

sultana

sarcastically

Somalia

In these words you can hear the vowel sound **ar** as in shark

T

*	* *	* * *	* * * *
tar(red)	target(ted)	ptarmigan	
tart	tarmac		
task	tarnish(es)	targetting	
	tarnished	tomato(es)	
trance	tarring		
	tartan		
tsar/czar			

V

*	* *	* * *	* * * *
vase	vantage	vibrato	
vast	varnish(es)		
	varnished		

Y

*	* *	* * *	* * * *
yard	yardstick		
yarn(ed)			

Z

*	* *	* * *	* * * *
czar/tsar		Zimbabwe	

In these words you can hear the vowel sound ar as in shark

*	* *	* * *	* * * *
*air (atmosphere / manner / feeling / tune)	affair	aerial	aeronautics
aired	aircraft	aerobics	
	Airedale	aerofoil	aquarium
*heir (next owner)	airfield	aerodrome	
	airline	aeroplane	
	airmail	aerosol	
	airport		
	airtight	airliner	
	airway		
		area	
	aware		
	Eire		

for H . . .
see page 238

heiress(es)
heirloom

B

*	* *	* * *	* * * *
*bare(d) (uncover)	barely	barium	Bulgaria
*bear (animal)	bearing		
*bear (carry)	bearer		
[bore]	beware		
[born/borne]			
blare(d)			

C

*	* *	* * *	* * * *
cairn	careful(ly)	canary(-ies)	
care(d)	careless	carefully	
		carelessly	
chair(ed)	chairman		
		comparing	
	compare(d)	contrary	

In these words you can hear the vowel sound air as in bear

D

✶

dare(d)

✶ ✶

dairy(-ies)
daring

declare(d)
despair(ed)

E

✶

*air (atmosphere / manner /
    feeling / tune)
aired

*heir (next owner)

✶ ✶

aircraft
Airedale
airfield
airline
airmail
airport
airtight

éclair

Eire

heiress(es)
heirloom

✶ ✶ ✶

aerial
aerobics
aerofoil
aerodrome
aeroplane
aerosol

airliner

area

✶ ✶ ✶ ✶

en- or in- ?

for H ...
see page 238

for I ...
see page 239

F

*	* *	* * *	* * * *
*fair (just / funfair / market / fine weather / light in colour)	fairground fairly fairy(-ies) farewell		
*fare (charge for ride / food / get on)			
fared	forbear [forbore] [forborne] forswear [forswore] [forsworn]		
*flair (natural skill)			
*flare (burst into flame / get wider at the bottom)			
flared	pharaoh		

G

*	* *	* * *	* * * *
glare(d)			

H

*	* *	* * *	* * * *
*hair(ed) (thread-like growth)	haircut hairy(-ier,-iest)	haircutting hairdresser hair-drier	hilarious
*hare (animal)			
hared	heiress(es) heirloom		Hungarian
*heir (next owner)			
*Herr (German for 'Mr.')			

In these words you can hear the vowel sound air as in bear

I

☆   ☆ ☆   ☆ ☆ ☆   ☆ ☆ ☆ ☆

ic- or ec- ?   invariably

for E ...
see page 237

L

☆   ☆ ☆   ☆ ☆ ☆   ☆ ☆ ☆ ☆

*lair (den)

M

☆   ☆ ☆   ☆ ☆ ☆   ☆ ☆ ☆ ☆

*mare (female horse)   mayoress(es)   malaria
*mayor (head of town
   or city)

P

☆   ☆ ☆   ☆ ☆ ☆   ☆ ☆ ☆ ☆

*pair (set of two)   parent   preparing
paired
*pare(d) (trim /   pharaoh
   peel)
                      prairie
*pear (fruit)   prepare(d)

prayer

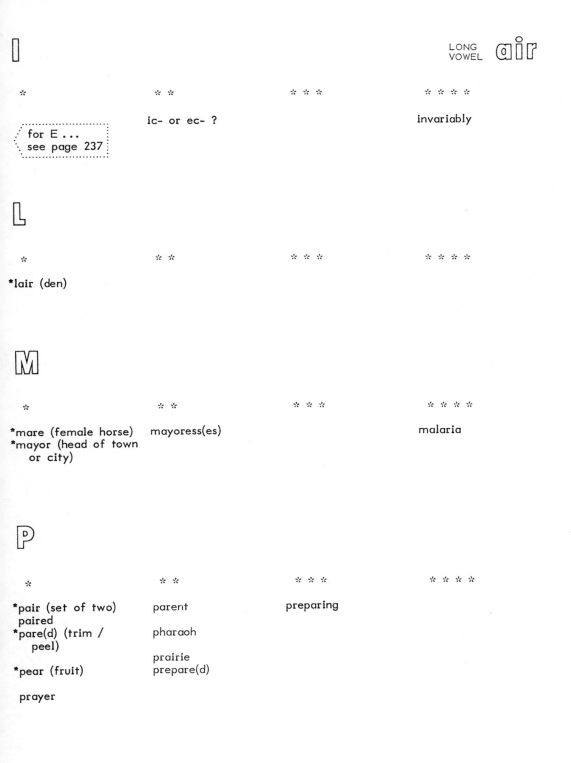

In these words you can hear the vowel sound air as in bear

239

*

rare

* *

rarely

repair(ed)

* * *

* * * *

S

*

scarce
scare(d)

share(d)

snare(d)

spare(d)

square(d)

*stair (step/s)
*stare(d) (look with
   fixed gaze)

swear
[swore]
[sworn]

* *

scarcely
scarecrow
scary(-ier,iest)

sharing

staircase
staring

* * *

scarcity

shareholder

* * * *

In these words you can hear the vowel sound a͡ir as in bear

T

*

tear
[tore]
[torn]

*their (belonging
   to them)
*theirs (something
   belonging to them)
*there (to/in that
   place / also used
   with 'is', 'are',
   'was', 'were' and
   other forms of
   'to be')
 there'd
 there'll
*there's (there is /
   there has)
*they're (they are)

* *

tearing

thereby
therefore
thereof
therewith

* * *

thereafter
thereupon

V

*

* *

vary(-ies)
   (varied)

* * ?

variant
various
varying

* * * *

variable
variation

W

*

*ware (products for
   sale / pottery)

*wear (carry on
   body / get worse
   with use)
   [wore]
   [worn]
*-were (form of verb
   'to be')
*where (to/in which
   place)

* *

warehouse
wary(-ier,-iest)

wearing

whereas
whereby
wherefore
wherein

* * *

whereupon
wherever

In these words you can hear the vowel sound air as in bear

*	* *	* * *	* * * *
*-air (atmosphere / manner / feeling / tune)	absurd	-aerial	adverbial(ly)
-aired	adjourn(ed)	-aerobics	advertisement
		-aerofoil	
*-heir (next owner)	-affair	-aerodrome	-aeronautics
	affirm(ed)	-aeroplane	
		-aerosol	alternative
	-aircraft		
	-Airedale	-airliner	-aquarium
	-airfield		
	-airline	alternate	
	-airmail		
	-airport	-area	
	-airtight		
	-airway	assertion	
		assertive	
	alert		
	assert		
	astern		
	-aware		
	-Eire		

for H . . .
see page 247

-heiress(es)
-heirloom

In these words you can hear the vowel sound er as in worm

☆   ☆ ☆   ☆ ☆ ☆   ☆ ☆ ☆ ☆

*-bare(ed) (uncover)   -barely   -barium

*-bear (animal)   -bearing   burglary(-ies)
*-bear (carry)   -bearer
 [bore]   -beware
 [born/borne]
*berth (bunk / place   birthday
    for ship at quay)   birthplace
 berthed

 birch(es)   blurring
 birched
*bird (feathered   burden(ed)
    animal)   *burger (sandwich)
*birth (delivery of   *burgher (citizen)
    child / origin)   burglar
                          burlap
 -blare(d)   burly(-ier,-iest)
 blur(red)   Burma
 blurt   burning
                          burring
 burn(ed)
 [burnt]
 burr/bur
*burred (murmured)
 burst
 [burst]

In this word 'er' has a neutral sound.

Bermuda

In these words you can hear the vowel sound er   as in worm

243

*	* *	* * *	* * * * [*]
-cairn	-careful(ly)	-canary(-ies)	circulation
-care(d)	-careless	-carefully	circulatory
		-carelessly	circumference
-chair(ed)	certain		circumstances
chirp(ed)		certainly	
church(es)	-chairman	certify(-ies)	commercially
churn(ed)	churchyard	(certified)	conservative
			convertible
*curb(ed) (restrain)	circle(d)	circular	
curds	circling	circulate	
curl(ed)	circuit	circumscibe(d)	
curse(d)	circus	circumstance	
curt			
curve(d)	clergy	clergyman	
*kerb (edge of pavement)	*colonel (army	commercial(ly)	
	officer)	-comparing	
kirk	-compare(d)	-contrary	
	concern(ed)	concerning	
	confer(red)	conferring	
	confirm(ed)	convergent	
	conserve(d)	conversion	
	converge(d)	courteous	
	converse(d)	courtesy(-ies)	
	convert		
	courteous	curlier	
	curdle(d)		
	curdling		
	curfew		
	curly(-ier,-iest)		
	cursor		
	curtain(ed)		
	curtsey		
	y(-ies)		
	(curtsied)		
	curvy(-ier,-iest)		

for Qu ... see page 251

*kernel (seed in nut)

> In these words 'er' and 'ir' have... er.... a neutral sound.
>
> certificate   circumference

In these words you can hear the vowel sound er as in worm

*	* *	* * *	* * * * [*]
-dare(d)	-dairy(-ies)	deserted	determination
	-daring	detergent	determining
dirt		determine(d)	
	-declare(d)	deterring	diversity
	*desert (leave)		
	deserve(d)	dirtier	
	-despair(ed)	dirtiest	
	*dessert (sweet dish)	disturbance	
	deter(red)		
	dirty(-ies)		
	(dirtied)		
	dirty(-ier,-iest)		
	discern(ed)		
	disperse(d)		
	disturb(ed)		
	diverge(d)		
	diverse		
	divert		

E

*	* *	* * *	* * * *
*air (atmosphere / manner / feeling / tune)	-aircraft	-aerial	emergency(-ies)
aired	-Airedale	-aerobics	
	-airfield	-aerofoil	en- or in- ?
	-airline	-aerodrome	
earl	-airmail	-aeroplane	eternally
*earn(ed) (get money by working)	-airport	-aerosol	
	-airtight		exterminate
earth(ed)		-airliner	externally
	early(-ier,-iest)		
err(ed)	earnest	-area	
	earnings		
*-heir (next owner)	earthquake	earlier	
	earthworm	earliest	
		earthenware	
urge(d)	-eclair		
*urn (vase / vessel)		emergence	
	-Eire		
		encircle(d)	
	emerge(d)		
		eternal(ly)	
for H ... see page 247	exert		
		excursion	
	-heirloom	exertion	
	-heiress(es)	external(ly)	
for I ... see page 247	urban	urgency	
	urchin		
	urgent		

In these words you can hear the vowel sound er as in worm

F

*

*-fair (just /
    funfair /
    market / fine
    weather / light
    in colour)
*-fare (charge for
    ride / food /
    get on)
 -fared

 fern

*fir (tree)
 firm(ed)
 first

*-flair (natural skill)
*-flare (burst into
    flame / get wider
    at the bottom)
 -flared

*fur (coat of animal)
 furred
 furl(ed)
*furs (coats of
    animals)
*furze (gorse)

* *

-fairground
-fairly
-fairy(-ies)
-farewell

ferment
fertile
fervour

firmly

-forbear
[forbore]
[forborne]
-forswear
[forswore]
[forsworn]
furnace
furnish(es)
furnished
furring
furry
further(ed)
furtive

pharaoh

* * *

fertilise(d)
    ze

furniture
furthermore

* * * * [*]

fermentation
fertilisation
    zation
fertiliser
    zer
fertility

> In this word 'er' has a neutral sound.
>
> ferment

: for th ...
: see page 253 :

G

*

jerk(ed)

germ

girl
girth

-glare(d)

* *

jerkin
jersey
Jersey

journal
journey(ed)

gerbil
German

girder
girdle(d)
girdling

Guernsey
gurgle(d)
gurgling

* * *

Germany
germinate

* * * *

germination

In these words you can hear the vowel sound er   as in worm

H

*   * *   * * *   * * * *

*-hair(ed) (thread-   -haircut   -haircutting
    like growth)   -hairy(-ier,-iest)   -hairdresser
*-hare (animal)   -hair-drier
-hared   -heiress(es)
                        -heirloom   herbaceous
*heard (did hear)   herdsman   herbivore
*-heir (next owner)   hermit
her
herb   hurdle(d)
*herd (group of   hurdling
    animals)   hurtle(d)
*-Herr (German for   hurtling
    'Mr.')
hers

hurl(ed)
hurt
[hurt]

> In this word 'er' has a neutral sound.
>
> herself

I

*   * *   * * *   * * * * [*]

irk(ed)   ic- or ec- ?   immersion   impersonal
                                       imperfect   impersonate
ir- or ear- ?   impersonation
ir- or er- ?   immerse(d)   impertinent
ir- or ur- ?   inertia
                 im- or em- ?   inferring   infirmary(-ies)
                                       internal(ly)   internally
                 inert   interpret(ed)   interpolate
                 infer(red)   inversion   interpretation
                 infirm   interpreted
                 insert   in- or en- ?   interpreter
                 invert   interpreting
                                       ir- or ur- ?   -invariably
                 irksome
                                       it- or et- ?   it- or et- ?
                 ir- or ear- ?
                 ir- or ur- ?   ix- or ex- ?   ix- or ex- ?

for E ...   ix- or ex- ?
see page 245

In these words you can hear the vowel sound er as in worm

J

*	* *	* * *	* * * *
germ	gerbil	Germany	germination
	German	germinate	
jerk(ed)			journalism
	jerkin	journalist	
	jersey		
	Jersey		
	journal		
	journey(ed)		

K

*	* *	* * *	* * * *
kerb(ed)	*kernel (seed in nut)		
kirk			
knurled			

> for C ...
> see page 244

> for Qu ...
> see page 251

L

*	* *	* * *	* * * *
*-lair (den)	learner		
	learning		
learn(ed)			
[learnt]			
lurch(es)			
lurched			
lurk(ed)			

In these words you can hear the vowel sound er as in worm

*	* *	* * *	* * * *
*-mare (female horse)	-mayoress(es)	mercenary(-ies)	-malaria
*-mayor (head of town or city)		merchandise	
	merchant	merciful(ly)	mercenary(-ies)
merge(d)	mercy(-ies)	merciless	mercifully
	merger	mercury	
	merging	Mercury	
mirth			
	murder(ed)	murderer	
myrrh	murky(-ier,-iest)	murderous	
	murmur(ed)	murmuring	

N

*	* *	* * *	* * * *
knurled	nervous	nasturtium	
	nervy(-ier,-iest)		
nerve		nursery(-ies)	
	nursing		
nurse(d)			

O

*	* *	* * *	* * * * [*]
	observe(d)	alternate	alternative
	occur(red)	observant	observatory(-ies)
		observer	
		observing	
		occurring	

*	* *	* * *	* * * * [*]
*-pair (set of two)	-parent	percolate	perforation
-paired		perfectly	perpendicular
*-pare(d) (trim /	perfect	perforate	persecution
peel)	perfume(d)	permanent	personality(-ies)
	person	permeable	personally
*-pear (fruit)	perspex	permeate	perspiration
*pearl (jewel)	perspire(d)	peroxide	
*per (for each)	perverse	persecute	purposefully
perch(es)		persevere(d)	
perched	-pharaoh	personal(ly)	
perm(ed)		personnel	
	-prairie	pertinent	
-prayer	prefer(red)	perversion	
	-prepare(d)		
purge(ed)	preserve(d)	preferring	
*purl (knitting		-preparing	
stitch)	purchase(d)		
*purr(ed) (sound of	purple	purposeful(ly)	
happy cat)	purpose	pursuer	
purse	purring		

In these words 'er' and 'ur' have... er.... a neutral sound.

'PERSISTENT' WORDS

perceive(d)	perfect(ion)	permissible	perplexing	persuasive
percentage	perform(ed)	permission	persist(ence)	pursue(d)
perception	performance	permit(ted)	persistent	pursuant
perceptive	performer	permitting	perspective	pursuit
perceptual(ly)	performing	perpetual(ly)	perspire(d)	
percussion	perfume(d)	perplex(es)	persuade	
percussive	perhaps	perplexed	persuasion	

for pre ...
see page 82

In these words you can hear the vowel sound er as in worm

Ⓠ

*	* *	* * *	* * * *
quirk			

Ⓡ

*	* *	* * *	* * * *
-rare	-rarely	referral	returnable
		referring	reverberate
	refer(red)	rehearsal	reversible
	rehearse(d)	researcher	
	-repair(ed)	returning	
	research(es)	reversal	
	researched		
	reserve(d)		
	return(ed)		
	reverse(d)		

S

*	* *	* * *	* * * *
-scarce	certain	certainly	certificate
-scare(d)		certify(-ies)	
scourge(d)	circle(d)	(certified)	circulation
scurf	circuit		circumstances
	circus	circular	
search(es)		circulate	**surgically**
searched	-scarcely	circumstance	
*serf (slave)	-scarecrow		
*serge (woollen	-scary(-ier,-iest)	-scarcity	
cloth)	scurvy		
serve(d)		-shareholder	
	searching		
-share(d)	searchlight	suburban	
shirk(ed)	sermon	surgery(-ies)	
shirt	serpent	surgical(ly)	
	servant		
Sir	service(d)		
	serviette		
skirt	servile		
	serving		
slur(red)			
	-sharing		
-snare(d)	sherbet		
	shirty		
-spare(d)			
sperm	sirloin		
spur(red)			
spurn(ed)	slurring		
spurs			
spurt	spurring		
-square(d)	-staircase		
squirm(ed)	-staring		
squirt	sterling		
	stirring		
*-stair (step/s)	sturdy(-ier,-iest)		
*-stare(d) (look with			
fixed gaze)	submerge(d)		
stern	surface(d)		
stir(red)	surfer		
	surfing		
*surf (foaming sea)	surform		
surfed	surgeon		
*surge(d) (rush	surging		
forward)	surmount		
	surname		
-swear	surpass(ed)		
[swore]	*surplice (gown worn		
[sworn]	in church)		
swerve(d)	*surplus(es) (excess)		
swirl(ed)	survey(ed)		

> In these words 'ur' has a neutral sound.
>
> 'SURPRISING' WORDS
>
> | | | |
> |---|---|---|
> | surmount | surprising | survive(d) |
> | surpass(ed) | surrender(ed) | survival |
> | surprise(d) | surround(ings) | survivor |

252

T

*   * *   * * *   * * * *

*	* *	* * *	* * * *
-tear	-tearing	terminal(ly)	terminally
[tore]		terminate	
[torn]	-thereby	tertiary	
term(ed)	-therefore		
*tern (bird)	-thereof	-thereafter	
	-therewith	-thereupon	
*-their (belonging	thermal(ly)	thermally	
to them)	thermos	thermostat	
*-theirs (something	thirsty(-ier,-iest)	thirtieth	
belonging to	thirteen(th)		
them)	thirty(-ies)	turbojet	
*-there (to/in that	Thursday	turbulence	
place / also		turbulent	
used with 'is',	*turban (head-	turmeric	
'are', 'was',	covering)	turpentine	
'were' and other	*turbine (engine)		
forms of 'to be')	turbot		
-there'd	turmoil		
-there'll	turtle		
*-there's (there is /	Turkey		
there has)	turkey		
*-they're (they are)	turning		
therm	turnip		
third	turnpike		
thirst	turnstile		
	turquoise		
turf(ed)			
Turk			
*turn(ed) (change			
direction)			
twirl(ed)			

In this word 'er' has a neutral sound.

thermometer

U

✻	✻ ✻	✻ ✻ ✻	✻ ✻ ✻ ✻

✻

earl
*earn(ed) (get money by
  working)
earth(ed)

err(ed)

urge(d)
*urn (vase / vessel)

✻ ✻

early
earthquake

urban
urchin
urgent

✻ ✻ ✻

earliest

urgency

> for H ...
> see page 247

V

✻

verb
verge(d)
verse(d)

✻ ✻

-vary(-ies)
- (varied)
verbal(ly)
verdict
verger
vermin
version
versus
vertex(-ices)

virgin
virtue
virtual(ly)

✻ ✻ ✻

-variant
-various
-varying

verbally
vermilion
vernier
vertebrate
vertical(ly)
vertices

virginal
virtually

✻ ✻ ✻ ✻ [✻]

-variable
-variation

vermiculite
vertically

virtually
virtuosity
virtuoso

In these words you can hear the vowel sound er as in worm

W

☆

-ware (products for
    sale / pottery)

-wear (carry on
    body / get worse
    with use)
[wore]
[worn]
*were (form of verb
    'to be')
weren't

-where (to/in which
    place)
*whirl(ed) (spin
    around)
*whirr(ed) (sound)
*whorl (turn of
    spiral)
*whorled (shaped in
    a spiral)

word
work(ed)
*world (the earth)
worm(ed)
worse
worst
worth

☆ ☆

-warehouse
-wary(-ier,-iest)

-wearing

-whereas
-whereby
-wherefore
-wherein
whirlpool
whirlwind
whirring
worker
working
workman
workshop
worldwide
worship(ped)
worsen(ed)
worthless
worthwhile
worthy(-ies)

☆ ☆ ☆

-whereupon
-wherever

workable
worshipper
worshipping

Y

☆

year
yearn(ed)

☆ ☆

☆ ☆ ☆

☆ ☆ ☆ ☆

In these words you can hear the vowel sound er as in worm

*

*all (every one)

*awe (fear and
   wonder)
awed
*awl (boring tool)

*oar (rowing blade)

*or (marks choice)
*ore (mineral)

ought

for H ...
see page 261

* *

aboard
abroad
absorb(ed)

accord

adore(d)
adorn(ed)

afford

almost
alright
also
*altar (holy table)
*alter(ed) (change)
although
always

appal(led)
applaud
applause

ashore
assault
assure(d)

auburn
auction(ed)
*auger (tool)
*augur (suggest for
   the future)
August
august
*aural(ly) (by the ear)
austere
author
autumn

award
awesome/awsome
awful(ly)
awkward

*oral(ly) (by the mouth)
orbit(ed)
orchard
orchid
ordeal
order(ed)
organ
orgy(-ies)
orphan(ed)

* * *

abortion
absorber
absorption

accordance
according

adsorption

almighty
already
alternate

appalling

assorted
assortment
assurance

audible
audience
auditory
*aurally (by the ear)
aurora
Austria
authentic(ally)
authoress(es)
authorise(d)
   ze
autograph(ed)

awfully

*orally (by the mouth)
orbital
orbited
orbiting
orchestra
ordeal
orderly(-ies)
ordinary
organic(ally)
organise(d)
   ze
organist
orgasm
ornament

* * * * [* * * *]

accordingly
accordion

adorable

alternating
alternative
alternator
altogether

auditory
authentically
authority(-ies)
autobiography(-ies)
autobiographical(ly)
automatic(ally)
automation
automobile
autonomic
autonomous
auxiliary(-ies)

ordinarily
ordinary
organically
organisation
   zation
organism
oriental
ornithologist
ornithology

In these words you can hear the vowel sound or as in horse

*

*bald (lacking hair)
balk/baulk(ed)
*ball (round
    object / dance)
*balled (made into a
    ball)
baulk/balk(ed)
*bawl (yell)
*bawled (did yell)

*boar (male pig)
*board (plank /
    daily meals /
    committee)
*boor (rough fellow)
*bore (drill /
    drilled hole /
    carried / fail to
    interest / tide-
    wave)
*bored (drilled /
    lacking an
    interest)
*born (delivered
    at birth)
*borne (carried)
bought

brawl(ed)
brawn
broad
brought

* *

balsa
balsam
Baltic
ballroom
basalt
bauxite

because
befall
[befell]
[befallen]
before
besought

*boarder (person who
    pays for food and
    bed)
borax
*border (edge /
    frontier)
bordered
boring

brawny
broadcast
[broadcast]
broadside

* * *

befallen
beforehand

broadcasting

* * * *

In these words you can hear the vowel sound **or** as in horse

*	* *	* * *	* * * *
call(ed)	calling	caustically	caustically
*caught (got / trapped)	cauldron causing	chloroform(ed)	conformity
*caulk(ed) (fill gaps with fibre and tar)	caustic(ally) caution(ed) cautious	chlorophyll conformist	cordially corporation
*cause (bring about / reason)	chloride	cordial(ly) corduroy	
caused	chlorine	cormorant	
*caw (harsh bird cry)	choral		
*cawed (did caw)	chorus(es)		
*caws (does caw)	chorused		
chalk(ed)	conform(ed)		
*chord (notes sounded together / term in geometry)	cordial(ly) corgi corner(ed)		
chore	cornet cornfield		
*clause (words in sentence / part of written agreement)	cornflakes courting courtyard		
claw(ed)	crawling		
*claws (curved nails or limbs)			
*coarse (rough)			
*cord (string)			
*core (central part / take out the core from)			
*cored (did core)			
*cork (bark of cork tree)			
corked			
corm			
corn(ed)			
*corps (group)			
corpse			
*course (track / direction / part of meal / of course)			
coursed			
*court (enclosed area / friends of sovereign / seek favour)			
crawl(ed)			

for Qu ...
see page 266

In these words you can hear the vowel sound **or** as in horse

D

*

daub(ed)
dawn(ed)

door

*draw (pull /
   sketch)
 [drew]
 [drawn]
*drawer (sliding
   container)
drawl(ed)

dwarf(ed)

* *

daughter
dawdle(d)
dawdling

deform(ed)
deport

distort
divorce(d)

doorway
dormant
dormouse(-mice)
dorsal

drawbridge
drawing

* * *

disorder(ed)

dormitory(-ies)

* * * *

dormitory(-ies)

E

*

* *

em- or im- ?

endorse(d)
enforce(d)
*ensure(d) (make
   certain)

en- or in- ?

escort

exalt
exhaust
explore(d)
export

* * *

em- or im- ?

enforcement
enormous

en- or in- ?

exalted
exhausted
exhaustion
explorer
exploring

* * * * [* * *]

extraordinarily
extraordinary

for I . . .
see page 262

In these words you can hear the vowel sound or as in horse

☆

fall
[fell]
[fallen]
false
fault
*faun (goat-God)
*fawn (young deer / colour / try to win favour)
fawned

fiord/fjord

flaunt
*flaw(ed) (fault)
*floor(ed) (levelled area)

*for (in place of / to belong to / because)
force(d)
ford
*fore (front / leading position)
forge(d)
fork(ed)
form(ed)
*fort (fortress)
*forth (forward)
*fought (contested)
*four (4)
*fourth (4th)

fraud

for th ...
see page 268

☆ ☆

falcon
fallen
falling
fallout
falter(ed)
faulty

fiord/fjord

floral
fluoride
fluorine

forbear
[forbore]
[forborne]
forceful(ly)
forearm
forecast
[forecast]
forefoot
foreground
forehand
foreman
foremost
foresee
[foresaw]
[foreseen]
foresight
foretell
[foretold]
forewarn(ed)
forfeit
forgo/forego
[forwent/forewent]
[forgone/foregone]
forlorn
formal(ly)
format(ted)
former
forming
forswear
[forswore]
[forsworn]
*forte (loud / strength)
fortnight
fortress(es)
fortune
*forty (40)
fourteen(th)
forward

Fräulein

☆ ☆ ☆

fluorescent

forcefully
forefather
forefinger
forgery
*formally (officially)
formation
formatted
formatting
*formerly (previously)
formula
formulate
fortieth
fortunate

☆ ☆ ☆ ☆ [☆]

fluorescent

fortification
fortunately

In these words 'or' is a neutral vowel. It sounds like the 'a' in 'astonish'.

'FORGOTTEN' WORDS

forbear
[forbore]
[forborne]
forbid
[forbad(e)]
[forbidden]
forbidding
forgave
forget(ting)
[forgot]
[forgotten]

forgetful(ly)
forgive
[forgave]
[forgiven]
forgiveness
forsake
[forsook]
[forsaken]

In these words you can hear the vowel sound **or** as in horse

G

*

gaunt
gauze

*gnaw(ed) (keep
   biting)

gorge(d)
gorse

* *

gaudy(-ier,-iest)

glory(-ies)
   (gloried)

gorgeous

* * *

Gibraltar

glorious

* * * *

H

*

*hall (large room /
   passage)
halt
*haul (drag /
   amount gained)
hauled
haunt
hawk(ed)

*hoar (white)
*hoard (store)
*hoarse (rough and
   husky)
*horde (gang /
   tribe)
horn(ed)
*horse (animal)

*whore (prostitute)

* *

halter
haughty(-ier,-iest)
haunches

hoarding
hormone
hornblende
hornet
horseback
horsehair
horseman
horsepower
horseshoe

* * *

haughtily

horsepower

* * * *

historian

In these words you can hear the vowel sound or as in horse

261

I

*	* *	* * *	* * * * [*]
	ignore(d)	immortal(ly)	immortality
		importance	immortally
	implore(d)	important	
	import		inaugural
		informal(ly)	inauguration
	indoors	informant	incorporat(ed)
	inform(ed)	installing	informally
	instal(led)	instalment/	informative
	*insure(d) (protect	installment	
	against loss)	insurance	ix- or ex- ?

for E ...
see page 259

in- or en- ?

in- or en-?

ix- or ex-?

J

*	* *	* * *	* * * *
jaunt	jaunty(-ier,-iest)	Gibraltar	Jordanian
jaw(ed)			
	Jordan		

K

*	* *	* * *	* * * *
	Koran		

for C ...
see page 258

for Qu ...
see page 266

In these words the 'o' may be neutral.

Koran   Korea(n)

In these words you can hear the vowel sound or as in horse

*	* *	* * *	* * * *
launch(es)	launcher	launderette	
launched	launder(ed)		
*law (rules enforced in a country)	laundry(-ies)		
lawn	laurel		
	lawyer		
lord			
*lore (traditions and facts)			

M

*	* *	* * *	* * * *
*mall (public walk)	Malta	Majorca	memorial
malt			
*maul (batter)	*morning (before midday)	Minorca	mortality
mauled	morpheme	misfortune	
mauve	morsel		
	mortal(ly)	moreover	
*moor (open land / fasten to land or to buoy)	mortar	mortally	
	mortgage(d)		
*more (additional / a larger amount)	mortice(d) se		
*morn (morning)	mournful		
Morse	*mourning (showing sadness at loss or death)		
*mourn (show sadness at loss or death)			

N

*	* *	* * *	* * * *
*gnaw(ed) (keep biting)	naughty(-ier,-iest)	nautical(ly)	nautically
		naughtier	
naught/nought	normal(ly)	naughtiest	notorious
	Norman	naughtiness	
*nor (and not)	northern		
norm	northward	normally	
north	Norway	northernmost	
nought/naught		Norwegian	

In these words you can hear the vowel sound or as in horse

✲	✲ ✲	✲ ✲ ✲	✲ ✲ ✲ ✲ [✲ ✲ ✲ ✲]

✲ | ✲ ✲ | ✲ ✲ ✲ | ✲ ✲ ✲ ✲ [✲ ✲ ✲ ✲]

*all (every one)

*awe (fear and wonder)
awed
*awl (boring tool)

*oar (rowing blade)

*or (marks choice)
*ore (mineral)

ought

almost
alright
also
*altar (holy table)
*alter(ed) (change)
although
always

auburn
auction(ed)
*auger (tool)
*augur
August
august
aural(ly) (by the ear)
austere
author
autumn

awesome/awsome
awful(ly)
awkward

*oral(ly) (by the
mouth)
orbit(ed)
orchard
orchid
ordeal
order(ed)
organ
ornate
orgy(-ies)
orphan(ed)

almighty
already
alternate

audible
audience
auditory
*aurally (by the ear)
aurora
Austria
authentic(ally)
authoress(es)
authorise(d)
        ze
autograph(ed)

awfully

*orally (by the mouth)
orbital
orbited
orbiting
orchestra
ordeal
ordering
orderly(-ies)
ordinal
ordinary
organic(ally)
organise(d)
        ze
organist
orgasm
ornament

alternating
alternative
alternator
altogether

auditory
authentically
authority(-ies)
autobiography(-ies)
autobiographical(ly)
automatic(ally)
automation
automobile
autonomic
autonomous
auxiliary(-ies)

ordinarily
ordinary
organically
organisation
        zation
organism
oriental
ornithologist
ornithology

....
: for H ...
: see page 261 :
....

In these words you can hear the vowel sound or as in horse

✵

*pause (brief gap /
   hesitate)
paused
*paw (foot of
   animal)
*pawed (examined by
   paw)
pawn(ed)
*paws (feet of
   animal)

*poor (badly off)
porch(es)
*pore (tiny hole /
   study closely)
*pored (studied
   closely)
*pores (tiny holes)
pork
port
*pour (flow out)
*poured (did pour)

prawn

✵ ✵

palfrey

perform(ed)

poorly
porous
porpoise
porter
porthole
portion
portrait
portray(ed)
pouring

✵ ✵ ✵

performance
performer
performing

porcelain
porcupine
portable
portcullis
Portugal
Portuguese

precaution
proportion

✵ ✵ ✵ ✵ [✵]

proportional(ly)

Q

*

quart
*quarts (more than
  one quart)
*quartz (mineral)

* *

quarter
quartet

* * *

* * * *

R

*

*raw (untreated /
  sore / chilly)

*roar (loud noise)
roared

wrath
wrought

* *

recall(ed)
record
reform(ed)
report
resort
resource(d)
restore(d)
retort
reward

roaring

* * *

recorded
recorder
recording
reported
reporter
resources

* * * *

In these words you can hear the vowel sound or as in horse

✢   ✢ ✢   ✢ ✢ ✢   ✢ ✢ ✢ ✢

salt
*sauce (tasty
    liquid / rude
    talk)
*saw (looked at /
    cutting tool)
*sawed (did saw)
[sawn]

scald
scorch(es)
scorched
score(d)
scorn(ed)
scrawl(ed)

shawl
*shore (coast)
shored
shorn
short
shorts

small

snore(d)

*soar (fly high)
*soared (flew high)
*sore (painful)
*sort (group)
*sought (looked for)
*source (origin)

spawn(ed)
spore
sport
sprawl(ed)

squawk(ed)

*stalk (stem /
    hunt / walk
    stiffly)
stalked
stall(ed)
staunch(es)
staunched
store(d)
*stork (bird)
storm
straw

-see next page

salty(-ier,-iest)
saucer
saucepan
saucy(-ier,-iest)
sauna
saunter(ed)

scornful(ly)
scorpion

shortage
shortening
shorter
shortest
shorthand
shortly

slaughter(ed)

smaller
smallest
smallpox

snorkel

stalling
stalwart
storage
storehouse
*storey (floor)
stormy(-ier,-iest)
*story(-ies) (tale)
strawberry(-ies)

support
surely

swarthy(-ier,-iest)

saucily

scornfully
scorpion

Signora

strawberry(-ies)

supported
supporter
supporting

subordinate

In these words you can hear the vowel sound **or** as in horse

*

*sure (certain)

swarm(ed)
*sword (weapon)
swore
sworn

T

*	* *	* * *	* * * *
*talk (speak)	talking	talkative	
talked	taller		
tall	tallest	thoughtfully	
*taut (tight)			
*taught (instructed)	thorax(es/-ces)	tornado(es)	
taunt	thoughtful(ly)	torpedo(es)	
thaw(ed)	torment		
thorn	torsion		
thought	torso(s)		
thwart	tortoise		
	torture(d)		
*tor (hill)	Tory(-ies)		
torch(es)	toward		
*tore (did tear)	towards		
torn			
*torque (turning			
force / necklace)			

V

*	* *	* * *	* * * *
vase			Victorian
*vault (gymnastic			victorious
leap /			
underground room /			
arched roof)			

In these words you can hear the vowel sound **or** as in **horse**

W

*

walk(ed)
wall(ed)
waltz(es)
waltzed
*war (conflict)
*warred (waged war)
*ward (part of
  hospital / person
  under legal
  protection)
warm(ed)
warmth
*warn(ed) (caution)
warp(ed)
wart

wharf(-ves)
*whore (prostitute)

*wore (was dressed
  in)
*worn (carried on
  the body / worse
  for wear)

wrath
wrought

* *

walking
walnut
walrus
warble(d)
warbling
warden
wardrobe
warfare
warlike
warmer
warning
warpath
warring
warship
wartime
water(ed)

* * *

wallpaper(ed)
waterfall
waterfowl
watershed

* * * *

walkie-talkie

Y

*

yawn(ed)

*yore (ancient times)
*your (belonging to
  you)
*you're (you are)
yours

* *

Yorkshire
yourself
yourselves

* * *

* * * *

In these words you can hear the vowel sound or as in horse

✻

✻ ✻

ahoy!

anoint
annoy(ed)

appoint

avoid

✻ ✻ ✻

adjoining

annoyance

appointment

avoided

✻ ✻ ✻ ✻

B

✻

boil(ed)
*boy (lad)

broil(ed)

*buoy (marker)
buoyed

✻ ✻

boiler
boiling
boycott

buoyant

✻ ✻ ✻

boisterous

buoyancy

✻ ✻ ✻ ✻

C

✻

choice

coil(ed)
*coin (money)
coined
coy

quoit

✻ ✻

cloister(ed)

✻ ✻ ✻

✻ ✻ ✻ ✻

for Qu ...
see page 274

In these words you can hear the vowel sound oi as in oyster-catcher

✻	✻ ✻	✻ ✻ ✻	✻ ✻ ✻ ✻
	destroy(ed)	destroyer	disloyally
			disloyalty
	disloyal(ly)	disloyally	
		disloyalty	
	doily(-ies)/		
	doyley(s)		

E

✻	✻ ✻	✻ ✻ ✻	✻ ✻ ✻ ✻
	embroil(ed)	embroider(ed)	embroidery
	employ(ed)	employee	
		employer	
	enjoy(ed)	employment	
	exploit	enjoying	
		enjoyment	

F

✻	✻ ✻	✻ ✻ ✻	✻ ✻ ✻ ✻
foil(ed)	foyer		
	Fräulein		

G

   *   * *   * * *   * * * *

*groin (part where
   legs join body)
*groyne (low
   structure built
   out into water)

H

   *   * *   * * *   * * * *

hoist

J

   *   * *   * * *   * * * *

join(ed)	joiner	joinery
joint	joining	joyfully
joist	joyful(ly)	
joy	joyous	

In these words you can hear the vowel sound oi as in oyster-catcher

L

*

loyal(ly)

* *

loyally
loyalty(-ies)

* * *

loyally
loyalty(-ies)

* * * *

M

*

moist

* *

moisture

* * *

* * * *

N

*

noise

* *

noisy(-ier,-iest)

* * *

noisier
noisiest
noisily

* * * *

O

*

oil(ed)

for H . . .
see page 272

* *

oilstone
ointment
oily

oyster

* * *

* * * *

In these words you can hear the vowel sound oi as in oyster-catcher

P

*	* *	* * *	* * * *
point poise(d)	poignant pointed pointer pointing poison(ed)	poisoner poisonous	

Q

*	* *	* * *	* * * *
*quoin (corner- stone) quoit			

R

*	* *	* * *	* * * *
royal(ly)	recoil(ed) rejoice(d) rejoin(ed) royally royalty(-ies)	royally royalty(-ies)	

In these words you can hear the vowel sound oi as in oyster-catcher

*

soil(ed)

spoil(ed)
[spoilt]

* *

soya

* * *

sequoia

* * * *

T

*

toil(ed)
toy(ed)

* *

toilet

* * *

* * * *

V

*

voice(d)
void

* *

voyage(d)

* * *

* * * *

In these words you can hear the vowel sound oi as in oyster-catcher

*   * *   * * *   * * * *

abound
about

account

allowance

announcement
announcer
astounded
astounding

*aloud (loud enough
   to be heard)
allow
*allowed (permitted)

amount

announce(d)

around
arouse(d)

B

*   * *   * * *   * * * *

blouse

*bough (branch)
bounce(d)
bound
bout
*bow (bend / front
   of ship)

brow
brown(ed)
*brows (more than
   one brow)
*browse(d) (nibble /
   dip into books)

bounty(-ies)

brownie

boundary(-ies)

In these words you can hear the vowel sound **ou** as in **owl**

*

chow

cloud
clout
clown(ed)

couch(es)
couched
count
cow(ed)
cower(ed)

crouch(es)
crouched
crowd
crown(ed)

* *

cacao

cloudless
cloudy(-ier,-iest)

*council (group for
   directing affairs)
*counsel (advice)
counselled
countdown
counted
counter
counting
countless
county(-ies)
*coward (person who
   lacks courage)
cowboy
cower
*cowered (did cower)
cowshed
cowslip

crowded

* * *

*councillor (member
   of a council)
counselling
*counsellor (person
   who gives advice)
countenance
counterfoil
countersink
cowardice

* * * * [*]

counterexample

In these words you can hear the vowel sound ou as in owl

*

doubt
*dour (unsmiling)
*douse/dowse (put
   into water /
   put out)
doused/dowsed
dowel(led)
*dower (property of
   bride or widow)
down(ed)
*dowse (use divining
   rod)

drought
drown(ed)

* *

denounce(d)
devour(ed)

discount
dismount

doubtful(ly)
doubtless
dowdy(-ier,-iest)
dowel(led)
dowelling
downfall
downhill
downland
downright
downstairs
downstream
downward
dowry(-ies)
dowser
dowsing

drowsy(-ier,-iest)

* * *

doubtfully
dowelling

* * * *

E

*

* *

endow(ed)

* * *

encounter(ed)

* * * *

In these words you can hear the vowel sound **ou** as in **owl**

F

    ✻   ✻ ✻   ✻ ✻ ✻   ✻ ✻ ✻ ✻

flounce(d)   flounder(ed)   foundation
*flour (ground
    grain)   *founded (established)
*flower (blossom)   founder
flowered   *foundered (sank /
                collapsed)
*foul (dirty)   foundry(-ies)
fouled   fountain
found
*fowl (bird)

Frau
frown(ed)

for th ...
see page 283

G

    ✻   ✻ ✻   ✻ ✻ ✻   ✻ ✻ ✻ ✻

gouge(d)   groundsel
gown

ground
*grouse(grouse)
    (bird)
growl(ed)
*growse (grumble)

H

    ✻   ✻ ✻   ✻ ✻ ✻   ✻ ✻ ✻ ✻

hound   hourglass(-es)   however
*hour (time)   household
house(d)   housing
how   housewife(-ves)
how'd   housework
howl(ed)

In these words you can hear the vowel sound ou as in owl

*

* *

* * *

* * * *

joust

L

*

* *

* * *

* * * *

Laos

louder

loudspeaker

loud
lounge(d)
louse
lout

loudest
loudly
lousy(-ier,-iest)

M

*

* *

* * *

* * * *

mound
mount
mouse
mouth
mouthed

miaow

mountainous

mountaineering

mountain
mounted
mousy(-ier,-iest)
mouthful
mouthpiece

mountaineer
mountainside
mountaintop

In these words you can hear the vowel sound OU as in owl

noun
now

nowadays

O

hour (time)

hourglass(es)

outbidding
outgoing
ounce   ourselves   outlying
*our (belonging to   outbid   outnumber(ed)
   us)   [outbid]   outsider
ours   outboard   outstanding
out   outbreak   outwitted
                      outburst   outwitting
owl   outcome
                      outdo
                      [outdid]
                      [outdone]
                      outdoors
                      outer
                      outfit
                      outing
                      outlaw(ed)
                      outlet
                      outline(d)
                      outlook
                      outpost
                      output
                      outrage(d)
                      outright
                      outrun
                      [outran]
                      outset
                      outshine
                      [outshone]
                      outside
                      outskirts
for H . . .
see page 279   outstretched
                      outward
                      outwit(ted)

*

plough(ed)

pouch(es)
pouched
pounce(d)
pound
pout
power(ed)

proud
prow
prowl(ed)

* *

powder(ed)
power(ed)

profound
pronounce(d)
proudly
prowess

* * *

powerful(ly)

pronouncement
pronouncing

* * * *

powerfully

R

*

round
rouse(d)
rout

* *

rebound
renown(ed)

rounded
rounders
rounding
roundup
router
rowdy(-ier,-iest)

* * *

roundabout

* * * *

In these words you can hear the vowel sound ou as in owl

scour(ed)
scout
scowl(ed)
scrounge(d)

shout
shower(ed)
shroud

slouch(es)
slouched

snout

sound
sour(ed)
south
sow

spout
sprout

stout

Saudi

scoundrel
scourer
scouring

shower(ed)
showery

sounded
sounding
southward

surmount
surround

showery

surrounded
surroundings

T

thou

towel(led)
tower(ed)
town

trout
trowel(led)

thousand
thousandth

tousle(d)

towel(led)
towelling
tower(ed)
towering

trousers
trowel(led)
trowelling

towelling
towering

trowelling

In these words you can hear the vowel sound ou as in owl

V

LONG
VOWEL OU

*	* *	* * *	* * * *

vouch(es)
vouched
vow(ed)
vowel

voucher
*vouchers (more than
  one voucher)
*vouches (does vouch)
vowel

W

*	* *	* * *	* * * *

wound

In these words you can hear the vowel sound ou as in owl

Use these pages to make a note of words you find especially useful.

Useful Words

Useful Words

Useful Words

Useful Words

Useful Words

Useful Words

Useful Words

Useful Words

Useful Words

Useful Words

Useful Words

Useful Words

Useful Words

Useful Words

Useful Words